P9-CKX-817

More praise for Kyoto2

'Informative and illuminating, this is a radical assessment of where we're going on climate change (ever further down the destructive slope) and where we could be headed with prompt and vigorous action (into a far healthier and still sustainable future).' – *Norman Myers, professor and visiting fellow at Green College and at the Said Business School, Oxford University*

'This is a fantastic book – timely, important and far-reaching, a key reference for anyone seeking to understand the complexities of dangerous climate change and current efforts to reduce it. Critical in tone and thought, *Kyoto2* sharply examines one of the most urgent issues of our time.' – *William F. Laurance, senior scientist, Smithsonian Tropical Research Institute, Panama, and former president, Association for Tropical Biology and Conservation*

'Analytical and prophetic, *Kyoto2* proposes a green economics of climate change that could just save our planet.' – *Miriam Kennet, Director, Green Economics Institute*

OLIVER TICKELL

KYOTO2

How to manage the global greenhouse

Zed Books
LONDON | NEW YORK

Kyoto2: How to manage the global greenhouse was first published in 2008 by Zed Books Ltd, 7 Cynthia Street, London N1 9JF, UK and Room 400, 175 Fifth Avenue, New York, NY 10010, USA

www.zedbooks.co.uk

Second imprint 2009

Set in OurType Arnhem and Futura Bold by Ewan Smith, London
Cover designed by Andrew Corbett
Printed in the UK by the MPG Books Group

Distributed in the USA exclusively by Palgrave Macmillan, 175 Fifth Avenue, New York, NY 10010, USA

A catalogue record for this book is available from the British Library
Library of Congress Cataloging in Publication Data available

ISBN 1-84813-025-2
ISBN 978-1-84813-025-8

Transferred to Digital Printing in 2009

1/09

Contents

Boxes

Acknowledgements

I am very grateful to the following people for their help, which has taken many forms – not least of which has been a willingness to enter into debate and discussion, so often the best way to test and advance thinking on complex issues such as those that are the subject of this book: Peter Barnes, Chloe Blackburn, Oriana Castello, Richard Douthwaite, Simon Fairlie, Jim Hansen, Roger Harrabin, Caspar Henderson, Cameron Hepburn, Chris Keene, Miriam Kennet, Paul Klemperer, John Latham, Diana Liverman, Larry Lohmann, James Lovelock, Mark Lynas, George Marshall, Alistair Martin, Mike Mason, George Monbiot, Pedro Moura Costa, Peter Newell, Tamsine O'Riordan, Jonathon Porritt, William Pouget, Matt Prescott, Beatrix Richards, Amanda Root, James Shaw, Craig Simmons, Robin Smale, Jeremy Smith, Crispin Tickell, John Topping, Susannah Trefgarne, Alistair Yeomans, Kenny Young, and, last but far from least, my wife and children, who have had to put up with me.

Introduction

> 'Up and and up they went, nearer and nearer to heaven's kingdom – until, disaster! The mirror shook so violently with its weird reflections that it sprang out of their hands and went crashing down to earth, where it burst into hundreds of millions, trillions of tiny pieces. And that made matters even worse than before, for some of these pieces were hardly bigger than a grain of sand. These flew here and there, all through the wide world; whoever got a speck in his eye saw everything good as bad or twisted – for every little splinter had the same power that the whole glass had. [...] The demon laughed until he nearly split his sides.' Hans Christian Andersen, *The Snow Queen*[1]

Economist Nicholas Stern famously described climate change as 'the greatest market failure the world has seen'.[2] But there is an exception: the attempts of the world's governments to redress that market failure, beginning with the Climate Convention's Kyoto Protocol. Far from overcoming the market failure identified by Stern, the Kyoto Protocol has created a whole new spectrum of market failures – like Hans Christian Andersen's demonic distorting mirror when it was smashed to smithereens.

First among the Protocol's failures is that its key objective – to reduce greenhouse gas emissions – is unmet, as reported by Michael Raupach in 2007.[3] Indeed, the rate of increase of global CO_2 emissions from burning fossil fuels and from industry has accelerated, from 1.1 per cent per year for 1990–99 to more than 3 per cent per year for 2000–04. The emissions growth rate since 2000, as Raupach writes, 'was greater than for the most fossil-fuel intensive of the Intergovernmental Panel on Climate Change emissions scenarios developed in the late 1990s'.

And as Gwyn Prins and Steve Rayner noted in *Nature*: 'The

Kyoto Protocol is a symbolically important expression of governments' concern about climate change. But as an instrument for achieving emissions reductions, it has failed. It has produced no demonstrable reductions in emissions or even in anticipated emissions growth. And it pays no more than token attention to the needs of societies to adapt to existing climate change.'[4]

At the heart of the Kyoto Protocol are its various 'flexibility mechanisms', which allow the 'Annex 1' rich countries to meet their emissions reductions targets by buying in emissions reductions or 'carbon credits' from elsewhere. But many of these reductions are in truth no such thing. Under the Protocol's rules, the reductions are meant to be additional to what would have happened anyway, and in the case of the Clean Development Mechanism (CDM) contribute to sustainable development in the host country.

It is now clear, however, that many of the projects are supporting human rights abuses and environmental destruction, while producing no additional emissions reductions (see Chapter 2). Indeed, the funds from the sale of carbon credits appear in some instances to be financing accelerated industrial development – and actually increasing emissions.

So what has gone wrong? The requirement that CDM projects contribute to sustainable development is policed by the government of the host country, which often receives direct financial benefit from the projects. There is no further oversight. As a result the sustainable development requirement might as well not exist. Then the Climate Convention's CDM Executive Board, which approves projects that generate carbon credits, has been more concerned to get the market moving than to subject projects to rigorous scrutiny.

All that is left to discriminate between 'good' and 'bad' carbon credits is the carbon market itself. But the carbon market is driven by its own economic logic, not by social or environmental concerns, as Jack Cogen, president of carbon asset manager Natsource, admitted with remarkable candour at a recent conference in Montreal: 'The carbon market doesn't care about sustainable development. All it cares about is the carbon price ... The carbon market is not going to be able to put sustainable development and everything else into one price.'[5]

One example of carbon malpractice is the growing role of carbon credits from hydropower, which now accounts for about a quarter of all the projects coming forward for approval. As International Rivers has documented, 35 per cent of the dams creating carbon credits were already built by the time the projects were approved, and 96 per cent were already under construction – making a mockery of the very idea that they produced any additional emissions reductions relative to business as usual.[6]

Another example is the sale of carbon credits worth some $4.7 billion from reducing emissions of 'F-gases' based on a capital investment of just $100 million. The F-gases are a by-product of the manufacture of HCFCs, powerful greenhouse gases used in refrigeration and air-conditioning even though benign alternatives exist – and the subsidy from abating the F-gases is worth more than the HCFCs themselves. So, the $4.7 billion (paid by taxpayers in industrial countries) may actually be supporting increases in greenhouse gas emissions.

The 'Bali Roadmap' which emerged from the December 2007 Climate Convention meeting at Nusa Dua, Bali, has applied a few emergency patches to the Kyoto Protocol, notably by recognizing the need to spend more money on technology transfer to poor countries, and on adaptation. But the potential inclusion of forests in the carbon trading system presents severe dangers of its own – among them the marginalization of traditional forest dwellers, owners and users, and a resulting increase in deforestation. And the Protocol's essential framework is set to persist despite its astonishing record of failure.

Governments have added to the economic distortions, inefficiencies and market failures created by the Kyoto Protocol with new ones of their own. Most iniquitous and absurd is the reckless dash into biofuels of the EU and the USA (see Chapter 2). The greenhouse gas emissions caused by biofuel production are in most cases greater than those associated with mineral petrol and diesel. These biofuels, which are costing OECD countries over $10 billion per year in subsidies, have created a worldwide food shortage that is pushing millions of people who were once merely hungry into starvation, and inflationary pressures that are corroding the entire global economy.

Biofuels are also accelerating the destruction of forests, especially the swamp forests of Indonesia, which are being logged, cleared, burnt and drained to make way for vast palm oil plantations. The biofuel policies of the EU and the USA are thus accelerating the extinction of the orang-utan and the destruction of the Asian peatlands, one of the Earth's greatest biological carbon reservoirs, containing 42Gt (gigatonnes) of embodied carbon (representing 155Gt of CO_2). This Asian peatland carbon is currently being released at 2Gt CO_2 per year – equal to the entire annual savings the Kyoto Protocol is expected to deliver during 2008–12.

And while vast sums are being spent in the carbon market and on biofuels, in many instances accelerating rather than reducing climate change, the urgent need for funding of the order of hundreds of billions of dollars per year (see Chapter 5) to support adaptation to inevitable climate change remains unmet. So far barely a few tens of millions have been raised, and the World Bank expects no more than $500 million by 2012. It sometimes seems that everyone is making fortunes out of the 'climate change business' – except those who really need the money.

This is perhaps most blatantly the case under the EU's Emissions Trading Scheme (EUETS), which gives huge power companies allowances to emit greenhouse gases at no cost – but the companies then pass the allowances on to their customers at the full market price, hidden in their electricity bills. This practice has produced a windfall for the power companies estimated at €30 billion per year across the EU. That represents an effective carbon tax of €60 per EU citizen, or €240 per typical four-person household – but one that is collected by power companies for the benefit of their shareholders.

Improvements to the EUETS are now in the pipeline – but

will not be fully implemented until 2013, and even then will leave loopholes which may (or may not) be removed in 2020. Perhaps the greatest loophole of all is that the EU's Linking Directive will allow the Kyoto Protocol's carbon credits to be traded within the EUETS as equivalent to EU allowances, and so undermine the integrity of EUETS emissions caps and soften prices – and so weaken incentives for long-term investments in cutting emissions.

Clearly the global response to climate change has been inadequate. Yet we know that governments can cooperate effectively to protect the global environment. This has been demonstrated by the Montreal Protocol, which phases out the chemicals responsible for damaging the stratospheric ozone layer using a direct regulatory approach backed by a 'multilateral fund' to pay for technology transfer to developing countries. Indeed, the Montreal Protocol has inadvertently done more in the fight against global warming than the Kyoto Protocol – and at modest cost and amid a total lack of controversy. A barely reported round of amendments to the Montreal Protocol in September 2007 has been estimated to result in greenhouse gas emissions reductions of 18–38Gt, compared to the Kyoto Protocol total of 8Gt – 2Gt a year for four years.

Other regulatory options that should be pursued with vigour are the setting of minimum standards for the energy performance of buildings, lighting, vehicles, appliances, electronic goods, electricity generation plant and industrial processes. McKinsey reported in 2007[7] that measures such as these – even pursuing only those options that deliver a return on investment of 10 per cent or more, so representing negative real costs – would more than halve global energy demand growth to 2020 from 2.2 per cent a year to under 1 per cent. This would reduce energy demand in 2020 by between a fifth and a quarter, and provide around half of the emissions reductions needed relative to 'business as usual' in order to stabilize greenhouse gases in the 450–500ppm (parts per million) range.

As for the Kyoto Protocol, its failure should not be allowed to overshadow the Climate Convention that gave rise to it; indeed, there is much to admire in the founding aims, principles and commitments. Faced with the uncomfortable but undeniable reality that the Kyoto Protocol is 'not fit for purpose', the governments of the world should revisit the Climate Convention and try to make it an effective treaty, adopting new mechanisms that harness the power of markets to tackle both the causes and the consequences of climate change, backed by appropriate direct regulation and funding in the manner of the Montreal Protocol.

There are formidable obstacles, not least the institutional momentum, political capital, entrenched mindset and economic vested interests that have accreted around the Kyoto Protocol. Thus the European Business Council for Sustainable Energy was calling at the Climate Convention meeting in Bali in December 2007 for a new climate agreement that would 'maintain continuity in the legally binding frameworks underpinning the carbon market' – in other words, to avoid change, no matter how grievously the present arrangements are failing. As Prins and Rayner argue:

> Kyoto has failed in several ways, not just in its lack of success in slowing global warming, but also because it has stifled discussion of alternative policy approaches that could both combat climate change and adapt to its unavoidable consequences. As Kyoto became a litmus test of political correctness, those who were concerned about climate change, but sceptical of the top-down approach adopted by the protocol, were sternly admonished that 'Kyoto is the only game in town'. We are anxious that the same mistake is not repeated in the current round of negotiations. [...] we acknowledge that those advocating the Kyoto regime will be reluctant to embrace alternatives because it means admitting that their chosen climate policy has and will continue to fail. But the rational thing to do in the face of a bad investment is to cut your losses and try something different.[8]

A window of opportunity is now open as the Kyoto Protocol

expires at the end of 2012, and negotiations under the Climate Convention as to its replacement are under way. But we need to move fast and effectively. The International Energy Agency's optimum trajectory towards a 450ppm CO_2 equivalent concentration sees emissions peaking in 2012, and no later than 2015. And the emergence of positive feedbacks in the climate system that increase warming (see Chapter 1) suggests that we should aim for stabilization at the lower level of 350ppm. As NASA climate scientist Jim Hansen puts it, 'If humanity wishes to preserve a planet similar to that on which civilization developed, paleoclimate evidence and ongoing climate change suggest that CO_2 will need to be reduced from its current 385 ppm to at most 350 ppm.'[9]

'It is still possible to avoid the worst impacts of climate change; but it requires strong and urgent collective action,' warned Nicholas Stern. 'Delay would be costly and dangerous.'[10] He was referring to the difficulties of achieving stabilization in the region of 450–550ppm. To achieve the considerably more demanding target of 350ppm, requiring an effective cessation of greenhouse gas emissions within four decades, will be all the more challenging. This book elaborates a set of proposals that would jump-start the necessary 'strong and urgent collective action', named 'Kyoto2'.

Kyoto2 summary

Purpose

Kyoto2's purpose is to deliver the objective of the Climate Convention, the most important outcome of the 1992 Earth Summit in Rio de Janeiro: 'stabilization of greenhouse gas concentrations in the atmosphere at a level that would prevent dangerous anthropogenic interference with the climate system ... within a time frame sufficient to allow ecosystems to adapt naturally to climate change, to ensure that food production is not threatened and to enable economic development to proceed in a sustainable manner'.

But what is the level of greenhouse gases at which we should aim to stabilize in order to 'prevent dangerous anthropogenic interference with the climate system'? The latest scientific findings (see Chapter 1) indicate that existing net greenhouse gas levels (including the negative contribution of reflective aerosols), calculated by the Intergovernmental Panel on Climate Change (IPCC) at 375 parts per million CO_2 equivalent (ppm CO_2 eq) in 2005, are already giving rise to positive feedback warming trends – and must therefore be considered dangerous. On a multi-century timescale only a rapid shift to climate neutrality will do the job.

Accordingly Kyoto2 proposes a set of mechanisms that aim to:

1 Progressively limit greenhouse gas emissions year by year in order to achieve global climate neutrality by mid-century, and long-term greenhouse gas stabilization at no more than 350ppm CO_2 eq.
2 Move decisively towards an equitable low-carbon economy, in which: energy is generated increasingly from renewable

and other clean sources; energy is used more efficiently; and 'energy poor' countries and people enjoy improved access to energy (Principle 4).

3 Support the advances in prosperity and quality of life that are so desperately sought across the world, and especially by the world's poorest people (Principles 2, 4 and 5).

4 Mobilize the funds with which to pay for human adaptation to such climate change that we are already committed to by virtue of lags in the climate system, and a 'best case' trajectory of future greenhouse gas emissions, with particular regard to the needs of the poorest countries and the poorest people, who are likely to be the principal victims of climate change, including climate-related health and emergency relief costs (Principles 2 and 3).

5 Give all countries endowed with carbon-rich ecosystems such as forests, swamps and peatlands financial incentives to conserve them: to keep the carbon they contain locked up; to enhance their ability to take up more atmospheric carbon; to preserve the biodiversity they embody; and to meet human needs (Principle 3).

6 Reduce the emissions from agriculture through reforms in agricultural practice, to enhance the role of farmed soils as sinks and long-term reservoirs of carbon, and to maintain and improve agricultural productivity in the face of climate change.

7 Give developed countries and their economies a leading role in providing the necessary finance, technology and know-how in order to bring all the above to fruition, in cooperation with developing countries, which also have their own important parts to play (Principle 1).

Main mechanism

The main mechanism is a market mechanism – since markets are generally the best means of allocating finite resources without unnecessary waste, while keeping as many people happy as possible. Kyoto2 has this in common with the Kyoto Protocol and the EUETS. Owing to poor design and implementation, however, the last two mechanisms have so far proved to be ineffective, wasteful and loaded with perverse incentives.

Reforms are under way which will in time bring about improvements in these systems. A more effective approach, however, is to design a new and better mechanism from scratch – learning from both the failures and the successes of the past, and drawing from climate science, economic theory, and principles of equity that apply across nations, peoples and generations. In particular it is essential to recognize the atmosphere as a global commons to be managed for the general benefit of humanity. Accordingly Kyoto2 proposes to:

1. Define a global cap, or a series of global caps, for greenhouse gas emissions, leading towards stabilization at 350ppm CO_2 eq in the atmosphere, and to allocate a proportion of that cap (based on current figures, 68 per cent) to greenhouse gases from fossil fuels and other industrial sources.
2. Regulate industrial greenhouse gas emissions 'upstream' at or close to production by requiring that the companies responsible surrender permits based on the greenhouse gas pollution implicit in their production, expressed in tonnes of CO_2 equivalent (tCO_2 eq). In the case of fossil fuels this would be at the points where flows are concentrated and easily measured, such as the oil refinery, coal washing station, gas pipeline or gas tanker. Other industrial greenhouse gases to be similarly controlled include:

   - CO_2 from calcinating lime in cement factories;
   - the mix of greenhouse gases emitted by aircraft which multiply the climate forcing of the CO_2 alone (by 36 times in the first year, down to 3.7 times over twenty years and 1.7 times over a century);
   - 'potent industrial greenhouse gases' (PIGGs), such as the F-gases from chemical factories and other industrial processes;
   - nitrous oxide (N_2O) of industrial origin, and based on vol-

ume of nitrate fertilizer production, since a proportion of the nitrate (3–5 per cent) is converted into nitrous oxide by soil and water bacteria.

3 Sell the permits by way of a global 'uniform price sealed bid' auction, subject to both reserve price and a 'safety valve' or ceiling price, with the proceeds accruing to a Climate Change Fund.
4 Credit permits when greenhouse gases are verifiably destroyed or sequestered into secure long-term storage, as with 'carbon capture and storage' (CCS).
5 Apply the Climate Change Fund to tackling both the causes and the consequences of climate change – that is, a combination of mitigation and adaptation, as set out below.

Non-market solutions

No matter how well the main market mechanism works, there is a complementary role for direct regulation to constrain greenhouse gas emissions, and additional, targeted taxes, levies and subsidies. These non-market methods will be most successful where they are designed to overcome specific market failures, and where the costs of the measures (no matter who has to pay them) reflect, to a reasonable approximation, a consistent long-term carbon price.

One great exemplar of this approach is the Montreal Protocol, whose regulatory role in phasing out 'ozone eater' chemicals is supported by financial assistance for technology transfer to developing countries through a 'Multilateral Fund'. This approach could well be extended to the full range of 'powerful industrial greenhouse gases' (PIGGs).

Energy labelling accompanied by demanding and progressive efficiency standards for cars, appliances, lighting, other energy-demanding goods and housing has also been highly effective. This approach, already widely used within the EU, should be extended to other countries, and extended to encompass new product types, such as computers and home entertainment systems.

As for diffuse land-based emissions from deforestation,

agriculture and soils, these are excluded from the market mechanism owing mainly to the difficulty of measuring and monitoring them. Instead, Kyoto2 proposes to finance global programmes to reduce emissions from these land-based sources, as detailed below.

Kyoto2 also adopts Jim Hansen's call for an end to coal-burning power plants that do not operate carbon capture and storage (CCS). This should be implemented soon in both developed countries (at the generator's expense) and in developing countries (with financial support from the Climate Change Fund). Other reforms are also needed in the power sector to encourage the development of combined heat and power (CHP) and to decentralize generation into smaller units closer to the demand for power and heat.

It is also important to bring an end to perverse subsidies to fossil fuel production, which have been estimated to amount to \$235–\$300 billion per year, and whose continuation would directly counter the operation of Kyoto2's main market-based mechanism described above.

Allocating resources

The auction of permits could credibly raise a sum of about €1 trillion per year for the Climate Change Fund (see Chapter 6). These funds would be allocated to:

1 finance human adaptation to the climate change to which we are already committed by way of lags in the climate system and unavoidable future greenhouse gas emissions;
2 pay countries that maintain their forests and other natural ecosystems in good condition (especially ecosystems that contain substantial embodied carbon in themselves or in underlying soils) and restore these ecosystems where lost or degraded, all subject to a requirement to respect the rights of traditional land/forest owners, users and dwellers;
3 research techniques for low-emissions agriculture and agricultural systems that will be resilient in the face of climate

change impacts, and so develop best-practice guidelines to be promoted worldwide to farmers, herders and ranchers by way of agricultural extension support;

4 finance research and development into renewable and other clean energy production, and the efficient use of energy;

5 provide supplementary finance to divert new energy infrastructure investments into renewable and other clean energy development, to retro-fit 'carbon capture and storage' (CCS) where appropriate, and to accelerate the phase-out of inefficient and polluting generation capacity and its replacement with renewable and other clean technologies;

6 support the development of appropriate standards in all countries for energy efficiency in industry, building, housing, transport, white goods, home entertainment, computer and other sectors, and in the case of poor countries to pay all or part of the supplementary costs so imposed;

7 investigate the potential of geo-engineering projects to reduce the global temperature and so prevent a 'runaway greenhouse effect' from taking hold, with particular focus on cost-effectiveness, careful evaluation of potential hazards and reversibility;

8 extend access to family planning services where such access is presently limited or denied;

9 finance emergency humanitarian relief related to extreme weather events;

10 finance programmes to address the health risks associated with climate change.

Box 0.1 Climate Convention – objective and principles

Objective The ultimate objective of this Convention and any related legal instruments that the Conference of the Parties may adopt is to achieve, in accordance with the relevant provisions of the Convention, stabilization of greenhouse gas concentrations in the atmosphere at a level that would prevent dangerous anthropogenic interference with the climate system. Such a level should be achieved within a time frame sufficient to allow ecosystems to adapt naturally to climate change, to ensure that food production is not threatened and to enable economic development to proceed in a sustainable manner.

Principles In their actions to achieve the objective of the Convention and to implement its provisions, the Parties shall be guided, *inter alia*, by the following:

1. The Parties should protect the climate system for the benefit of present and future generations of humankind, on the basis of equity and in accordance with their common but differentiated responsibilities and respective capabilities. Accordingly, the developed-country Parties should take the lead in combating climate change and the adverse effects thereof.
2. The specific needs and special circumstances of developing-country Parties, especially those that are particularly vulnerable to the adverse effects of climate change, and of those Parties, especially developing-country Parties, that would have to bear a disproportionate or abnormal burden under the Convention, should be given full consideration.
3. The Parties should take precautionary measures to anticipate, prevent or minimize the causes of climate

change and mitigate its adverse effects. Where there are threats of serious or irreversible damage, lack of full scientific certainty should not be used as a reason for postponing such measures, taking into account that policies and measures to deal with climate change should be cost-effective so as to ensure global benefits at the lowest possible cost. To achieve this, such policies and measures should take into account different socio-economic contexts, be comprehensive, cover all relevant sources, sinks and reservoirs of greenhouse gases and adaptation, and comprise all economic sectors. Efforts to address climate change may be carried out cooperatively by interested Parties.

4 The Parties have a right to, and should, promote sustainable development. Policies and measures to protect the climate system against human-induced change should be appropriate for the specific conditions of each Party and should be integrated with national development programmes, taking into account that economic development is essential for adopting measures to address climate change.

5 The Parties should cooperate to promote a supportive and open international economic system that would lead to sustainable economic growth and development in all Parties, particularly developing-country Parties, thus enabling them better to address the problems of climate change. Measures taken to combat climate change, including unilateral ones, should not constitute a means of arbitrary or unjustifiable discrimination or a disguised restriction on international trade.

Box 0.2 In a nutshell

1 Kyoto2 is a global system to auction transferable permits to pollute the atmosphere with industrial greenhouse gases up to a series of annual caps defined at levels that would prevent dangerous interference with the Earth's climate system.

2 As a global system it would apply equally in all countries. There would be no national emissions allocations and no need for the 'territorial accounting' that characterizes the Kyoto Protocol and the EUETS.

3 Greenhouse gas emissions would be regulated 'upstream' – that is, as near as possible to the point of production, and in the case of emissions from fossil fuels, as close as practical to the point of production of the fuels themselves.

4 This system would create market incentives for the wide scale and systematic reduction of greenhouse gas emissions and the development of alternatives, to be supported in turn by regulations and standards aimed at overcoming specific market failures.

5 The funds raised at auction would be invested to tackle both the causes and the consequences of climate change, with an emphasis on addressing the needs of the poor and of those most adversely impacted, including to:

- help adaptation to such climate change as is already inevitable;
- accelerate progress towards a clean, energy-efficient, low-carbon global economy;
- reform land use so as to conserve biological carbon within soils, peatlands, forests and other ecosystems, and reduce emissions from land of other greenhouse gases;
- research low-cost and environmentally benign geoengineering options that could *in extremis* prevent a 'runaway greenhouse effect' from taking hold.

1 | What's the problem?

'The primary scarcity facing the planet is not of natural resources nor money, but time.' International Energy Agency[1]

'We would be taking a great risk with future generations if, having received this early warning, we did nothing about it or just took the attitude: "Well! It will see me out!"' Margaret Thatcher[2]

'Society may be lulled into a false sense of security by smooth projections of global change.' Tim Lenton[3]

'The doomsday clock of climate change is ticking ever faster towards midnight.' Prince Charles[4]

'Moderate slowing of fossil fuel use will not appreciably reduce long-term human-made climate change. Preservation of climate requires that most remaining fossil fuel carbon is never emitted to the atmosphere.' Jim Hansen[5]

The Earth is heating up, and fast. The Intergovernmental Panel on Climate Change (IPCC) has reported that eleven of the last twelve years (1995–2006) rank among the twelve warmest years since 1850.[6] Meanwhile greenhouse gases have been building up in the atmosphere faster than even the highest 'emissions scenarios' put forward by the IPCC in 1995.[7]

So have temperatures and sea level rises – as reported by Stefan Rahmstorf, Professor of Ocean Physics at Potsdam University, himself an IPCC lead author on the physical science of climate change.[8] Sea levels have risen by an average of 1.8mm per year since 1961, rising to 3.1mm per year since 1993, as a result of melting glaciers, ice caps and the polar ice sheets, and the thermal expansion of ocean waters. Rahmstorf's analysis of climate trends compared to the projections of the IPCC's 2001

Assessment Report shows that temperature rise is at the top end of the predicted range, while sea level rise is significantly greater than even the highest predictions.

Thus 'the climate system, in particular sea level, may be responding more quickly to climate change than our current generation of models indicates', he writes, adding that the IPCC's climate projections 'have not exaggerated but may in some respects even have underestimated the change, in particular for sea level'.[9]

One sign of this temperature rise is the rapid growth of the tropical climate zone – since 1980 it has expanded by 275 kilometres to north and south, as described by Dian Seidel of the US National Oceanic and Atmospheric Administration.[10] Again, Seidel notes that the observed recent rate of expansion is greater than predicted by climate model projections. This could lead to 'profound changes in the global climate system'. In particular the poleward movement of atmospheric circulation systems, such as jet streams and storm tracks, 'could result in shifts in precipitation patterns affecting natural ecosystems, agriculture, and water resources'.

There are now many indications that the world is entering into a phase of accelerated global heating – one in which 'positive feedback' processes in the Earth's climate system play an increasingly important role as drivers of further heating. This danger was highlighted by James Lovelock, originator of Gaia theory, at a packed Royal Society public lecture in which he spoke of the unprecedented melting of Arctic sea ice during the 2007 summer. Because ice reflects 80 per cent of the sun's heat, while open water absorbs 95 per cent, the melting sea ice creates a positive feedback that leads to even more heating, which in turn leads to even more melting, and so on. Thus:

> We have to understand that the Earth System is now in positive feedback and is moving ineluctably towards the stable hot state of past climates. I cannot stress too strongly the dangers inherent in systems in positive feedback. Imagine a wooden

> house whose occupants have built too large a fire to warm them and the furniture near the fire was smouldering. If they did not act immediately, positive feedback would ensure that the whole house was consumed by fire in minutes.[11]

This heating is self-reinforcing and the effects carry over from year to year, as Jim Hansen – director of the NASA Goddard Institute for Space Studies and Professor of Earth and Environmental Sciences at Columbia University – explained to the Iowa Utilities Board. 'As the warming global ocean transports more heat into the Arctic, sea ice cover recedes and the darker open ocean surface absorbs more sunlight,' he said. 'The ocean stores the added heat, winter sea ice is thinner, and thus increased melting can occur in following summers, even though year-to-year variations in sea ice area will occur with fluctuations of weather patterns and ocean heat transport.'[12]

And the heating of the Arctic Ocean is especially dangerous as it will also heat up the Greenland Ice Sheet and cause it to melt faster than anticipated. This could cause some metres of sea level rise during this century, and would ultimately lead to 7 metres of sea level rise once its 3 billion cubic kilometres of ice have melted away. It has always been assumed that the melting or disintegration of this massive volume of ice would take millennia to occur, but recent observations show that this is not so. While it takes millennia for an ice sheet to build up, writes Hansen, it can give way with surprising speed since multiple positive feedbacks accelerate the process once it is under way. 'Snow-covered ice reflects back to space most of the sunlight striking it. However, as warming causes melting on the surface, the darker wet ice absorbs much more solar energy. Most of the resulting melt water burrows through the ice sheet, lubricates its base, and thus speeds the discharge of icebergs to the ocean.'[13]

Further positive feedbacks take place where ice sheets meet the sea or ocean. Warming sea water accelerates melting, and rising sea levels tend to lift the ice and destabilize it further:

effects that may be at work at the massive Pine Island ice sheet in West Antarctica, where the British Antarctic Survey reports a surge in the speed of its seaward descent.[14]

The rate of ice sheet melt in West Antarctica along the Bellingshausen and Amundsen seas has also increased by 59 per cent in ten years to reach an estimated 132 Gt/y (gigatonnes per year) in 2006, according to Eric Rignot, Principal Scientist for the Radar Science and Engineering Section at NASA's Jet Propulsion Laboratory, while ice sheet losses on the Antarctic peninsula increased by 140 per cent to reach an estimated 60 Gt/y. 'Losses are concentrated along narrow channels occupied by outlet glaciers and are caused by ongoing and past glacier acceleration,' he reports. 'Changes in glacier flow therefore have a significant, if not dominant, impact on ice sheet mass balance.'[15]

Likewise in Greenland, ice sheets are melting away at unprecedented rates, as reported by Edward Hanna of Sheffield University's Department of Geography.[16] Summer 2003 was the warmest since at least 1958 in coastal southern Greenland, 2005 was the second warmest and 2006 the third warmest. In 2005 Hanna observed 'the most extensive anomalously warm conditions over the ablation zone of the ice sheet, which caused a record melt extent', and 2006 saw the third-highest run-off in forty-nine years from ice sheet melting. He and his co-authors 'attribute the significantly increased Greenland summer warmth and Greenland Ice Sheet melt and runoff since 1990 to global warming'.

Hansen notes that these dramatic increases in polar ice melt have taken place under a warming of under 1°C since pre-industrial times. Thus 'Global warming of several more degrees, with its polar amplification, would have both Greenland and West Antarctica bathed in summer melt for extended melt seasons.'[17] He concludes that we need to constrain greenhouse gas emissions far more sharply than is presently considered feasible by policy-makers. While recognizing that sea level changes from ice melt are inherently unpredictable, he writes,

> I find it almost inconceivable that BAU [business as usual]

> climate change would not yield a sea level change of the order of meters on the century timescale. The threat of a large sea level change is a principal element in our argument that the global community must aim to keep additional global warming less than 1°C above the 2000 temperature, and even 1°C may be too great. In turn, this implies a CO_2 limit of about 450 ppm, or less. Such scenarios are dramatically different than BAU, requiring almost immediate changes to get on a fundamentally different energy and greenhouse gas emissions path.[18]

This view is supported by Rahmstorf, who projects a sea level 0.5m to 1.4m higher in 2100 than in 1990. He also believes that the uncertainties over future sea-level rise are larger than previously estimated. 'A rise of over 1m by 2100 for strong warming scenarios cannot be ruled out,' he argues, 'because all that such a rise would require is that the linear relation of the rate of sea-level rise and temperature, which was found to be valid in the 20th century, remains valid in the 21st century.' As such the very low sea-level rise values reported in the IPCC's Third Assessment Report 'now appear rather implausible in the light of the observational data'.[19]

Arctic heating will also warm the tundra regions of the Canadian, Siberian and Alaskan Arctic, with the risk of emitting billions of tonnes of methane – a greenhouse gas some thirty times more powerful than carbon dioxide – presently locked up in the permafrost (see also Chapter 7). Indeed, this process may already be under way in western Siberia, which has warmed by 3°C over the last forty years, as reported by Fred Pearce in *New Scientist*:

> An area stretching for a million square kilometres across the permafrost of western Siberia is turning into a mass of shallow lakes as the ground melts, according to Russian researchers just back from the region. The sudden melting of a bog the size of France and Germany combined could unleash billions of tonnes of methane, a potent greenhouse gas, into the atmosphere. [...] The warming is believed to be a combination of man-made

> climate change, a cyclical change in atmospheric circulation known as the Arctic oscillation, plus feedbacks caused by melting ice, which exposes bare ground and ocean. These absorb more solar heat than white ice and snow.[20]

Likewise in the interior of Alaska, reports F. Stuart Chapin, Professor of Ecology at Alaska University, warming has triggered pronounced ecological and social change. Since 1950 air temperatures have increased by 0.4°C per decade, and are projected to rise even faster in the future; the growing season has lengthened by 2.6 days per decade, and permafrost has warmed by 0.5°C per decade.[21] A large part of the problem is that warming 'is amplified at high latitudes as reflective sea ice, glaciers, and snow cover are replaced by heat-absorbing water, land, and forests'.

If these trends continue and spread to other Arctic regions, the 'runaway greenhouse effect' – in which cascades of positive feedback cycles become the main, and growing, drivers of heating – will be well out of control. And if that point is reached, humanity can reduce its greenhouse gas emissions to zero without making any difference: the 'climate roller-coaster' (to borrow a phrase from George Marshall's *Carbon Detox*)[22] will be well and truly under way, and we had better hold on tight.

Another positive feedback process now under way is that oceans are absorbing less of the CO_2 that we put into the atmosphere. That leaves more in the atmosphere to contribute to global heating – the so-called 'airborne fraction'. As Josep Canadell, Executive Director of the Global Carbon Project, reports, CO_2 emissions are rising sharply thanks to a combination of economic growth and the increasing carbon intensity of the global economy since 2000, which means that 'comparing the 1990s with 2000–2006, the emissions growth rate increased from 1.3% to 3.3% per year'.[23]

But the trend is accentuated because oceans and forests are also taking up less of the CO_2 we emit, leading to an increased airborne fraction. This is currently about 57 per cent, with the remaining 43 per cent absorbed in soils, oceans and biomass.

Canadell cites convincing evidence of a long-term trend over the last fifty years of 'a decline in the efficiency of CO_2 sinks on land and oceans in absorbing anthropogenic emissions'. The effect is hard to quantify, but could be responsible for as much as a third of the increase in atmospheric CO_2. 'An increasing [airborne fraction] is consistent with results of climate-carbon cycle models,' he concludes, 'but the magnitude of the observed signal appears larger than that estimated by models. All of these changes characterize a carbon cycle that is generating stronger-than-expected and sooner-than-expected climate forcing.'[24]

Specific information has emerged regarding the reduced absorption of CO_2 by tropical forests, as reported by Kenneth Feeley, Fellow of Harvard University's Center for Tropical Forest Science,[25] with significant declines in stem growth rates at tropical forest sites in Panama and Malaysia. Changes in growth were 'significantly associated with regional climate changes', and growth rates went down as average mimimum temperatures went up. 'While the underlying cause(s) of decelerating growth is still unresolved,' he reports, 'these patterns strongly contradict the hypothesized pantropical increase in tree growth rates caused by carbon fertilization.'

The findings are consistent, however, with a new coupled atmosphere–vegetation model of the world's greatest tropical forest, the Amazon, by Kerry Cook and Edward Vizy of Cornell's Department of Earth and Atmospheric Sciences, which also indicates that rising atmospheric CO_2 will lead to significant declines in forest cover. If atmospheric CO_2 levels rise to 757ppm, the model projects reduced rainfall, alterations in seasonal cycles and a weakening of tropical circulation systems, resulting in 'a 70% reduction in the extent of the Amazon rain forest by the end of the twenty-first century and a large eastward expansion of the caatinga vegetation that is prominent in the Nordeste region of Brazil today'.[26]

The role of the Southern Ocean as a carbon sink is also weakening, according to Corrine Le Quéré, Professor of Environmental Sciences at the University of East Anglia, who estimates that its capacity to absorb carbon from the atmosphere is reducing at a rate of 80Mt (megatonnes) of carbon (about 300Mt of CO_2) per year each decade. She puts this down to the increasing wind speeds over the Southern Ocean – itself a result of global warming. 'Consequences include a reduction of the efficiency of the Southern Ocean sink of CO_2 in the short term (about 25 years) and possibly a higher level of stabilization of atmospheric CO_2 on a multicentury time scale.'[27]

These are all examples of 'tipping points' in the Earth's climate system – defined by Le Quéré's colleague at UEA, climate scientist Tim Lenton, as 'critical thresholds at which a tiny perturbation can qualitatively alter the state or development of a system'. Thus, 'at a particular moment in time, a small change can have large, long-term consequences for a system'.[28]

'Human activities may have the potential to push components of the Earth system past critical states into qualitatively different modes of operation, implying large-scale impacts on human and ecological systems,' warns Lenton. 'Our synthesis of present knowledge suggests that a variety of tipping elements could reach their critical point within this century under anthropogenic climate change. The greatest threats are tipping the Arctic sea-ice and the Greenland ice sheet, and at least five other elements could surprise us by exhibiting a nearby tipping point.'[29]

These other tipping points include disruptions to ocean circulation – which could, for example, cause the North Atlantic Drift or Gulf Stream current, which warms northern Europe (including Britain), to submerge farther south than it now does. The failure of the Gulf Stream could bring glacial conditions to northern Europe, even while the rest of the Earth warms. And we know from analysis of ancient ice layers in the Greenland ice sheet that temperature swings of 8–10°C (known as 'Dansgaard-Oeschger' events) have taken place more than twenty times during the past glacial period.[30] As Rahmstorf warns, 'The Greenland ice contains a clear warning: the climate system is by no means a sluggish, good-natured sloth – it can react very abruptly and violently.'

The increasing evidence of positive feedback cycles in global warming leads Lovelock to conclude that reducing our carbon emissions is not enough. We also need to restore our increasingly damaged biosphere, since 'by abrading the skin of our planet to provide farm land we have destroyed more than 40 percent of the Earth's natural ecosystems and these were what previously served to sustain a stable climate'. He also believes that we must research 'geoengineering' solutions (see Chapter 6), because these may represent our final line of defence against the 'runaway greenhouse effect'.[31]

The alternative to effective global measures was set out by the International Energy Agency's *World Energy Outlook 2007*,[32] whose 'business as usual' reference scenario projects that the world's primary energy needs will grow by 55 per cent between 2005 and 2030 (1.8 per cent per year). Energy-related CO_2 emissions go up by 57 per cent, thanks to the growing importance of coal. 'In line with the spectacular growth of the past few years, coal sees the biggest increase in demand in absolute terms, jumping by 73% between 2005 and 2030 and pushing its share of total energy demand up from 25% to 28%.' In all 74 per cent of the increase in primary energy demand comes from developing countries, whose economies and populations are growing fastest, and 45 per cent comes from China and India alone.

Based on IPCC projections, this reference scenario would lead to a global heating of 6°C – enough to transform the world we know into a very different and far less pleasant place (see Chapter 7 to see just how unpleasant it could be). Even under the International Energy Agency's (IEA) 'alternative policy scenario' in which OECD emissions decline after 2015, global emissions would still be 27 per cent higher in 2030 than in 2005. This would lead to a long-term CO_2 equivalent concentration in the atmosphere of 550 parts per million, believed to correspond to an average temperature 3°C above pre-industrial levels. To stabilize at 450ppm and limit the temperatures increase to a projected maximum of 2.4°C,

> CO_2 emissions would need to peak by 2015 at the latest and to

> fall between 50% and 85% below 2000 levels by 2050. [...] Emissions savings come from improved efficiency in fossil-fuel use in industry, buildings and transport, switching to nuclear power and renewables, and the widespread deployment of CO_2 capture and storage (CCS) in power generation and industry. Exceptionally quick and vigorous policy action by all countries, and unprecedented technological advances, entailing substantial costs, would be needed to make this case a reality.[33]

The European Commission has adopted similar targets as its climate change policy. 'By 2050 global emissions must be reduced by up to 50% compared to 1990, implying reductions in developed countries of 60–80% by 2050,' states the Commission's 2007 paper *Limiting global climate change to 2 degrees Celsius: The way ahead for 2020 and beyond*. 'Many developing countries will also need to significantly reduce their emissions.'[34]

Both the Commission's and even the IEA's proposal targets are, however, inadequate. As shown above, the world is already experiencing positive feedback forcings and the serious danger of a 'runaway greenhouse effect' with a temperature rise of just 0.8°C from pre-industrial levels, following a rise in CO_2 from a historic 280ppm to 379ppm in 2005 (or 375ppm CO_2 eq including the contributions of other greenhouse gases and reflective aerosol particles).[35] A further temperature rise of up to 1°C is 'in the pipeline' for 2100 even if emissions stop now, owing mainly to the thermal lag of the oceans, with longer-term warming of 1.4°C as other slow feedbacks kick in.[36]

The available options are set out by Andrew Weaver, Professor at the School of Earth and Ocean Sciences at Victoria, BC. Using a coupled atmosphere–ocean–carbon cycle computer model to examine the long-term implications of various 2050 greenhouse gas emission targets, he finds that

> All emission targets considered with less than 60% global reduction by 2050 break the 2.0°C threshold warming this century, a number that some have argued represents an upper bound on manageable climate warming. Even when emissions are stabil-

ized at 90% below present levels at 2050, this 2.0°C threshold is eventually broken. Our results suggest that if a 2.0°C warming is to be avoided, direct CO_2 capture from the air, together with subsequent sequestration, would eventually have to be introduced in addition to sustained 90% global carbon emissions reductions by 2050.[37]

To keep temperature rise below 2°C in 2500, Weaver shows, we need to adopt the 100 per cent emissions reduction trajectory in which net CO_2 emissions are reduced from the current (2006) 9Gt per year to just 0.2Gt per year in 2050. This scenario alone produces a long-term reduction in CO_2 levels: they begin at 380ppm in 2007, rise to 407ppm in 2050, and then slowly decline to 368ppm in 2500. Even the ambitious-sounding 90 per cent reduction scenario fails to deliver the goods: CO_2 emissions rise to 413ppm in 2050, and then continue to rise, reaching 445ppm in 2500, acompanied by a 2.3°C temperature rise.

The IPCC's Fourth Assessment Report[38] supports Weaver in offering little comfort from either the 500ppm or the 450ppm figures. Stabilization at 535–590 ppm CO_2 eq is predicted to result in a dangerous 2.8–3.2°C temperature rise above pre-industrial levels. Even stabilization at 445–490 ppm CO_2 eq would limit temperature rise only to the 2.0–2.4°C range. The conclusion is clear: the world needs to go 'carbon neutral', and the sooner the better, as much of the CO_2 we are emitting now will still be in the atmosphere in centuries' time – 20 per cent even after 1,000 years.[39] And by doing this we will head, long term, for a CO_2 concentration tending towards 350ppm.

Jim Hansen argues a similar case: that current levels of greenhouse gases are already 'too high to maintain the climate to which humanity, wildlife, and the rest of the biosphere are adapted', and that we need to stabilize at 300–350ppm CO_2 eq if we are to restore the planetary energy balance, maintain sea ice and ice caps, prevent the shifting of climatic zones, preserve Alpine water supplies and avoid ocean acidification.[40]

Our current analysis suggests that humanity must aim for an

> even lower level of GHGs. Paleoclimate data and ongoing global changes indicate that 'slow' climate feedback processes not included in most climate models, such as ice sheet disintegration, vegetation migration, and GHG release from soils, tundra or ocean sediments, may begin to come into play on time scales as short as centuries or less. Rapid on-going climate changes and realization that Earth is out of energy balance, implying that more warming is 'in the pipeline', add urgency to investigation of the dangerous level of GHGs.[41]

Thus he proposes an initial target of 350ppm, arguing that this is technically feasible provided that we 'phase out coal use except where CO_2 is captured and sequestered', and halt development of unconventional fuels such as tar sands and shales. To bring down CO_2 in the atmosphere to a more desirable long-term 300ppm, close to pre-industrial levels, he argues for substantial carbon storage in soils and ecosystems, which could ultimately reduce atmospheric CO_2 by a further 50ppm. As for the alternative,

> We must realize that there is a limit on the total fossil fuel CO_2 that we inject into the atmosphere. We cannot burn all of the fossil fuels (oil, gas, coal and unconventional fossil fuels such as tar shale and tar sands) and release the CO_2 into the air without creating a different planet. Burning all fossil fuels, if the CO_2 is released into the air, would destroy creation, the planet with its animal and plant life as it has existed for the past several thousand years, the time of civilization, the Holocene, the period of relative climate stability, warm enough to keep ice sheets off North America and Eurasia, but cool enough to maintain Antarctic and Greenland ice, and thus a stable sea level. We cannot pretend that we do not know the consequences of burning all fossil fuels.[42]

To fulfil with confidence the objective of the Climate Convention to 'prevent dangerous anthropogenic interference with the climate system', we need to stabilize greenhouse gases at a level lower than today's rather than contemplate further increases.

Specifically we must achieve a complete cessation of net greenhouse gas emissions by 2050, and preferably sooner – delivering a long-term stabilization target of 350ppm CO_2. Accordingly Kyoto2 adopts Hansen's 300–350ppm as its stabilization target – a science-based figure that stands in contrast to the current political debate between a 'tough but realistic' 550ppm stabilization target (as adopted by Nicholas Stern in his *Review*)[43], and a 'desirable but impractical' 450ppm target.

We know what we have to do: keep the great bulk of our fossil fuel reserves, or at least the carbon they contain, in the ground where nature put them; redesign the global economy to achieve climate neutrality by around 2050; protect and restore forests, woodlands, grasslands, peatlands, soils and other biological carbon stores and sinks; and deal with the unavoidable human and environmental impacts of climate change. But how? Kyoto2 provides one answer.

2 | The policy response

> 'Our ability to come together to stop or limit damage to the world's environment will be perhaps the greatest test of how far we can act as a world community. No one should underestimate the imagination that will be required, nor the scientific effort, nor the unprecedented cooperation we shall have to show. We shall need statesmanship of a rare order. It's because we know that, that we are here today.' Margaret Thatcher[1]

> 'I find it puzzling that conservatives, and I consider myself to be a moderate conservative, are not more concerned about preserving creation.' Jim Hansen[2]

The Climate Convention

> 'There are those who say that the leaders of the world do not care about the Earth and the environment. Well, let them all come here to Rio. Mr President, we have come to Rio. We've not only seen the concern, we share it. We not only care, we're taking action. We come to Rio with an action plan on climate change. It stresses energy efficiency, cleaner air, reforestation, new technology. I am happy to report that I have just signed the Framework Convention on Climate Change. [...] Let us join in translating the words spoken here into concrete action to protect the planet. [...]
>
> It's been said that we don't inherit the Earth from our ancestors, we borrow it from our children. When our children look back on this time and this place, they will be grateful that we met at Rio, and they will certainly be pleased with the intentions stated and the commitments made. But they will judge us by the actions we take from this day forward. Let us not disappoint them!' President George Bush Senior[3]

The Climate Convention – in full the United Nations Framework

Convention on Climate Change or UNFCCC – was negotiated at the Earth Summit in Rio de Janeiro in 1992, and came into force on 21 March 1994. Its objective is the 'stabilization of greenhouse gas concentrations in the atmosphere at a level that would prevent dangerous anthropogenic interference with the climate system'.

This central objective is followed by five Principles (see the Summary) in which signatories agreed to 'protect the climate system for the benefit of present and future generations of humankind' and 'take precautionary measures to anticipate, prevent or minimize the causes of climate change and mitigate its adverse effects'. The treaty also states that 'Where there are threats of serious or irreversible damage, lack of full scientific certainty should not be used as a reason for postponing such measures'.

Subsequent developments in the Climate Convention have left the treaty's early promise unfulfilled. The very moderate targets it contained to constrain greenhouse gas emissions – that the industrialized countries should constrain emissions to 1990 levels – were unmet. Its main product to date is the failed Kyoto Protocol (see below). Nevertheless, it defines a landscape within which an effective and equitable system can be constructed – subject to one important exception: the country-based or 'territorial accounting' approach it embodies for allocating responsibility for greenhouse gas emissions.

Territorial accounting The targets set by the Climate Convention are allocated to countries, an approach inherited by the Kyoto Protocol and by implication the Bali Roadmap. The whole idea of territorial accounting is hard to justify, however – it has rather just been assumed that this is how it should be done. This may simply be because the parties to international climate negotiations are governments, and governments have a natural tendency to see themselves as the key players.

In fact there are many good reasons for abandoning this approach. 'Embodied carbon' is freely traded across national boundaries, in energy, energy products, electricity, manufactured goods and services from telecoms to tourism. There is no particular reason to hold responsible the country in which the actual emission takes place. It could just as well be the country where the end product is consumed, or where the factory emitting the carbon is owned.

As Richard Wing asks in a letter to *New Scientist*,[4] 'If a Japanese company owns a factory in China which is making goods to sell to customers in the US, then whose emissions are they?' Adding to the complexity of the problem, the factory might be burning Australian coal and Iranian oil, produced by corporations domiciled in Europe or Singapore, owned by shareholders scattered across the globe.

Under the UNFCCC system Wing's question has a clear answer, if not a fair one: the emissions 'belong' to China. This approach has unhelpful consequences. For example, it has encouraged rich countries to deindustrialize and shift their manufacturing base to developing countries such as China, India, Malaysia, Mexico and Brazil. Most of the incentive for this has probably come from lower labour costs, but the avoidance of controls on greenhouse gas emissions has also played a part.

The products are still consumed in the rich countries, yet the emissions associated with their production have moved to the developing countries, so absolving the rich countries of formal responsibility, and moving those emissions outside the scope of controls on industrialized-country emissions. Additional emissions will also be generated from air and sea freight. This entire process has been examined by economists Dieter Helm, Robin Smale and Jonathan Phillips, who find that

> On the UNFCCC basis, UK greenhouse gas emissions have fallen by 15% since 1990. In contrast, on a consumption basis, the illustrative outcome is a rise in emissions of 19% over the same period. This is a dramatic reversal of fortune. It merits an immediate, more detailed and more robust assessment. It suggests that the decline in greenhouse gas emissions from the

UK economy may have been to a considerable degree an illusion. Trade may have displaced the UK's greenhouse gas appetite elsewhere. This illustration of consumption-based measurement delivers a total for UK emissions that is 72% higher in 2003 than under the UNFCCC method.[5]

One solution would be to create a more sophisticated system of territorial accounting, in which the emissions associated with a product or service are transferred with the product from country to country until accounted in the territory of consumption. To do this, however, would involve an enormous carbon audit and accounting exercise which would be both error prone and highly costly.

The solution proposed by Kyoto2 is therefore to do away with territorial accounting altogether, and replace it with 'upstream accounting' based on the production of fossil fuels, and of other industrial non-fossil greenhouse gases (see Chapter 4).

The Kyoto Protocol

> 'The genius of the market system is that it responds flexibly, if imperfectly, to a future that will not have been predicted. But when it is created through political action, rather than emerging spontaneously, business will seek to influence its design for commercial advantage.' John Kay, *Financial Times*[6]

When the Kyoto Protocol, a treaty subordinate to the Climate Convention, was adopted on 11 December 1997, it looked like a positive step. It committed industrialized 'Annex 1' countries to legally binding reductions in greenhouse gas emissions of – on average – 5.2 per cent below 1990 levels between 2008 and 2012, with the US target set at 7 per cent. But from the moment it was agreed, it has been beset by problems.

Delays and non-ratification The Kyoto Protocol only came into force over seven years after it was agreed, on 11 February 2005. The world's biggest greenhouse gas emitter, the USA, never ratified it, however, and in June 2001 George W. Bush's administration rejected it entirely – despite the original Climate Convention having been signed by Bush's father, George Bush Senior.[7]

The other major non-ratifier has been Australia (despite being allowed to increase its greenhouse gas emissions by 8 per cent from 1990 levels). Australia formally ratified in early 2008, however, following a change of government. Canada, which ratified on 17 December 2002, has since announced its intention not to fulfil its obligations; its emissions have risen by about 30 per cent since that time.

No targets for developing countries Non-Annex 1 countries, including China, India, Brazil, Mexico and Indonesia, where greenhouse gas emissions are rising fastest, have no obligations to limit their greenhouse gas emissions and no targets to achieve. The phenomenal rate of increase of their emissions has shocked the world. From 2005 to 2006 China's CO_2 emissions rose by an astonishing 7.5 per cent, and in 2006 China overtook the USA as the world's biggest producer of the gas by an 8 per cent margin, thanks largely to soaring coal-fired power generation and cement production.[8]

As noted by Michael Raupach, leader of CSIRO's Continental Biogeochemical Cycles research team,

> The growth rate in emissions is strongest in rapidly developing economies, particularly China. Together, the developing and least-developed economies (forming 80% of the world's population) accounted for 73% of global emissions growth in 2004 but only 41% of global emissions and only 23% of global cumulative emissions since the mid-18th century.[9]

Ineffective, inefficient and abuse-prone flexibility mechanisms The Kyoto Protocol includes three 'flexibility mechanisms' that allow Annex 1 countries that miss their targets to fulfil their treaty obligations by buying in reductions in greenhouse gas emissions from other countries. These are:

1 The Clean Development Mechanism (CDM) under which projects to reduce greenhouse gas emissions in developing countries can generate 'Certified Emission Reductions' (CERs). This is the most important mechanism. It has two objectives: to contribute to the sustainable development of the host country; and to allow Annex 1 countries to meet their emissions reductions targets in a cost-efficient way.
2 Joint Implementation (JI), which operates in the same way as the CDM but between Annex 1 countries, producing 'Emissions Reduction Units' (ERUs). Typically the JI projects take place in 'transition economies' such as those of the former Soviet Union, where emissions reductions can be obtained most cheaply.
3 Emissions Trading (ET), which allows Annex 1 (industrialized) countries undershooting their Kyoto Protocol greenhouse gas emissions targets to sell their surplus rights to other Annex 1 countries that are exceeding their targets. These are denominated in 'Assigned Amount Units' (AAUs). In practice ET applies primarily to the huge reduction in CO_2 emissions in Russia and Ukraine following the collapse of the Soviet Union and the ensuing economic decline (now partially reversed). Such emissions reductions are widely known as 'hot air'.

These mechanisms have created a dynamic and for some highly profitable business sector, with a substantial trade in an assortment of instruments related to reductions in greenhouse gas emissions currently worth over $10 billion per year, and rising. In some cases, however, the emissions reductions are entirely notional, and in the worst cases greenhouse gas emissions are actually being stimulated by the Kyoto Protocol, rather than reduced. In general, the flexibility mechanisms have achieved meagre benefits at a high cost. (See below for a description of how dubious CERs with a market value of $4.7 billion were produced for a technology investment of $100 million.)

There have also been widespread accusations of fraud and deception over projects for the CDM. For example, hydropower now accounts for a quarter of projects submitted to the CDM Executive Board (EB). Thus International Rivers[10] finds that 96 per cent of the Chinese hydropower projects submitted for CDM registration, or already registered, are expected to start generating credits within two years of their validation comment period, while 35 per cent of projects were complete by the time of registration. Large hydro projects typically take several years to prepare, however, and four to eight years to build. Barbara Haya's report for IR concludes:

> More than a third of the hydros approved ('registered') by the EB were already completed at the time of registration and almost all were already under construction. In China, the world's most prolific dam-builder, the majority of large hydro projects nearing completion are now applying for CDM credits. Yet there has been no substantial increase in the number of hydros under construction compared to recent years when hydros did not receive any credits. Most credits that may be generated by these projects should therefore be considered to be 'hot air' – fake credits which will increase global greenhouse gas emissions.[11]

Furthermore, many of these hydro projects are incompatible with the 'sustainable development' purpose of the CDM – which is entirely self-policed by the governments of the countries in which projects take place, with no further oversight. Several are implicated in serious human rights abuses, and considerable environmental destruction.

CERs derived from industry projects are in many cases no better, contributing to neither emissions reductions nor sustainable development. For example, numerous CDM projects are taking place in the sponge iron operations of Jindal Steel and Power Limited (JSPL), based at Raigarh, India, including four at Patrapali, the largest sponge iron plant in the world, as described by Kevin Smith.[12] In 2005 some ten thousand people protested against its $412 million expansion plans, amid accusations of land-grabbing and gross pollution.

One element of JSPL's expansion plans is an 800,000-tonne-per-year steel plant with a 'non-recovery' coke oven – one which does not recover and reuse the waste heat emitted at a temperature of about 1,100°C.[13] The CDM project is to recover the heat, representing about a quarter of the coal-fired thermal input, and use it to generate power for in-house consumption and export to the grid. The emission of such high-temperature gases is, however, forbidden under India's Energy Conservation Act 2001, while heat recovery is standard industry practice and considered essential to the plant's financial viability. The project is therefore generating no emissions reductions, as claimed. Indeed, the sale of CERs is helping to finance the plant's expansion and thus increase its pollution and combustion of fossil fuels.

An academic appraisal of early CDM projects confirms that few achieved the CDM's twin goals. Christoph Sutter and Juan Carlos Parreño analysed the sixteen CDM projects approved by August 2005: nine renewable power projects, three landfill gas recovery, two HFC-23 reduction, one fuel switch and one energy efficiency measure in housing. They find that eleven of the sixteen projects were failing to deliver additional emissions reductions, while

> So far, there are no registered CDM project activities that have a high rating in additionality and sustainable development. This means that projects registered so far do in the best case contribute to one of the two CDM objectives, but none is contributing to both objectives. In addition, more than 40% of all projects neither have a relevant contribution to sustainable development nor are they likely to generate real emission reductions. That means, they serve none of the two CDM objectives as stated in the Kyoto Protocol.[14]

The amount of Russian and Ukrainian 'hot air' overhanging the market is estimated at 615Mt CO_2 eq.[15] This is four times the UK's entire emissions in 2000. If valued at \$15 per tonne, the Russian/Ukrainian hot air would be worth approaching \$10 billion – the price of Russia's and Ukraine's participation in the Kyoto Protocol. The sale of this hot air would, however, allow many Annex 1 countries to meet their Kyoto obligations without doing anything to reduce their own, or indeed anyone else's, emissions.

The dubious and in some cases wholly negative nature of the benefits arising out of the carbon markets created by the Kyoto Protocol is for many people, however, including some senior politicians, unimportant: it is the carbon market itself which is the point. Gordon Brown made his own position clear when he spoke to WWF in autumn 2007 – that climate policy should conform to the needs of the carbon market:

> Built on the foundation of the EU Emissions Trading Scheme, with the city of London its centre, the global carbon market is already worth 20 billion euros a year, but it could be worth 20 times that by 2030. And that is why we want the 2012 agreement, the post-2012 agreement, to include a binding emissions cap for all developed countries, for only hard caps can create the framework necessary for a global carbon market to flourish.[16]

The F-gas fiasco The Montreal Protocol (see below) has proved to be a powerful instrument for controlling the gases that destroy stratospheric ozone, which are also important greenhouse gases. There are, however, other halogenated hydrocarbons that fall outside the Montreal Protocol as they are not ozone-depleting. These include the HFCs or 'F-gases', which are powerful greenhouse gases: they are now responsible for 1.5 per cent of all global warming, and their contribution is expected to rise to over 8.6 per cent by 2025 if present trends continue.

The most important of these, HFC-23, arises as a by-product of HCFC manufacture (also a powerful greenhouse gas, and a weak ozone depleter that is being phased out under the Montreal Protocol). Other HFCs are manufactured for applications in refrigeration and air-conditioning, such as HFC134a. Measurements on Mount Zeppelin on the Arctic island of Ny-Alesund show that the atmospheric concentration more than doubled between 2001 and 2004.[17]

HFCs are controlled by the Kyoto Protocol, but this has brought little or even negative environmental benefit. In Annex 1 countries the Protocol has been ineffective in accelerating an HFC phase-out. And in developing countries, notably China and India, it is providing a multibillion-dollar windfall for industrialists. By investing the relatively small sum of $100 million in abating HFC-23 emissions from HCFC manufacture, they (and their carbon entrepreneur partners) have been able to sell $4.7 billion worth of carbon credits under the CDM. This has created a perverse incentive to persist with the production of HCFCs – which are, remember, powerful greenhouse gases – for as long as possible, rather than switch to benign alternatives.

The problem was clearly set out by Michael Wara, writing in *Nature*:

> The largest volume of credits, almost 30 percent of the entire market, come from capturing and destroying trifluoromethane (HFC-23), a potent greenhouse gas that is a by-product of the manufacture of refrigerant gases. At current carbon market prices (€10 [US$13] per tonne of CO_2) and neglecting taxes, these HFC-23 credits amount to €4.7 billion up to 2012 (the end of the first compliance period of the Kyoto Protocol). In fact, HFC-23 emitters can earn almost twice as much from CDM credits as they can from selling refrigerant gases – by any measure a major distortion of the market. The distortion exists because it is extremely cheap to cut HFC-23 emissions from these facilities. Indeed, in the industrialized world similar manufacturers have chosen to reduce their emissions voluntarily. An alternative approach to cutting HFC-23 emissions from the small number of refrigerant producers in the developing world (17 at the last count) would be to pay them for the extra cost of installing the simple technology needed to capture and destroy HFC-23. This technological solution would cost the developed world less than €100 million, saving an estimated €4.6 billion in CDM credits that could be spent on other climate-protecting uses.[18]

And as Kevin Smith[19] points out, the windfall profit 'has not gone to the companies and communities who are taking action on clean energy and energy reduction projects, but rather to big, industrial polluters who are then at liberty to reinvest the profits into the expansion of their operations'. He cites the example of Indian industrial conglomerate SRF, which recorded an $87 million profit from HFC-23 credits in 2006/07. Ashish Bharat Ram, the managing director, told the *Economic Times* that 'strong income from carbon trading strengthened us financially, and now we are expanding into areas related to our core strength of chemical and technical textiles business'.[20]

Wara's damning verdict is unarguable: as a subsidy, the CDM 'should be judged by how effectively it reduces emissions for each dollar expended. In these terms, the CDM is a very inefficient subsidy.'[21]

No long-term incentives for investment The Kyoto Protocol has failed to provide the long-term, secure price signals needed to encourage significant investments in low-carbon energy infrastructure, in that:

- The flexibility mechanisms operate in a market fraught with price instability owing to uncertainty over both the demand for, and the supply of, CERs and related instruments, so there is no secure sense of a long-term carbon price.
- No replacement has been agreed to the Kyoto Protocol's first 2008–12 compliance period, and emissions reductions to be sold into that market need to be secured by 2012. Projects delivering emissions reductions beyond 2012 can sell those future credits only into post-2012 markets, which are at present not underpinned by a global climate agreement. This undermines intrinsically viable projects that deliver their returns over a longer period, and so restricts the supply of CERs, raises the CER price, and encourages a 'quick buck' approach among project developers.

This accounts in part for the fact that the Kyoto Protocol has failed to mobilize any significant new funding for energy research; indeed, funding for energy research has declined by 40 per cent since 1980. As the IEA reports,

> ... climate policy uncertainty does weaken investment incentives for low-carbon technologies. Uncertainty could also lead to investment choices that would appear sub-optimal in a world of greater policy certainty. Unfavourable effects of policy uncertainty could include extending the life of existing plant rather than investing in more efficient new plant, modest increases in electricity prices, and the creation of investment cycles that may exacerbate short-term peaks and troughs in generation capacity.[22]

Shipping and aviation omitted Fast-rising emissions from shipping and aviation are exempt from the Kyoto Protocol. Shipping is estimated[23] to produce CO_2 emissions of 1.2Gt/y, while the emissions volume may rise by 75 per cent by 2020 as the volume of world trade increases.

By contrast the entire aviation sector[24] burnt 222Mt of jet fuel in 2004, producing 700Mt of CO_2, about half the amount generated by shipping, and about 1.6 per cent of the global total, while aviation fuel use is projected to rise at 3 per cent per year.[25] The contribution of aviation is greater than that of the CO_2 alone, however, thanks to nitrous oxide and other contrail (exhaust fume) constituents, and a factor between two and three is normally applied to the CO_2 emissions from aviation to account for the additional warming impact.

Thus shipping and aviation combined are contributing about 8 per cent of the overall human climate forcing. These sectors are also fast-growing sources of greenhouse gases, and their percentage contribution is expected to increase. To omit them from any control under the Kyoto Protocol is a substantial failure by any reckoning.

This does not tell the whole story, however. The warming impact of aviation emissions is strongly 'front-loaded', making their short-term impact especially severe, as described by Carey Newsom and Sally Cairns. They consider an aircraft flying in the year 2000:

> For the year 2000 alone, the calculations suggest that the overall

> effect of those emissions is 36 times greater than those of the CO_2 emissions. However, because of their different lifespans, over a 20 year time frame, the effects of all emissions would only be 3.7 times greater than the CO_2 emissions, whilst over a 100 year time frame, the effects would be 1.7 times greater.[26]

This has significant implications for our policy response to climate change. In particular, it means that a drastic curtailment of aviation emissions would rapidly reduce short-term climate forcing. In the event of a 'runaway greenhouse effect' we should be ready to respond in this way – all the more reason for the Climate Convention to take control of aviation emissions.

It is worth noting that shipping emissions have an opposite, short-term cooling effect: the result of the reflective sulphate particles emitted as a result of burning high-sulphur fuel. (See also the discussion of transport sector emissions in Chapter 5.)

Deforestation The Climate Convention highlights the need to preserve and enhance forests and their ability to soak up carbon in Article 4(d), with all parties committing to 'promote and cooperate in the conservation and enhancement, as appropriate, of sinks and reservoirs of all greenhouse gases ... including biomass, forests and oceans as well as other terrestrial, coastal and marine ecosystems'. Yet the clearance and burning of forests have reached unprecedented levels from Brazil to Indonesia, and it is estimated[27] that 18 per cent of global emissions of CO_2 arise from this source.

Although forestry projects are in principle admissible in the CDM, only a single such project has been approved to date. The main reasons for the lack of forestry projects are the bureaucratic burden and the fact that only carbon absorbed by 2012 can be sold into the first commitment period, and forestry projects typically achieve their carbon drawdown over a timescale of about a century. The conservation of existing forests is not accommodated within the CDM, only the establishment of new forests.

The December 2008 meeting of the Climate Convention in Bali

agreed to find a way of incorporating credits based on reduced deforestation into carbon markets. This approach is, however, fraught with danger (see below).

Weak compliance mechanisms The Kyoto Protocol essentially runs on the 'honour system'. In theory countries that fail to comply with their treaty obligations face cuts in their future allocations, but in practice, since future allocations are negotiable, there is no meaningful sanction. The position is stronger only in the EU, as the EU's targets are now reflected in the Union's own legislation. As noted by Scott Barrett, Professor of Environmental Economics at Johns Hopkins University, 'The compliance mechanism, negotiated years after the emission limits were agreed upon, essentially requires that non-complying countries punish themselves for failing to comply – a provision that is unlikely to influence behavior.'[28]

This casts additional uncertainty on the market for CERs and related instruments since some Annex 1 governments may fail to fulfil their obligation to buy CERs, etc., if they have not met their emissions reduction targets. For example, Canada, which has ratified the Kyoto Protocol, is expected to increase its emissions to 38 per cent above 1990 levels by 2010, when it should have cut them by 6 per cent. It has also stated that it will not buy compensatory CERs (or equivalent instruments). Yet as Fred Pearce writes,[29] it may escape any sanction, as the price of its participation in a future agreement.

Rising greenhouse gas emissions As a result of these multiple failures, the Kyoto Protocol has failed to constrain the overall rise of global greenhouse gas emissions, as shown by Raupach:

> CO_2 emissions from fossil-fuel burning and industrial processes have been accelerating at a global scale, with their growth rate increasing from 1.1 percent per year for 1990–1999 to >3 percent per year for 2000–2004. The emissions growth rate since 2000 was greater than for the most fossil-fuel intensive of the Inter-

governmental Panel on Climate Change emissions scenarios developed in the late 1990s. Global emissions growth since 2000 was driven by a cessation or reversal of earlier declining trends in the energy intensity of gross domestic product (GDP) (energy/GDP) and the carbon intensity of energy (emissions/energy), coupled with continuing increases in population and per-capita GDP. Nearly constant or slightly increasing trends in the carbon intensity of energy have been recently observed in both developed and developing regions. No region is decarbonizing its energy supply.[30]

Inadequate funding for adaptation Under the Climate Convention's Principle 1 developed countries 'should take the lead in combating climate change and the adverse effects thereof'. The Kyoto Protocol created three funds to support adaptation:

- The Adaptation Fund (AF), which exists 'to finance concrete adaptation projects and programmes in developing countries that are Parties to the Kyoto Protocol'. It is funded by a 2 per cent tax on transactions under the CDM except those arising from 'least developed countries'. It contained about $3 million by the time of the Climate Convention talks in Nairobi in November 2006, and is likely to contain no more than $500 million by 2012.[31]
- The Least Developed Countries Fund (LDCF), aimed specifically at the LDCs to help them prepare and implement national adaptation programmes of action (NAPAs). The LDCF is operated by the Global Environment Facility (GEF), and funded by voluntary contributions. As of May 2006 receipts and pledges amounted to $87.5 million,[32] rising to 'over $150 million'.[33]
- The Special Climate Change Fund (SCCF), to finance projects relating to adaptation, technology transfer, capacity building, energy, transport, industry, agriculture, forestry, waste management and economic diversification. The SCCF is operated by the GEF, and funded by voluntary contributions. As of May 2006 receipts and pledges amounted to $45.4 million.[34]

These sums are inadequate in the face of likely demand for climate change adaptation funding of the order of $100 billion per year (see Chapter 6).

No scientific or economic basis The Kyoto Protocol has no firm scientific or economic basis, having emerged from a maelstrom of negotiation and horse trading dominated by national, political and commercial vested interests. The Kyoto targets relate to neither environmental nor economic objectives, as described by William Nordhaus:

> The most fundamental defect of the Kyoto Protocol is that the policy lacks any connection to ultimate economic or environmental policy objectives. The approach of freezing emissions at a given historical level for a group of countries is not related to any identifiable goals for concentrations, temperature, costs, or damages. Nor does it bear any relation to an economically oriented strategy that would balance the costs and benefits of greenhouse-gas reductions.[35]

In conclusion The Kyoto Protocol was almost certainly the best that could be agreed to at the time – as evidenced by the slow pace of subsequent ratification and the continued non-participation of the USA. But it has failed. Most fundamentally, it is a 'cap and trade' system, but without an overall cap – leaving only the 'trade' element. So while it has given rise to a multibillion-dollar carbon trading sector, actual emissions of greenhouse gases have remained on a steep upwards trajectory. In creating the global carbon trading business, the Kyoto Protocol has created a powerful institutional vested interest for the continuance of the fundamentally flawed approach that it represents.

The Bali Roadmap

The agreements that emerged from the December 2007 meeting of the Climate Convention in Bali, Indonesia, are collectively known as the Bali Roadmap. It is important to realize that the roadmap is not about actual policy on climate change, but about what can be talked about in further talks over what is to happen when the first 'commitment period' of the Kyoto Protocol expires in 2012: in Poznan, Poland, in December 2008, then in Copenhagen, Denmark, in December 2009.

The main advances in the roadmap are the commitments to be negotiated: reducing emissions from forest destruction by somehow including forest conservation in the carbon trading regime; financing the adaptation needs of developing countries; and funding the transfer of low-carbon technologies to developing nations. This certainly looks like progress, if of a limited nature.

While there is an urgent need to reduce emissions from deforestation, there are considerable dangers in including forests within the carbon trading regime. We need to cut industrial greenhouse gas emissions, and to save the world's forests, not one or the other. By putting carbon credits from 'reduced emissions from forest degradation and destruction' (REDD) into the Kyoto Protocol's carbon trading regime, we are accepting that the Annex 1 countries will be able to continue to pollute at will, provided they offset their pollution by reducing emissions from deforestation elsewhere.

And the negative experience of the CDM in the relatively straightforward areas in which it has operated to date inspires little confidence in its ability to encompass the far trickier area of emissions from deforestation. Will the reductions in emissions from deforestation that are traded be genuinely additional? Our experience of the CDM suggests not. Will the projects contribute to sustainable development? Again, the human rights abuses and environmental destruction that have characterized many CDM projects to date indicate that sustainability will not be a high priority.

Will the rights of the world's 1.6 billion traditional forest owners, users and dwellers, including indigenous peoples, be strengthened or weakened? Without strong rules for their protection, diligently upheld at every level, their interests are likely to be swept aside – just as they would be for a dam, a plantation or an industrial zone. As Friends of the Earth International states in its *Forests Declaration*, there is a danger of 'further displacement, conflict and violence' as forests increase in value and 'are declared off-limits to communities that live in them or depend on them for their livelihoods'.[36]

The danger is well expressed by Deepak Rughani and Almuth Ernsting when they warn of likely support for

> vast industrial tree plantations, which are wrongly classified as 'afforestation and reforestation'. Clear-felling followed by the planting of eucalyptus monocultures will continue to be classified as 'reforestation' and 'forest protection' will thus continue to drive the destruction of the biodiverse natural forests and other essential ecosystems – and of the livelihoods of ever larger numbers of communities.[37]

There are also valid concerns about the framework under which forestry emissions reductions are likely to be assessed. The most likely way in which forest carbon credits will be generated under a REDD system is by demonstrating reductions in emissions against a historic baseline. This gives countries with large forest endowments an interest in increasing deforestation in order to establish a high baseline, and so increase future payments.

In order to preserve the principle of 'additionality' this approach would also exclude from the carbon market the protection of forests already deemed to be 'safe' by virtue of protected status. But such designations confer little or no real protection on the ground in many tropical countries, notably in Indonesia (host of the Bali conference). Paradoxically, this means that areas designated for special protection as national parks, nature reserves, etc., by virtue of their biological importance, are likely to be specifically excluded from protection under REDD carbon trading.

Holding rather greater promise were the agreements among the Annex 1 countries about what they plan to achieve after 2012, which took place during parallel discussions in the 'Ad Hoc Working Group on Further Commitments for Annex 1 Parties Under the Kyoto Protocol' (AWG). As reported by David Steven, the Annex 1 countries (except the USA) accepted that:[38]

- globally, emissions need to peak in the next ten to fifteen years, before falling to 'very low levels' – well under half of 2000 levels by 2050;
- industrialized countries must take the lead and reduce their emissions by 25–40 per cent in 2020–30, and show that they are taking things seriously;
- developing countries will have to come into the agreement, inspired by the rich countries' example, to deliver far greater global cuts by 2050.

So where is the post-2012 process really going? It is hard to feel optimistic so long as the framework for future agreement is that of the failed Kyoto Protocol. As Deepak Rughani argues, all that the Bali Roadmap really promises is 'an exercise in more extensive emissions trading and offsetting' under 'inherently dysfunctional' regimes.[39] There is some hope, however, in the emergence of a new willingness to move forward collectively and solve the problem of global warming. The challenge will be to get a new framework in place that can be effective, just and attract broad international support, and it will not be easy.

The EU's Emissions Trading Scheme (EUETS)

> 'The sensible concept is that some business and industrial sectors will find it easy to achieve lower carbon, others will not. If those that can make above average reductions are able to sell permits to those that struggled to reach that target, the overall result will be greater effect at lower cost. But lawyers were needed to give effect to this broad principle with audited and enforceable rules. Lobbyists followed. Investment banks salivate at the prospect of new speculative markets. So instead of a simple mechanism for transferring credits between businesses, we have an online, real-time market in which the price of carbon fluctuates wildly to the benefit of day traders and the detriment of long-run guidance on investment.' John Kay, *Financial Times*[40]

The EUETS is the means by which the EU aims to meet the 8 per cent emissions reduction allocated to it in the Kyoto Protocol. Unlike the Protocol itself, the EUETS is a proper cap-and-trade system; it has been damaged, however, by a number of serious flaws since its inception on 1 January 2005.

- Phase 1 of the EUETS applies only to the emissions from the largest greenhouse gas emitters, such as power stations and other major industrial plant, responsible for only about 40 per cent of all emissions in the EU.
- The 'allowances' to emit greenhouse gases were 'grandfathered' – given away to the biggest polluters in proportion to their historic emissions. This both reduced the incentive for technological innovation, and handed electricity generators as much as €30 billion per year in surplus profits as they traded their surplus allowances, and passed the price of their allowances (EUAs) on to electricity consumers, although they were received at no cost. In the UK alone Ofgem estimates the cost to consumers will be £9 billion from 2008 to 2012, or 17 per cent of the wholesale price of electricity.[41] It has also estimated that the EUETS will add £31 per year to the average British electricity bill for 2008.[42]
- In Phase 1 of the EUETS (2005–07), EUAs were over-allocated by national governments under pressure from their industries by 65Mt CO_2 eq more than actual emissions in 2005, and 30Mt in 2006. So the system produced no reduction in emissions. Following a price spike of €30/t CO_2 eq in April 2006 the price declined below €1 in February 2007 and fell to €0.7–0.8 in late 2007, seriously undermining investor confidence in the market.
- Cross-linkages with the Kyoto Protocol market, under which countries will be able to buy in CERs and ERUs from Kyoto markets to meet their EUETS obligations, threaten to undermine the stability of the EUA market and the long-term price signals necessary to stimulate long term investments.
- Emissions from aviation and shipping are not part of the

> EUETS, much as they are omitted from the Kyoto Protocol. From 1990 to 2003, the EU's greenhouse gas emissions from international aviation increased by 73 per cent, or 47Mt CO_2 eq (a growth rate of 4.3 per cent per year).[43]

Thus Peter Atherton of Citigroup, in answer to the question of whether EUETS Phase 1 had achieved its policy goals, replied: 'Prices up, emissions up, profits up ... so, not really. Who wins and loses? All generation-based utilities – winners. Coal and nuclear-based generators – biggest winners. Hedge funds and energy traders – even bigger winners. Losers ... ahem ... consumers!'[44] There have, however, been some important and positive reforms to the EUETS. In Phase 2 (2008–12), more EUAs are to be auctioned rather than grandfathered, allocations are being tightened (by 7 per cent from 2005) to force down greenhouse gas emissions, the scheme is being extended to cover medium-sized emitters, and the Commission has proposed that emissions from aviation (but not shipping) be included from 2011. One possibility is that transport emissions may be regulated 'upstream' at the level of the fuel supplier.

The post-2012 extension of the EUETS (Phase 3) is also agreed in principle, whether or not agreement is reached over a successor to the Kyoto Protocol: in March 2007 all twenty-seven EU leaders agreed to a 20 per cent cut in the EU's greenhouse gas emissions by 2020, and the first trade in 'shadow market' Phase 3 EUAs swiftly following when 50,000 EUAs for delivery in 2013 were traded between Morgan Stanley and RNK Capital LLC at €20.05 on 13 March 2007.

The EC's proposals for EUETS Phase 3 are for 100 per cent auctioning of EUAs to utilities, but with allowances still handed out free of charge to a small number of exempted energy-intensive industries, such as cement, steel and aluminium makers. In all, about 60 per cent of allowances would be auctioned. Only post-2020 in a Phase 4 would this rise to 100 per cent. The scheme will take in additional industries equivalent to an extra 6 per cent of emissions, and will also regulate PFC gases and nitrous oxide. Furthermore, the overall allocation will be down 21 per cent from 2005 levels by 2020. A cap will be set on the volume of EUAs that may be substituted by CERs and ERUs generated under the Kyoto Protocol's CDM and JI, and will exclude forestry-based credits altogether, forcing the majority of emissions reductions to be achieved within Europe.

The EU has also encouraged member states to use the receipts from the auction of EUAs to invest in renewable energy. This is up to member states, however, and the UK for a start has said it has no intention of doing so.[45]

These proposals represent a vast improvement over Phases 1 and 2, and over the Kyoto Protocol itself. One intriguing possibility is that the EUETS itself may provide the basis of an improved future climate regime, if non-EU countries and states are permitted (and want) to join. The EUETS has created a far bigger marketplace than the Kyoto Protocol: the global carbon market turns over about 1Gt of CO_2 eq a year, worth some $30–50 billion, of which over 80 per cent is traded under the EUETS, and only 10 per cent under the Kyoto Protocol's flexibility mechanisms. And the EUETS reforms now under way demonstrate its ability to learn from past errors. A reformed and globalized EUETS may offer one route towards an effective global climate mechanism.

But there remain major obstacles to overcome. We need 100 per cent auctioning well before 2020. And we need to dispense with the archaic system whereby EUAs are allocated by the Commission to member states, whose governments then grant them or sell them to their industries. The entire process of national allocations is unnecessary, inefficient and undermines the principle of a single European carbon market. Indeed, as the EUETS moves towards 100 per cent auctioning of EUAs, the perpetuation of national allocations comes to represent nothing more than an income stream for governments, incentivizing them to clamour for greater allocations and collectively undermine moves towards tightening overall caps.

The Montreal Protocol

The most effective international treaty for controlling greenhouse gas emissions to date is the 'Montreal Protocol on Substances that Deplete the Ozone Layer', an international treaty under the 1987 'Vienna Convention for the Protection of the Ozone Layer'. The Montreal Protocol, which came into force on 1 January 1989, uses a 'direct regulation' approach to phase out the production of chlorinated and brominated hydrocarbons responsible for depleting the stratospheric ozone that protects the Earth's surface from dangerous UV-B radiation, with timetables set for each chemical. It gave the '5(1)' developing countries more time to comply, and created a Multilateral Fund with some US$2 billion to invest in technology transfer to help the 5(1) countries achieve their targets.

The Montreal Protocol has been highly effective. The extent of ozone depletion now appears to have peaked in the late 1990s[46] and the chemicals responsible are on a downward trend, although recovery will not be complete until the late twenty-first century. It has also proved highly effective in reducing global warming owing to the fact that the controlled gases are powerful greenhouse gases, up to ten thousand times stronger than CO_2. Indeed, as the Netherlands Environmental Assessment Agency (NEAA) reported on 5 March 2007:

> The 1987 Montreal Protocol – restricting the use of ozone-depleting substances – has helped to both reduce global warming and protect the ozone layer. Without this protocol, the amount of heat trapped due to ozone-depleting substances would be double that of today. The benefits to the climate, achieved by the Montreal Protocol alone, at present greatly exceed the initial target of the Kyoto Protocol.[47]

Guus Velders[48] estimated that the Kyoto Protocol will, by 2012, reduce annual greenhouse gas emissions by 2Gt CO_2 eq, compared to 8Gt for the Montreal Protocol – subject to a 30 per cent reduction to account for ozone's role as a greenhouse gas and other factors, giving us a net 5.6Gt CO_2 eq. 'This reduction, most of which has already occurred, is substantially greater than the first Kyoto reduction target,' he observes. And as the NEAA pointed out,

> New measures under the Montreal Protocol can result in additional, significant climate benefits, compared to the Kyoto Protocol reduction target. These new measures consist of removing CFCs present in existing applications (refrigerators, foams), and of limiting the production of not fully halogenated fluorocarbons (HCFCs), and/or of implementing the use of alternative gases with lower global warming potentials.[49]

Their call was taken up in September 2007 when, combining options proposed by Argentina, Brazil, Norway, Switzerland, the USA, Mauritania, Mauritius and Micronesia, the world's governments signed up to an accelerated freeze and phase-out of HCFCs at the Montreal Protocol's twentieth anniversary meeting, bringing existing deadlines forward by a decade. UNEP's research indicates that the agreement

> could, over the coming decades, deliver cumulative emission reductions over the equivalent to perhaps 18 to 25Gt CO_2eq depending on the success of governments in encouraging new ozone and climate-friendly alternatives. Annually, it could represent a cut equal to over 3.5 percent of all the world's current greenhouse emissions.[50]

Indeed, the benefits could prove even greater, according to the Montreal Protocol's Technology and Economic Assessment Panel:

> Close to 38 Gt CO_2eq [could be abated] if the acceleration is accompanied by the recovery and destruction of old equipment and insulating foam and improvements in energy efficiency. For example a faster switch to alternatives to HCFCs may well stimulate technological innovation including a more rapid introduction of energy efficient equipment that in turn will assist in reducing greenhouse gas emissions even further.[51]

This record of genuine achievement compares favourably with the Kyoto Protocol (see above), which is expected to cause reductions in greenhouse gas emissions of no more than 2Gt CO_2 eq per year by 2012.[52] This relatively easy and rapid success of the Montreal Protocol in tackling greenhouse gas emissions stands in stark contrast to the slow, meagre and expensive gains achieved under the Kyoto Protocol. This strongly suggests that there is a role for direct regulation, also backed by a 'Multilateral Fund' or similar instrument, in a future climate protocol. More on this in Chapter 6.

The biofuel disaster

From 2008, all UK fuel suppliers must get 2.5 per cent of their fuel from plants, rising to 5 per cent in 2010. In the EU as a whole, biofuels are to provide 5.75 per cent of transport fuel by 2010, and 10 per cent by 2020. And as Ronald Steenblik reports for the Global Subsidies Initiative in *Biofuels – At What Cost?*, the cost to taxpayers is enormous: €3.7 billion in 2006, mainly in reduced tax rates.[53]

In the USA tax breaks are driving a similar rush into biofuels, mainly ethanol fermented from grain crops. Current world production of bioethanol is 40 billion litres, of which 48 per cent is produced in the USA – backed by more than two hundred support measures costing $5.5–7.3 billion a year or US$0.38–0.49 per litre of petroleum equivalent for ethanol.[54]

These measures are largely justified by the perception of biofuels as 'carbon neutral'. But even on the most optimistic figures biofuels are a very expensive way of reducing carbon emissions. For the EU, *Biofuels – At What Cost?* reports costs/tCO_2 of 'between €575 and €800 for ethanol made from sugarbeet, around €215 for biodiesel made from used cooking oil, and over €600 for biodiesel made from rapeseed'. For corn-based ethanol in the USA the cost is 'some $500 in federal and state subsidies'. These figures compare with current prices in the EUETS of about €20/tCO_2, and $20 under the CDM.[55]

But the truth is even worse. Bioethanol from corn, wheat or

barley appears to be 'carbon negative' – demanding an energy input representing 129 per cent of its energy content, taking in the energy cost of fertilizers, tractor fuel, fermentation, distillation and industrial plant, as found by David Pimentel.[56]

Critics do not consider Pimentel's study as definitive, however. In his useful 'study of studies' on the efficiency of biofuels, Simon Fairlie finds a consensus that the energy cost of biodiesel is between 40 and 60 per cent of its final yield, while estimates for bioethanol are higher and more divergent, ranging up from the US Department of Agriculture's figure of 74 per cent to the British Association of Biofuels and Oils figure of 90 per cent and Pimentel's 129 per cent.[57]

This is not the whole story, however: add in the bacterial decomposition of nitrate in soil and groundwater to the greenhouse gas nitrous oxide (N_2O) and the figures get considerably worse. This was shown in 2007 by Nobel Prize-winner Paul Crutzen:

> When the extra N_2O emission from biofuel production is calculated in 'CO_2-equivalent' global warming terms, and compared with the quasi-cooling effect of 'saving' emissions of fossil fuel derived CO_2, the outcome is that the production of commonly used biofuels, such as biodiesel from rapeseed and bioethanol from corn (maize), can contribute as much or more to global warming by N_2O emissions than cooling by fossil fuel savings. [...] the relatively large emission of N_2O exacerbates the already huge challenge of getting global warming under control.[58]

Biodiesel has also become a major driver of deforestation in South-East Asia, especially Indonesia, as thousands of square kilometres of rainforest – much of it on deep peat soils – are burnt to make way for palm oil plantations every year. A Wetlands International study shows that to save 1 tonne of fossil CO_2 emissions with oil palm biodiesel means emitting eleven times more from forest and peatland destruction.[59] Similar figures apply to soya oil from South American forests. 'Drainage of peatland results in very rapid peat decomposition, causing emissions of 70 up to 100 tonnes of carbon dioxide per year per hectare.

The production of one tonne of palm oil therefore results in carbon dioxide emissions of up to 33 tonnes.'[60] Another study by Joseph Fargione of the Nature Conservancy finds that every hectare of rainforest cleared for growing soya to make biodiesel creates a 'biofuel carbon debt' that would take 300 years of biodiesel production to pay off. If the rainforest is cleared in Indonesia to grow palm oil, the carbon debt would take 400 years to repay.[61]

And the rush into biofuels is creating a humanitarian crisis as food prices rise – which is only to be expected since the current 'first generation' biofuels are derived from food crops that would normally be eaten by people and livestock. George Monbiot reports: 'Swaziland is in the grip of a famine and receiving emergency food aid. Forty per cent of its people are facing acute food shortages. So what has the government decided to export? Biofuel made from one of its staple crops, cassava. [...] This is one of many examples of a trade described last month by Jean Ziegler, the UN's special rapporteur, as "a crime against humanity".'[62]

Or, as the *World Development Report 2008* explains:

> Biofuel production has pushed up feedstock prices. The clearest example is maize, whose price rose by over 60 percent from 2005 to 2007, largely because of the US ethanol program combined with reduced stocks in major exporting countries. Feedstock supplies are likely to remain constrained in the near term. [...] Rising agricultural crop prices caused by demand for biofuels have come to the forefront in the debate about a potential conflict between food and fuel. The grain required to fill the tank of a sports utility vehicle with ethanol (240 kilograms of maize for 100 liters of ethanol) could feed one person for a year; this shows how food and fuel compete. Rising prices of staple crops can cause significant welfare losses for the poor, most of whom are net buyers of staple crops.[63]

As for the future, further increases in biofuel use will further squeeze food supplies and increase greenhouse gas emissions – and at huge public cost, according to *Biofuels – At What Cost?*:

Already, the level of support enjoyed by the industry in OECD countries in 2007 is probably of the order of US$13–15 billion a year, for a pair of fuels that account for less than 3 percent of overall liquid transport fuel demand on an energy-equivalent basis. Bringing that share to 30 percent – a level frequently suggested by proponents – without making radical changes to the current support system, and without substantially reducing the demand for transport fuels, would imply annual subsidies of US$100 billion a year or more.[64]

Speaking in early 2008 on the BBC's *Today* programme, EU Environment Commissioner Stavros Dimas admitted that social and environmental problems had emerged and that there was a need to 'move ahead very carefully' and apply 'sustainability criteria' to palm oil used in biodiesel to ensure that rainforest was not destroyed in order to produce it – even at the expense of missing the EU's biofuel targets.[65]

Such is the nature of global commodity markets, however, that the move, however well intentioned, may make little difference. The EU's exports of rapeseed oil to China for food have fallen as the oil is diverted into biofuel, and China is consequently buying more palm oil to supply its food needs. Indeed, it now appears that much of the palm originally planted for biofuels is now being diverted into food use since the price is higher.

The effect has been studied by Timothy Searchinger and colleagues with reference to the USA, and they find that previous analyses have 'failed to count the carbon emissions that occur as farmers worldwide respond to higher prices and convert forest and grassland to new cropland to replace the grain (or cropland) diverted to biofuels'. Taking into account this effect, corn-based ethanol 'nearly doubles greenhouse emissions over 30 years and increases greenhouse gases for 167 years'. Even biofuels from switchgrass, grown on former corn lands, increase emissions by half. 'This result raises concerns about large biofuel mandates and highlights the value of using waste products.'[66]

This implies that the EU's application of sustainability criteria will have little effect, if any, in reducing rainforest loss in Indonesia and other palm oil producing countries. World production of edible oils is already struggling to meet food demand and any diversion of that supply into biofuels – no matter how sustainable that particular element of the supply – will push at the 'agricultural envelope' and force its expansion into forests. This is evidenced by the recent increase in deforestation in the Amazon, where as many as 7,000 square miles of forest were cleared for cattle and soya farming between August and December 2007.[67]

So where did it all go wrong? The answer lies in the origins of the biofuel support measures, which were assiduously pushed by two powerful lobbies. First, the car manufacturers: facing public and regulatory pressure to reduce their cars' contribution to global warming, they worked hard to shift the emphasis on to the fuel their cars burnt. Second, big agriculture, including giant agro-industrial combines such as Archer Daniels Midlands (ADM), backed by powerful farming and landowning constituencies in the USA and Europe. As Matthew Wald wryly observed in *Scientific American*, 'Unfortunately, net energy and pollution considerations may not have played much of a role in the federal government's 2005 setting of a "renewable fuel standard" for 2012 or in giving ethanol a 51-cent-per-gallon tax break. "Congress didn't do a life-cycle analysis; it did an ADM analysis", says one federal official with long-term experience in energy and pollution.'[68]

UK taxes, levies and subsidies

The UK has a number of taxes and levies of various sorts relevant to greenhouse gas emissions. They are listed here – at the risk of appearing parochial – because they provide an exemplar of how policies, programmes and initiatives can accrete over time into a complex interacting web, prone to unforeseen consequences of various sorts.

- The Climate Change Levy on the use of energy by business, which creates carbon savings at a cost of £18–40/tC (£5–11/tCO_2).

- Air Passenger Duty, raised on flights leaving UK airports. Current levels are set in bands between £10 and £80 depending on the type of flight. Costs imposed vary from over £100/tCO_2 eq to under £15/tCO_2 eq.
- Vehicle Excise Duty (road tax), raised at a higher rate on high-emission vehicles of up to £215 (due to rise to £400) per year.
- Fuel Duty of about 50p/litre (or 57p for diesel), plus VAT, bringing total tax on a litre of petrol to about 64p. At 2.315 Kg of CO_2/litre, the effective greenhouse tax on petrol (excluding VAT) is £216/tCO_2.
- The UK's 'Renewables Obligation' (RO), which requires electricity retailers to buy a growing proportion of their electricity from renewable sources, or pay a penalty that is recycled to other retailers (see Box 4.1).
- The UK's Non Fossil Fuel Obligation (NFFO), a now-superseded policy dating back to 1990. A a substantial part of the UK's renewable electricity, however, is provided under NFFO contracts. This production also counts towards the RO, in the process producing an unanticipated financial surplus worth £550 million to £1 billion by 2010,[69] which has been commandeered by the Treasury for general expenditures. The long-term contracts now being proposed by Ofgem would represent a return to an NFFO-like system.
- The anomalous subsidy on domestic fuel and electricity by way of the reduced rate of VAT of 5 per cent (in effect a negative tax compared to other purchases – such as those of insulation materials), worth about 1p per unit of electricity, producing 0.2Kg CO_2, so a 'tax' of -£50/tCO_2.
- The 'Energy Efficiency Commitment' (EEC), which requires energy suppliers to invest in reducing energy demand among customers by raising their efficiency. Costs have ranged from negative (that is, bringing a direct economic benefit) to £60/tC (£16/tCO_2).
- The Carbon Emissions Reduction Target (CERT), which in April 2008 replaced the EEC, approximately doubling the

activity under the EEC to produce a lifetime reduction in carbon dioxide emissions of 154 million tonnes. Under CERT energy suppliers must direct at least 40 per cent of carbon savings at low-income and elderly consumers in order to reduce 'fuel poverty'.

- A commitment to refund stamp duty on the sale of new homes that achieve the 'zero-carbon' standard, up to £15,000, until 2012 – a scheme which now appears unlikely to benefit more than a handful of people following a surprise tightening of the 'zero carbon' definition.

This complex mix of taxes, levies, obligations and subsidies sends out confused signals, creates unintended interactions and opportunities for double or treble counting. In particular no consistent 'carbon price' emerges, and the carbon prices reflected by these different mechanisms cover a wide range, between £216/tCO_2 for fuel duty (on the admittedly unsustainable assumption that 100 per cent of the fuel duty reflects climate change costs) and around £100/tCO_2 for the Renewables Obligation, down to -£50/tCO_2 (that is, a £50 'carbon subsidy') through the reduced rate of VAT on domestic fuel and electricity.

As Steven Sorrell and Jos Slim comment,

> The complex, elaborate and interdependent mix of climate policies developed in the UK provides a particularly rich example of the challenges to be faced. [...] The net result may be a mix of overlapping, interacting, and conflicting instruments which lack any overall coherence. In short, a policy mix may easily become a policy mess.[70]

The unsatisfactory situation led the House of Commons Select Committee on Environmental Audit to call for a strategic review of government actions on climate change and to create a new policy framework:

> The organic process by which the Government has sought to address climate change has led to a confusing framework that cannot be said to promote effective action on reducing emis-

sions. There is now a need for a strategic review of Government action to ensure that the leadership and responsibility for the development and delivery of climate change mitigation and adaptation policies is clear. This is especially important given the myriad different bodies involved. In addition to this it is essential to develop a new long-term policy framework to ensure that policies introduced today do not undermine our ability to reduce emissions in the future.[71]

To this complex mix must now be added the Climate Change Act (Climate Change Bill at the time of writing), which creates a legal obligation for the UK government to achieve emissions cuts of 60 per cent by 2050 from 1990 levels, with an intermediate target at 2020 (excluding international shipping and aviation). A national 'carbon budget' will be set every five years, and government ministers must publish an annual progress report. The Act aims to achieve a global stabilization of greenhouse gases at 550ppm CO_2 eq by 2050, widely considered too high. Many NGOs are consequently calling for 80 per cent emissions cuts consistent with stabilization at 450ppm.

The Climate Change Act is a unique and ambitious example of environmental legislation. It contains no actual measures to achieve its objectives, however. As we have seen above, the UK's approach to achieving cuts in greenhouse gas emissions is at best paradoxical. If the Act is to be effective, more coordinated, consistent and effective approaches will need to be adopted, perhaps along the lines that are being pioneered in California.

California

The saying goes that whatever California is doing now, the rest of the USA will be doing in ten or twenty years' time. In the case of climate change, this prospect offers some hope for the future. While the US federal government, under President George W. Bush, has done its best to block progress on tackling climate change, the Republican 'Governator' of California, Arnold Schwarzenegger, has enacted an astonishing series of measures

Box 2.1 The Renewables Obligation

The UK's Renewables Obligation represents an excellent example of how market mechanisms can go wrong. Designed by clever economists no doubt motivated by the very best of intentions, the RO began in 2002 and has emerged as among the most expensive and least effective support mechanisms for renewables generation in Europe. It represents a cost to electricity consumers of £50–130/tCO_2 saved, as against the EUETS price of €20 or so[72] – with a total price tag of around £1 billion per year, or £10 per year on the typical electricity bill for 2008, Ofgem estimates.[73]

The RO works by defining increasing year-on-year targets for electricity retailers to meet in sourcing their electricity from renewable sources, which will reach around 20 per cent by 2020. Retailers demonstrate adherence by submitting sufficient Renewables Obligation Certificates (ROCs), which they buy from renewables generators, who are awarded ROCs in proportion to their output. Those retailers submitting insufficient ROCs have to pay a 'buy-out price' to Ofgem, which goes into a pot redistributed to all generators on a per ROC basis.

One reason why the RO is so inefficient is that the main obstacle to new renewables generation arises from 'bottlenecks in the planning system', as reported in the *Financial Times*.[74] As a result willing new entrants are barred from the market while 'cash injections are enriching the operators of existing wind farms well beyond their expectations': in 2007 427MW (megawatts) of new renewable capacity was erected, compared with 650MW in 2006. 'So while the amount paid in subsidy by consumers increases steadily, the amount of electricity produced from wind, and other renewables, is rising only slowly. Existing wind farms are therefore making bigger profits than ever, from a combination of higher subsidies and a higher electricity price. Indeed, according to calculations made by Ofgem, the electricity regulator, the high electricity price of more than £50 per megawatt hour means wind farms in favourable locations with strong winds could be profitable without the subsidy.'

Another factor is that many of the ROCs arise from old renewable plant contracted under the Non Fossil Fuel Obligation (NFFO), which predates the RO. In this case the income from ROCs, and any premium on the price of electricity, accrues to the NFFO Fund, operated by Ofgem. The Treasury now considers this highly profitable fund to constitute a 'hereditary revenue of the Crown' (along with revenues from the Crown's traditional rights to treasure trove, swans and sturgeons), and so carries out an annual raid on NFFO Fund surpluses. It has been estimated by the National Audit Office[75] that these will amount to £550 million to £1 billion by 2010. Much of the sum paid by consumers to finance the RO is therefore in effect a tax, which goes directly into general government revenues rather than supporting renewable energy.[76]

By contrast, renewable electricity in Germany is supported by the use of 'feed-in tariffs' under the Renewable Energy Law, guaranteeing generators a long-term elevated electricity price. The climate of certainty this creates means that investors demand a lower rate of return, reducing the cost relative to the UK's RO, in which returns are highly uncertain – leading investors to seek a risk premium. Ofgem is now proposing a similar system based on 'long term contracts', which would give renewables generators a fixed, long-term, guaranteed electricity price.

designed to reduce the state's greenhouse gas emissions to just 20 per cent of 1990 levels by 2050. These include:

- A 'million solar roofs' programme.
- The 'Hydrogen Highway' initiative, to catalyse a move towards hydrogen-fuelled transport.
- Plans to increase energy recovery from farm waste and other biomass.
- The 2002 'Pavley law', due to take effect in 2009, which requires car manufacturers to reduce emissions from their vehicles by 30 per cent. This has been challenged in the federal courts by manufacturers, who claim that the state has no power to mandate such standards. If they are upheld, they 'are expected to achieve the greatest absolute emissions reductions from any policy in the world'. The standards have also been adopted by another eleven US states.[77]
- A programme to make the state government's 70,000 vehicles 'the cleanest, greenest in the nation'.[78]
- An energy efficiency investment of $2 billion by the California Public Utilities Commission aimed at cutting energy demand by the equivalent of the output of three large coal-fired power stations, saving 3Mt of CO_2 emissions.
- A 'greenhouse gas performance standard', set by the California Energy Commission, which requires that new power stations emit no more CO_2 per kilowatt hour than a new combined-cycle gas turbine (CCGT).
- A regulation (effective early in 2007) to prevent California's utility companies from buying electricity from inefficient sources elsewhere in the USA, which would lead to CO_2 'leakage'.
- A target to make 20 per cent of California's electricity renewable by 2010, and 33 per cent by 2020.
- The Green Building Initiative, which aims to make state buildings among the most energy efficient in the nation – part of measures to reduce the state government's energy use by 20 per cent over ten years.

These measures are notable for the approach taken – one of

setting demanding standards, and spending public money, in order to achieve a tough but realistic objective.

Direct regulation – other examples

We have already examined the effectiveness of the direct regulation approach of the Montreal Protocol applied at a global level. But there are many other examples of direct regulation in many countries. These include:

- the EU's compulsory energy efficiency labels on domestic appliances, with minimum standards for refrigeration equipment and boilers;
- energy efficiency standards for refrigerators in China;
- the EU's forthcoming restrictions on HFCs in air-conditioners, and the tighter restrictions imposed by Denmark;
- building standards that raise the energy efficiency of buildings in many countries (but which are often inadequate and poorly enforced);
- compulsory energy efficiency surveys on houses for sale in the UK, resulting in an Energy Performance Certificate to be given to prospective buyers in a Home Information Pack;
- car efficiency standards, in place in the USA since 1975, but updated only in 2007 to undemanding levels;
- forthcoming car efficiency standards in the EU of 130g CO_2/km by 2012 (following an ineffective voluntary agreement with the car industry to achieve an average of 140g CO_2/km by 2008) – the UK is now advocating a 100g CO_2/km standard for 2020;
- progressively more stringent car efficiency standards in China, agreed in 2004;
- impending restrictions on the sale of inefficient incandescent light bulbs in Australia, the UK, China and other countries;
- impending UK and EU bans on 'stand-by' buttons, and more efficient circuitry for devices left permanently plugged in on charge;
- impending EU energy efficiency standards for computers, routers and home entertainment systems;

- the UK's Climate Change Act, which commits the government and future governments to reduce the UK's greenhouse gas emissions by 60 per cent by 2050 according to a series of five-year carbon budgets. Gordon Brown is also to consult on a more ambitious target to cut emissions by 80 per cent.

These approaches have been and will continue to be an important aspect of reducing greenhouse gas emissions. They are of particular value where market failures exist, limiting the market signal of fuel and energy costs on purchasers of energy-consuming goods. This theme is pursued in Chapter 5.

The Climate Neutral Network

In February 2007 countries, cities and companies anxious to act seriously on climate change came together under the auspices of UNEP in Monaco to create the Climate Neutral Network (CNN), whose aim is to 'federate the small but growing wave of nations, local authorities and companies who are pledging to significantly reduce emissions en route to zero emission economies, communities and businesses'.[79]

At its founding it included five countries (Costa Rica, Iceland, Norway, New Zealand and Monaco), four cities (Arendal, Norway; Rizhao, China; Vancouver, Canada; and Växjö, Sweden) and five companies (Co-operative Financial Services, UK; Interface Inc., United States; Natura, Brazil; Nedbank, South Africa; and Senoko Power, Singapore).

Each member is adopting its own strategies towards carbon neutrality. Thus Iceland is shifting towards the use of hydrogen derived from geothermal energy, Costa Rica is conducting large-scale reforestation of lands cleared for ranching, New Zealand is developing a wide range of renewable energy sources, and Norway (which already has huge hydroelectric generation capacity) will be capturing CO_2 emissions and storing them in reservoirs beneath the North Sea.

Since the world needs to move rapidly towards zero net greenhouse gas emissions (see Chapter 1), this voluntary initiative appears enormously promising. It appears certain that the founder members will be joined by many others in the months and years to come, as the CNN is opened up to intergovernmental bodies, organizations, civil society groups and even individuals. It is also very interesting as far as Kyoto2 is concerned: the country members of the CNN could develop into a broad carbon-neutral economic zone that could operate Kyoto2 (or a similar system) as a mechanism to deliver its aims and harmonize the activities of its members.

3 | The atmospheric commons

> 'Everyone knows what private wealth is, even if they don't have much of it. [...] But there's another trove of wealth that's not so well-known: our common wealth. Each of us is the joint recipient of a vast inheritance. This shared inheritance includes air and water, habitats and ecosystems, languages and cultures, science and technologies, social and political systems, and quite a bit more. Common wealth is like the dark matter of the economic universe – it's everywhere, but we don't see it. One reason we don't see it is that much of it is, literally, invisible. Who can spot the air, an aquifer, or the social trust that underlies financial markets? The more relevant reason is our own blindness: the only economic matter we notice is the kind that glistens with dollar signs. We ignore common wealth because it lacks price tags and property rights.' Peter Barnes, *Capitalism 3*[1]

Commons or free-for-all?

> '... that which is common to the greatest number has the least care bestowed upon it. Every one thinks chiefly of his own, hardly at all of the common interest; and only when he is himself concerned as an individual. For besides other considerations, everybody is more inclined to neglect the duty which he expects another to fulfil ...' Aristotle, *Politics*[2]

The Kyoto2 approach recognizes the atmosphere as a 'global commons' – a resource that is the common property of humanity, and for that matter of non-human life forms whose needs we also need to recognize and respect. Our present situation is that of a 'tragedy of the commons', to borrow the title of biologist Garrett Hardin's famous essay[3] – or, as he later modified his resonant phrase, 'the tragedy of the unregulated commons'.

The example set out by Hardin was that of grazers sharing a pasture, each receiving a marginal personal benefit by increasing the size of their herd, but all losing as a result as the productivity of the overgrazed pasture diminishes:

> Adding together the component partial utilities, the rational herdsman concludes that the only sensible course for him to pursue is to add another animal to his herd. And another; and another [...] But this is the conclusion reached by each and every rational herdsman sharing a commons. Therein is the tragedy. Each man is locked into a system that compels him to increase his herd without limit – in a world that is limited. Ruin is the destination toward which all men rush, each pursuing his own best interest in a society that believes in the freedom of the commons. Freedom in a commons brings ruin to all.[4]

The situation he describes does not perfectly fit actual grazing commons, which are typically managed cooperatively and where precise rights and limitations apply. As George Monbiot writes, 'Hardin's paper had one critical flaw. He had assumed that individuals can be as selfish as they like in a commons, because there is no one to stop them. In reality, traditional commons are closely regulated by the people who live there. [...] In a true commons, everyone watches everyone else, for they know that anyone over-exploiting a resource is exploiting them.'[5]

Hardin's analysis, however, applies well to the atmospheric commons and its pollution with greenhouse gases. Each country, company or individual benefits in some way from their individual production of greenhouse gases, but the global good suffers from the resulting climate change. And indeed, Hardin himself extended his discussion to the 'negative commons' of pollution:

> In a reverse way, the tragedy of the commons reappears in problems of pollution. Here it is not a question of taking something out of the commons, but of putting something in – sewage, or chemical, radioactive, and heat wastes into water; noxious and dangerous fumes into the air, and distracting and unpleasant

> advertising signs into the line of sight. The calculations of utility are much the same as before. The rational man finds that his share of the cost of the wastes he discharges into the commons is less than the cost of purifying his wastes before releasing them. Since this is true for everyone, we are locked into a system of 'fouling our own nest', so long as we behave only as independent, rational, free-enterprises.
>
> The tragedy of the commons as a food basket is averted by private property, or something formally like it. But the air and waters surrounding us cannot readily be fenced, and so the tragedy of the commons as a cesspool must be prevented by different means, by coercive laws or taxing devices that make it cheaper for the polluter to treat his pollutants than to discharge them untreated. [...] The law, always behind the times, requires elaborate stitching and fitting to adapt it to this newly perceived aspect of the commons.[6]

And while it is possible (whether or not desirable) to enclose a grazing commons and convert it into private property, the atmosphere is of its nature a shared resource which we all inhabit. As Margaret Thatcher put it: 'The fact is that you cannot divide the atmosphere into segments and say: "All right! We will look after our bit and you look after yours!" We shall only be able to deal with the problems by a giant international effort in which we all cooperate.'[7]

But what form should that cooperation take? One answer comes from Aubrey Meyer and Nicholas Hildyard in a Corner House Briefing:

> Equity and everybody's rights to equal ecological space, however, are surely the starting points. No individual should be denied the possibility of surviving climatic change because of their poverty, race, class, gender, religion or geographical location. Likewise, any 'solution' that denies people in the South the resources and technologies that they may seek to build (or rebuild) sustainable livelihoods in a rapidly warming world, whilst permitting the use of those resources and technologies in the North, would be pro-

foundly hypocritical. [...] The developing countries are not the ones which have created the problem of global warming – and expecting them to forgo development options in order to correct a problem caused mainly by others is patently unfair. [...] Equity also presupposes, however, that everyone takes responsibility for keeping their future emissions within ecological limits. [...] A willingness on the part of all countries to accept future limits on greenhouse emissions is therefore necessary. But on what basis should emission cuts, now and in the future, be allocated?[8]

Contraction and Convergence

Several proposals have been made for tackling the problems of global heating which recognize the atmosphere as a global commons. The best known of these is known as 'Contraction and Convergence' (C&C), so named by its principal advocate, Aubrey Meyer of the Global Commons Institute. He and Nicholas Hildyard elegantly frame the parameters we need to bear in mind. But rather than setting out the many possible approaches to managing the atmospheric commons to achieve their declared objectives, they leap immediately to their solution:

> Many Southern countries argue for emission targets to be set on a per capita basis, rather than merely a percentage increase or reduction over 1990 levels. The aim would be for per capita emissions globally to converge, allowing developing countries to increase their per capita emissions upwards, while those of developed countries would contract to meet them. This jointly-agreed pattern of carbon use would take place under an agreed carbon ceiling. Accepting per capita emissions as the cornerstone of any future framework for controlling emissions may open the way for negotiating a long-term agreement that takes account of the differing circumstances and means of all countries; meets the developing countries' demands for fairness; accepts the need for eventual limits by developing countries; and meets the prerequisite for an effective long-term international agreement to avoid dangerous climatic change.[9]

In reaching this conclusion, they skip over a host of assumptions without, apparently, even realizing that they are doing so. Here is my attempt to specify those underlying assumptions, together with the other defining characteristics of C&C:

1 greenhouse gases should be regulated at the country level;
2 based on the country in which any given emission takes place;
3 a series of global caps on emissions should be set for given periods;
4 and divided into tradable greenhouse gas emissions permits;
5 to be allocated free of charge to national governments;
6 on a per capita of adult population basis;
7 as of a fixed date to avoid any perverse incentive for population increase.

In so doing they follow environmental economist Michael Grubb, who, in 1990, was the first to set out the theory that became C&C:

> There is only one really solid basis for allocation. That is to recognize equal per capita entitlements to carbon emissions: and, consequently, initially to allocate carbon emission permits in proportion to national population. The moral principle is simple, namely that every human has an equal right to use the atmospheric resource. The economic principle follows directly – those who exceed their entitlement should pay for doing so. The practical effect is obvious: it would require the industrialized world, with high per capita energy consumption, to assist the developing world with efficient technology and technical services. [...] The net effect is to achieve in concrete terms what most economists argue for in theory: the polluter pays the cost of exploiting the atmospheric resource.[10]

Such an allocation system, argues Michael Jacobs in *The Green Economy*, 'would have the great advantages of simplicity and fairness, resting on a principle against which it is difficult to argue, namely that each person in the world should have an equal entitlement to use the atmosphere's assimilative capacity'.[11]

These authors assume that the allocation of per capita greenhouse gas emission rights arises spontaneously out of the recognition of the atmosphere as a global commons. Their approach is, however, in fact, quite the opposite: a proposal to 'enclose' the atmospheric commons and make it the tradable property of national governments – the equivalent of the conversion of clan lands in the Scottish Highlands, originally owned by the chieftain in trust for the clan as a whole, into the chieftains' private property. As Karl Marx explained in *The People's Paper* in 1853:

> Every one of the usages and traditions of the Scottish Gaels reposes on the supposition that the members of the clan belong to one and the same family. The 'great man', the chieftain of the clan, is on the one hand quite as arbitrary, on the other quite as confined in his power, by consanguinity, etc, as every father of a family. To the clan, to the family, belonged the district in which it had established itself, exactly as in Russia, the land occupied by a community of peasants belongs, not to the individual peasants, but to the community. Thus the district was the common property of the family. [...] The division and subdivision of the land corresponded to the military function of the single members of the clan.[12]

The conversion of clan land into the chieftains' private property began before the decisive battle of Culloden in 1746 but greatly accelerated thereafter with the conversion of military service into money rent. This process later led to the infamous 'Highland Clearances' which took place over the ensuing century or so.

This historical precedent indicates that there are potential dangers in the approach advocated by C&C. For example, oppressive governments might keep their people in a state of deliberate 'carbon poverty' in order to maintain a supply of surplus emissions rights for 'export' – much as subsistence Highland agriculture was cleared away in favour of an export-oriented economy supplying buoyant English markets for wool, mutton, beef, kelp, whisky, fish and timber.[13] This possibility is explored by William Nordhaus, Sterling Professor of Economics at Yale University, who argues that such a system

> in essence prints money for those in control of the permits. Such wealth creation is potentially dangerous because the value of the permits can be used for non-environmental purposes by the country's leadership rather than to reduce emissions. It would probably become common practice for dictators and corrupt administrators to sell part of their permits, pocket the proceeds, and enjoy first-growths and song along the Riviera.[14]

And as Charlie Kronick, climate campaigner at Greenpeace UK, observes,

> Both the contraction and convergence targets are negotiable, not fixed and leave the delivery to trading a global commodity – in this case carbon – in a market over which the poorest have little control. It is hard to cite an example of a single trade in a global commodity – oil, tin, coffee, soya beans, timber, etc, etc – that has resulted in a measurable increase in wealth for most communities in the developing world or improvement in levels of livelihood.[15]

C&C's proposed atmospheric enclosure also lacks justification by reference to actual commons regimes, which reveal diverse ways of allocating temporary property rights to commonly owned assets; for example:

1 plots for arable cultivation may be allocated to commoners by random lot;
2 grazing rights for particular numbers of sheep, cattle and horses, in various combinations, may be attached to the ownership of specific houses and cottages, or be inherited within families;
3 rights to graze cattle, or to cultivate land, for any given year, may be rented at fixed prices, or sold at auction to the highest bidders, and the money so raised applied to the community's general benefit, or to specific causes such as the care of orphans, widows and retired soldiers;

4 no more animals may be grazed on common pasture than farmers can overwinter on their own land – as widely practised in Switzerland;
5 stipulating the type of crab pot that may used in a coastal crab fishery, so controlling the size of crab that can be caught;
6 in the Northumberland sea-coal commons, where local people gather sea coal at low tide, restricting beach access to horses and banning the use of four-wheel drive vehicles;[16]
7 in the case of England's urban commons, the land is maintained by the local authority for general public access, recreation, landscape and wildlife, and not for any form of economic exploitation;
8 the right to fish in the rivers of England and Wales is controlled by the Environment Agency through licences, for which fees must be paid, and subject to 'closed seasons' coincident with the main spawning periods to protect stocks.

It would also rule out more cooperative international approaches to manage the atmosphere for the common good, and thus represents an enormous opportunity cost. We need to raise substantial sums of money of the order of €1 trillion per year (see Chapter 6) to:

- pay for adaptation to climate change;
- finance the development and broad application of efficient and low-carbon technologies;
- reward countries that conserve their soils, forests and other ecosystems, and finance associated projects;
- and to research and if necessary deploy geo-engineering solutions to constrain global heating within tolerable limits.

The only apparent source for these funds, capable of delivering them on the required scale, is the sale of greenhouse gas production permits. Ordinary aid budgets are already committed and in any case insufficient: only a handful of developed countries (Norway, Luxembourg, Denmark, Sweden and the Netherlands) have met the UN's target to provide 0.7 per cent of gross national income (GNI) to official development assistance, set in a 1970 General Assembly Resolution. The weighted average level is 0.25 per cent, amounting to a total of $78.6 billion.[17] Give the permits away, and the opportunity is lost. Hence the Kyoto2 approach: to sell the permits to the polluters and to reinvest the funds so raised.

By contrast C&C would transfer large sums of money from governments of countries such as the USA, EU nations and Japan, which would need to buy permits, to governments of (mainly populous) countries with relatively low greenhouse gas emissions. This money would then be theirs to spend as they wished.

It is easy to see why the beneficiary governments would favour this arrangement, but hard to see how donor governments would justify the transfers of tens or hundreds of billions of taxpayers' funds to electorates clamouring (as electorates always will) for tax cuts and higher spending on health, education, pensions and housing – all the more so as these vast intergovernmental transfers would do nothing in themselves to mitigate or adapt to climate change.

Cap and Share

The 'Cap and Share' (C&S) approach has been developed by a group of economists, green intellectuals and other free-thinkers, among them Richard Douthwaite (author of *The Growth Illusion* and *The Ecology of Money*) and Molly Scott Cato (economics speaker for the England and Wales Green Party). It is in effect a variant of C&C, and proposes that, each year:

1 an independent trust sets a cap for the year based on scientific advice;
2 'production authorization permits' (PAPs) are distributed equally to all global citizens;
3 people can then sell their PAPs, give them away or withdraw them to reduce the effective cap;
4 primary fossil fuel producers have to buy PAPs to the volume of their production;

5 inspectors enforce the cap by comparing companies' fossil fuel production to the number of PAPs submitted.

This system represents a significant improvement on C&C in that:

- it is a genuine system for allocating rights to the atmospheric commons, with the rights going directly to individuals and communities rather than governments;
- it avoids the focus on countries and governments which is key to C&C;
- emissions are regulated 'upstream' at or close to the point of production of fossil fuels, not at the points of emission;
- while its ultimate aim is to become global, the system could initially be adopted by individual countries and groups of countries;
- the approach is not fixed in stone – on the contrary, its authors and supporters are open to new ideas and happy to modify their thinking in order to reach the best possible system.

The plan (as it is now), however, has some drawbacks:

- It includes no mention of the role of other industrial gases and industrial CO_2 of non-fossil fuel origin; this could, however, easily be remedied within its framework.
- In distributing the rights equally to all global citizens, the benefits are distributed per capita rather than according to need, and the benefits offered by Kyoto2 of a substantial (of the order of $1 trillion, as we see in Chapter 6) per year fund to spend directly on addressing the causes and the consequences of climate change are forgone.
- Emissions from deforestation, agriculture and other land-based sources would similarly not be addressed by the cap (which applies to fossil fuels only) or by spending measures (since there are none).
- It includes no 'safety valve' system to prevent PAP price spikes, and no 'reserve' to prevent price troughs, weakening long-term price signals, and threatening adverse short-term economic

consequences. Again, this could easily be remedied without prejudice to the core model.

The latest discussion version (5) of C&S does, however, allow for up to 5 per cent of greenhouse PAPs to be sold for the benefit of a Transition Fund to finance capital projects related to climate change:

> Countries might receive grants to improve the energy efficiency of their buildings and transport systems, or to take precautions against the increasing storms, drought or rising sea levels brought about by climate change. Or they might qualify because they had a greater need than other countries to enable their industries to adopt new, low-energy technologies. Both rich countries and poor ones would be able to apply.[18]

This moves C&S significantly closer to the Kyoto2 model – the difference being one of how much money should be put into the Transition Fund, which is broadly equivalent to Kyoto2's Climate Change Fund, rather than one of strict principle. The gap between the two approaches, such as it is, may yet be bridged.

C&C does now seem to be gaining significant traction: in particular Ireland is considering adoption of C&S as a means of achieving its domestic targets to reduce greenhouse gas emissions, as reported by Mark Lynas in *New Statesman*.[19]

Cap and Dividend

'Cap and Dividend' (C&D) is essentially a variant of C&S (see above), proposed by social entrepreneur Peter Barnes in *Carbon Capping: A citizen's guide*.[20] This approach is proposed for application on a country basis with a particular view to the USA; the principles, however, are globally applicable. It proposes that citizens never actually receive the permits, which are instead auctioned by governments, and the revenues are then distributed equally to residents of the country. Those who use least fossil fuels will therefore receive a net benefit, and those who use most will incur a net loss.

Unlike C&S, which would allow people to voluntarily withhold their PAPs from the market, C&D does not allow this choice. People could of course buy 'their' permits back in the market if they so chose.

This scheme appears well designed to appeal to US sensibilities – and in particular the antipathy of US citizens to anything that looks, smells or feels like a tax. It is not designed as a global system.

Carbon rationing with tradable quotas

A further variant of this general approach calls for a system of carbon rationing with tradable 'personal carbon quotas' or 'domestic tradable quotas' (DTQs), to be allocated equally to citizens within a country or indeed the world to 'spend' on fossil fuels and fossil-fuel-intensive services, such as electricity, flights and heating and automotive fuels. Each citizen's quota would be paid into an 'account' similar to a bank account. When puchasing an energy product such as gas, petrol or coal, they would have to pay the associated number of DTQs, perhaps using a plastic 'swipe card'. They could also sell surplus DTQs to others with a more profligate lifestyle.

In the original versions of the idea, independently conceived by economist David Fleming and social innovator Mayer Hillman, individuals would be allocated a proportion of the national DTQs on a per capita basis, while the remainder would be sold to companies and other organizations in a government-run auction. The concept has since been extended by Richard Starkey of the Tyndall Centre for Climate Change Research, and others, and accommodates the possibilities that all DTQs should be allocated to individuals who could then sell on to organizations; and that individuals not wanting to participate actively in the market should sell all their DTQs on receipt and buy them back as required with fuels and energy products. This would be, in effect, Cap and Share.

The main disadvantage of a DTQ system is the huge associated accounting exercise. Most people already have trouble enough managing their money and find it hard to face up to tax returns, pension plans, debt problems, etc. To impose yet more administrative obligations on the public might – for all but enthusiasts – be a step too far. Author Mark Lynas is one long-term supporter of the principle of carbon rationing with DTQs, but he concedes that the system would 'not be easy to implement':

> Because carbon rations would have to be tradable in order to be economically efficient, the government would need to set up and police 48 million carbon accounts. This presents privacy as well as administrative problems. It also establishes carbon as a kind of parallel currency: people who are over their ration limit (or have already sold their share) would have to buy carbon at market prices in order to purchase fuel. We would, in effect, need to become a nation of carbon currency speculators – quite a tall order, when most people can barely even manage their mortgage.[21]

Despite the difficulties it is conceivable that such a system might be created in countries such as Denmark that maintain accurate and up-to-date centralized records of their citizens and residents. It is harder to envisage in the UK, however, where government records are in a state of relative chaos and insecurity, and impossible to imagine in less developed countries, where the very existence of many citizens passes without official record. As a global system carbon rationing with DTQs would be unworkable owing to:

- the poor quality of information held by governments about their citizens and other residents in most countries of the world;
- the sheer scale of information collection, maintenance and processing that would be required to maintain the necessary database of the entire human population;
- the possibilities for fraud, for example by way of multiple registrations;
- security and human rights implications.

4 | Applying market economics

> 'Standards of living are fundamentally related to how much knowledge we have of how to use the World's resources.
>
> 'It is very clear that the complexity of the World is such that our ability to actually forecast is limited by our inability to see all the ramifications of all the various permutations and combinations.' Alan Greenspan, former chairman of the Federal Reserve[1]

> 'Now, we don't make agreements on hot air, but on solid science and what is practical and what is reasonable for our people.' Margaret Thatcher[2]

This chapter sets out Kyoto2's core market mechanism, including a full discussion of the economic principles and arguments that underlie the choices made:

1. The definition of a global cap (or a series of global caps) on greenhouse gas emissions aimed at stabilizing their concentration at a level and on a timescale consistent with the Climate Convention's Objective.
2. Holding those companies responsible for industrial greenhouse gas emissions accountable, through market mechanisms, consistent with the 'polluter pays' principle.
3. Assessing industrial greenhouse gas emissions 'upstream' – that is, as close as practical to the source of the emissions, and for emissions from burning fossil fuels, close to the point of production of the fossil fuels themselves.
4. The allocation of greenhouse gas permits by sale.
5. Preference for a sealed-bid auction mechanism, subject to a reserve price reflecting the social cost of carbon, and a ceiling price at which unlimited permits will be sold, sufficient to fund additional investments in low-carbon development that will

more than offset the extra permits beyond the allocated cap being sold now, and so allow the extra permits to be clawed back in future years.

6 The use of the funds raised from the sale of permits to fund a full suite of measures to address the causes and the consequences of climate change (see Chapter 6).

While market-driven approaches are powerful and necessary in the battle against global heating, non-market approaches also have a significant role. These are the subject of Chapter 5.

Another important question is that of cost. Are the measures proposed affordable? Kyoto2 proposes a system that would raise about $1 trillion per year from an auction of carbon permits (see Chapter 6). This sum represents about 1.5 per cent of current world product, currently some $66 trillion. But this does not mean it would cost the economy $1 trillion. The money would not be locked away, but spent on tackling the causes and consequences of climate change and so recirculated within the global economy.

In this way it would have many beneficial effects, including the employment of many millions of people in the building trades, exploiting negative-cost energy-efficiency opportunities, creating a new, decentralized and mainly renewable global energy infrastructure, extending the scope of electricity supply, raising the sustainablity of agriculture and forestry, conserving biodiversity, and reducing health-damaging exposure to fossil-fuel pollution. By financing an early transition to a low-carbon global economy no longer held to ransom by the rising cost of ever-scarcer and lower-grade fossil fuels, and building a world no longer subject to the security risks created by competing access to fossil fuels, Kyoto2 would in fact underpin sustainable, long-term growth.

Nicholas Stern is among those who believe that greenhouse gas emissions can be constrained at modest cost and that such action is the economically advantageous option. 'Tackling climate change is the pro-growth strategy for the longer term, and it can be done in a way that does not cap the aspirations for growth of rich or poor countries,' he writes in his famous *Review*. 'The earlier effective action is taken, the less costly it will be.'[3] Thus, he concludes,

> Comparing the social costs of carbon on a BAU [business as usual] trajectory and on a path towards stabilisation at 550ppm CO_2e, we estimate the excess of benefits over costs, in net present value terms, from implementing strong mitigation policies this year, shifting the world onto the better path: the net benefits would be of the order of $2.5 trillion. This figure will increase over time. This is not an estimate of net benefits occurring in this year, but a measure of the benefits that could flow from actions taken this year; many of the costs and benefits would be in the medium to long term.[4]

The sentiments were echoed in the Bali Communiqué, signed by 150 business leaders shortly before the Bali meeting of the Climate Convention in December 2007, which stated: 'We believe that tackling climate change is the pro-growth strategy. Ignoring it will ultimately undermine economic growth.'[5]

Further support comes from the OECD in its 2008 report *OECD Environmental Outlook to 2030*,[6] which concludes that 'protecting the environment can go hand-in-hand with continued economic growth'. In the *Outlook*, the OECD envisages a baseline projection with no policy changes, under which the economy grows 99 per cent between 2005 and 2030, but with significant environmental consequences. An environmental (EO) policy package that would reduce emissions of nitrogen and sulphur oxides by one-third, however, and constrain greenhouse gas emissions growth to 13 per cent (rather than 52 per cent), would have a barely perceptible impact on growth. 'The EO policy package would imply a reduction of just over 1% in world GDP in 2030, such that world GDP would be about 97% higher in 2030 than today, instead of nearly 99% higher. On average, this would mean a loss of 0.03 percentage points in annual GDP growth globally to 2030.'[7]

The OECD also developed a more ambitious policy package designed to stabilize the atmospheric concentration of greenhouse gases at 450ppm CO_2 eq, in which global emissions would reduce by 39 per cent by 2050 relative to 2000 levels. 'Such action would reduce GDP by 0.5% and 2.5% below Baseline estimates in 2030 and 2050 respectively, equivalent to a reduction in annual GDP growth of about 0.1 percentage points per annum on average.' These projected reductions in long-term GDP are so small as to be imperceptible against the imprecision inherent in such long-term projections.

The OECD does not provide a costing for policies designed to stabilize greenhouse gases at the Kyoto2 target of 350ppm CO_2 eq, but even if this were to cost the global economy twice as much as the 450ppm trajectory, the costs would be manageable: a reduction in annual GDP growth of 0.2 per cent. And as described above, there are good reasons to believe that Kyoto2 would actually increase long-term economic growth (and, no less important, human welfare) rather than diminish it.

So, as a first approximation, the cost to global economic growth of taking serious action on climate change is zero. By contrast, not taking action bears very real risks of catastrophic climate change on such as scale as to threaten the survival not just of the economy but of humankind (see Box 4.6).

Why a cap on greenhouse gas emissions?

> 'The shift to a low-carbon global economy will take place against the background of an abundant supply of fossil fuels. That is to say, the stocks of hydrocarbons that are profitable to extract (under current policies) are more than enough to take the world to levels of greenhouse-gas concentrations well beyond 750ppm CO_2e, with very dangerous consequences. Indeed, under BAU [business as usual], energy users are likely to switch towards more carbon-intensive coal and oil shales, increasing rates of emissions growth.' Nicholas Stern[8]

The need for a cap – that is, an absolute limit – on greenhouse gas emissions arises not so much out of economic theory as out of the science of climate change, which needs to be the ultimate determinant of climate policy. The global climate system is not expected to respond smoothly to climate forcing by greenhouse gases. On the contrary, there is a danger of sudden and extreme discontinuities, often accompanied by the emergence of positive feedback cycles creating a 'runaway greenhouse effect', marked by such events as:

- large-scale release of methane, itself a powerful greenhouse gas, from warming seas and from melting permafrost in the Arctic;
- rapid retreat of tundra vegetation in the Arctic, which is under snow and ice for much of the year and thus reflective of solar radiation, and its replacement with forest, which is more absorptive of solar radiation;
- large-scale melting of polar sea ice, especially in the Arctic, leading to an increase in the absorption of solar radiation (this process appears already to be under way in the Arctic summer);
- accelerated melting of grounded ice caps such as the Greenland Ice Sheet, releasing vast volumes of water into the ocean which would cause severe and rapid sea-level rise;
- large-scale drought and high temperatures in currently forested regions such as the Amazon, leading to enormous fires, in turn releasing immense volumes of greenhouse gases into the atmosphere.

Indeed, some of these processes (see Chapter 1) may already be upon us. The main objective of climate policy must therefore be to prevent a runaway greenhouse effect from taking hold – an event that would overwhelm conventional cost–benefit analysis and approaches to discounting future liabilities (see Box 4.6).

As shown by the IPCC in 2007,[9] stabilization at 535–590ppm CO_2 eq is predicted to result in a 2.8–3.2°C temperature rise – very likely to trigger a 'runaway greenhouse effect' scenario. Stabilization at 445–490ppm CO_2 eq would limit temperature rise to 2.0–2.4°C – still an uncomfortably high figure, given the positive feedback climate forcings that are already kicking in now after just a 0.8°C average temperature rise. To be reasonably sure of maintaining climatic stability, we need to reduce greenhouse gases below their present level (375ppm CO_2 eq in 2005, including the contribution of reflective aerosol particles) as quickly as possible – rather than countenance further increases.

In this situation, the sum of damages inflicted by greenhouse gas rises disproportionately to the volume emitted. Hence the damages per tonne of CO_2 (or equivalent) depend on our chosen emissions trajectory and stabilization target. The per tonne cost is lowest on a low-emissions trajectory and target, and rises as we move to higher-emissions trajectories and targets. Hence Stern suggests per tonne damages of $85 in a 'business as usual' scenario, falling to $30 in a 550ppm scenario and to $25 in a 450ppm scenario. These figures may or may not be 'right' – but they do illustrate the principle at work.

The science also suggests that beyond a certain level of emissions, the per tonne cost will fall: once a 'runaway greenhouse effect' is well under way, any additional human greenhouse gas contributions would be swamped by those from positive feedbacks within the climate system, and so bear only a small per tonne cost as the main damage would already have been done. But there is no need to dwell on this: we don't want to go there. The key point is that in order to put a price on carbon we first need to choose a trajectory and target – best defined by way of a cap on emissions, or rather a series of caps, for the years ahead.

As shown in Chapter 1, Stern's choice of stabilization targets is at fault in that both the 450ppm and 550ppm targets endanger climate stability. A precautionary approach suggests that we should adopt a lower 300–350ppm target. The Kyoto2 analysis suggests that an initial carbon cost in the region of €20–40/tCO_2 – equivalent to the social cost estimated by Stern for his 550ppm target – emerges as sufficient to fund a full suite of adaptation and mitigation measures (see Chapter 6) if backed up by direct regulatory measures aimed at overcoming market failures (see Chapter 5).

It has been argued (for example, by the US government) that

no emissions constraints are needed to bring about any required emissions reductions because the rapid development and widespread deployment of energy-saving and low-carbon technologies could, without a cap, achieve the same objective. This argument, however, runs foul of the 'Khazzoom-Brookes postulate', which has recently been brought to public attention by George Monbiot in his book *Heat: How to stop the planet burning*:[10]

> As efficiency improves, people or companies can use the same amount of energy to produce more services. This means that the cost of energy for any one service has fallen. This has two effects. The first is that money you would otherwise have spent on energy is released to do something else. The second is that as processes which use a lot of energy become more efficient, they look more financially attractive than they were before. So when you are deciding what to spend your extra money on, you will invest in more energy-intensive processes than you would otherwise have done. The extraordinary result is that, in a free market, energy efficiency could *increase* energy use.

The theory is supported by a recent analysis by Nick Hanleya of raising energy efficiency in Scotland:

> Making 'more with less' intuitively seems to be good for the environment, and this is the presumption of current UK policy. However, in a system-wide context, improvements in energy efficiency lower the cost of energy in efficiency units and may even stimulate the consumption and production of energy measured in physical units, and increase pollution. Simulations of a computable general equilibrium model of Scotland suggest that an across the board stimulus to energy efficiency there would actually stimulate energy production and consumption and lead to a deterioration in environmental indicators. The implication is that policies directed at stimulating energy efficiency are not, in themselves, sufficient to secure environmental improvements: this may require the use of complementary energy policies designed to moderate incentives to increased energy consumption.[11]

The definition of a cap on greenhouse gas emissions, or rather a series of annual caps, is therefore the essential tool for constraining both our greenhouse gas emissions and the per tonne social cost of those emissions. Energy efficiency and low-carbon development are laudable objectives so long as we understand what they are for – to enable continued economic growth and human welfare gains under a greenhouse gas emissions cap, and so making the cap consistent with economic and political imperatives.

Who should be held accountable for greenhouse gas emissions?

In today's globalized economy, goods, energy, energy products and energy embodied within goods are traded more or less freely across international boundaries. Under the Climate Convention's 'territorial accounting' system, emissions 'belong' to the country in which they take place. So if a product is made in China, in a Japanese-owned factory using oil from Iran supplied by a US oil company, and finally consumed in the UK, the greenhouse gas emissions are China's (see Chapter 2). But which country is truly responsible and should be accountable? The lack of a clear answer suggests that the entire territorial accounting approach is faulty.

The approach is also ineffective. Under the Kyoto Protocol, it is national governments which are responsible for achieving any targets they have been set for greenhouse gas emissions within their territories. They must in turn act upon those companies and individuals that are actually doing or causing the emitting. As Geoffrey Heal, Professor of Finance and Economics at Columbia Business School, points out,

> Carbon dioxide is produced as a result of billions of decentralised and independent decisions by private households for heating and transportation and by corporations for these and other needs, all outside the government sphere. The government can influence these decisions, but only indirectly through regulations or incentives.[12]

This makes governments interpreters of global policy, creating in each country a separate policy and fiscal framework, multiplying complexity and, in the process, cost and inefficiency. In view of the above, Kyoto2 proposes to abandon the territorial accounting system altogether, and instead create a single global framework that applies equally in all countries. We may then hold accountable either:

- the companies that command the business processes giving rise to greenhouse gas emissions; or
- the individual consumers who may be held ultimately responsible for all supply chain emissions leading up to the end point of consumption of goods and energy products.

One economic principle to apply here is the Coase Theorem (see Box 4.3), which holds that it does not really matter which party in such a situation carries the cost, provided that property rights are well defined and transaction costs are nil. The main conclusion to be drawn is that our choice of party to hold accountable should minimize transaction costs. This points towards holding companies rather than consumers directly accountable as they are smaller in number and easier to regulate. In any event, consumers will end up bearing the costs in their purchases, which will inevitably include an element reflecting any additional costs of production. (See also the discussion of personal carbon rations in Chapter 3.)

It is reassuring to see that companies already are held responsible for their emissions in the world's single largest carbon market, the EU's Emissions Trading Scheme (EUETS). The EUETS is in many ways flawed; holding companies accountable for their greenhouse gas emissions, however, is one aspect of the EUETS that has proved effective and enforceable. Companies, as opposed to individual consumers, emerge as the most appropriate actors to hold accountable for greenhouse gas emissions.

Upstream or downstream – where should greenhouse gas emissions be assessed?

Energy arises from many different sources, is converted into a wide range of energy products, which may then be used to produce goods, all embodying their energy of production, or indeed secondary energy products (electricity, batteries), and all the while these goods and energy products are being moved around all over the world.

The greenhouse gases associated with the fossil fuels that drive these complex processes are emitted at many different points – oil-well gas flares, refineries, chemical plants, power stations, aircraft, cars, motorbikes, domestic boilers, etc. The picture that emerges is one of near-unfathomable complexity – a complexity best avoided by moving to one end or other of the greenhouse gas production process:

- 'upstream': at or close to the point of production; for example, of the fossil fuels that ultimately give rise to greenhouse gas emissions;
- 'downstream' or 'end of pipe': at or close to the point at which greenhouse gases are actually released.

The approach that has so far been adopted by regulators is the 'downstream' approach – regulating greenhouse gases at the point of emission. This is, for example, the way the Kyoto Protocol applies, by measuring (or attempting to measure) the greenhouse gases emitted in each country. But there is a problem: greenhouse gases are released at a huge number and diversity of locations. Every home, every car and motorbike, every office, factory and power station is releasing greenhouse gases.

The picture can be greatly simplified by moving the regulation upstream: for example, accounting for the greenhouse gases from burning petrol at the filling station rather than the individual vehicle. But the logic of moving upstream does not stop there. Ideally we want to carry on upstream until we reach those bottlenecks in the chain of processes ultimately leading to greenhouse gas releases, at which flows are concentrated into a small number of channels where they may easily be measured and controlled. The logic is well described by Peter Barnes in *Carbon Capping: A citizen's guide*:

> Carbon dioxide doesn't trickle from a few smokestacks, it gushes from virtually everywhere. That makes it hard to cap where it enters the atmosphere. Fortunately, there's a much easier place to cap carbon: where it enters the economy. Think of carbon as flowing through the economy the way water flows through a garden sprinkler. To reduce the flow of water, you wouldn't plug holes in the sprinklers; you'd turn a valve at the spigot. In like manner, to reduce the flow of carbon, we can crank down a valve where carbon enters the economy.[13]

Examples of appropriate points of regulation include:

- for oil and oil products, refineries (with a muliplier for aviation fuel as it exits refineries to account for the extra radiative impacts of aviation emissions);
- for coal, coal washing stations;
- for natural gas, pipelines and gas tankers carrying the gas out of production areas;
- for the extra CO_2, over and above that of fossil fuel burning, from the calcination of lime for cement, the cement factory (there are currently about 1,500 factories worldwide);
- for the nitrous oxide (N_2O, a greenhouse gas almost three hundred times more powerful than CO_2 and the third-most important greenhouse gas after CO_2 and methane) arising from agriculture, at the factory producing nitrate fertilizer, which is converted into N_2O in soils and water by bacterial action;
- for potent industrial greenhouse gases (PIGGs) such as HFCs, HCFCs, SF6 and perfluorocarbons (PFCs), the chemical plants or factories at which they are produced (subject to the possibility of direct regulation as set out in Chapter 6).

This would mean that much of the global inventory of industrial and fossil-fuel-based greenhouse gas production could be closely regulated at some thousands of locations worldwide. This would have two main benefits:

- elimination of fraud and accidental error: the close scrutiny would make it very hard for companies to avoid paying the dues commensurate to their throughput or production;
- low cost: by concentrating regulation at a small number of locations, compliance costs would be kept to a minimum.

Allocation of greenhouse gas permits – allocation or sale?

> 'Greenhouse gases are, in economic terms, an externality: those who produce greenhouse gas emissions are bringing about climate change, thereby imposing costs on the world and on future generations, but they do not face the full consequences of their actions themselves. Putting an appropriate price on carbon – explicitly through tax or trading, or implicitly through regulation – means that people are faced with the full social cost of their actions. This will lead individuals and businesses to switch away from high-carbon goods and services, and to invest in low-carbon alternatives.' Nicholas Stern[14]

The example of the EUETS is instructive. In its current form, which will last until 2013, no more than 10 per cent of allowances (EUAs) may be sold, and the remaining 90 to 100 per cent must be allocated to existing polluters at no cost based on their historic levels of pollution, in a process known as 'grandfathering'.

As Gerard Wynn reported for Reuters in August 2007, the result is that 'European power companies will directly earn from the scheme nearly $30 billion a year in windfall profits' – by charging electricity customers all or part of the market value of EUAs even though they received them for free.[15] The free allocation of permits to polluters does not reduce costs to business and consumers – the effect is rather to create windfall profits for the biggest polluters. Hopes that the power companies would use the surplus revenues to invest in renewable generation remain unfulfilled.

This situation is very much in accord with social entrepreneur Peter Barnes's views in *Capitalism 3*.

> Giving away pollution permits, instead of auctioning them to the highest bidders, is like handing out free leases to an office building. Worse, it's like handing out free leases and letting the freeloaders sublease to others and pinch the rent. And we're not talking about pocket change, either. When it comes to carbon dioxide emissions, the assignment of property rights is potentially worth trillions of dollars. That's money consumers will inescapably pay in higher prices for energy. To whom they pay it depends on who gets the property rights to the sky.[16]

Barnes has economic theory on his side – as set out in 2002 by Peter Cramton, Professor of Economics at the University of Maryland, and Suzi Kerr, Director of Motu Economic and Public Policy Research:

> Advocates of grandfathering usually fail to point out that, if the permits are given to energy companies, consumers will still pay the higher energy prices. It is the carbon cap itself that will determine the price increase. Regardless of whether the government auctions permits or gives them away for free, the same energy price should be expected. [...] The energy price rise depends only on the carbon permit price and the relative elasticities of energy demand and supply. The only difference between grandfathering and auctioning is that in grandfathering the energy companies, not the taxpayers, pocket the extra revenue.[17]

We also need to consider the effectiveness of different approaches in terms of their potential to promote technological innovation. The 1989 analysis of resource economists Scott Milliman and Raymond Prince

> reveals that free and auctioned permits, which seem economically similar at first glance, may provide different technological change incentives, and that auctioned permits may be the preferred instrument [...] It appears that direct controls, emission

subsidies, and free permits, relative to emission taxes and auctioned permits, are often inferior with respect to promoting abatement technological change.[18]

A further advantage of selling permits is that the revenues so arising can be 'recycled' to reduce the levels of other taxes, and so reduce the economic distortions they create, giving rise to the so-called 'double dividend hypothesis'. The question was addressed in 2006 by environmental economist Cameron Hepburn, Associate Editor of the *Oxford Review of Economic Policy*, who concluded that the imposition of environmental charges is the most efficient from a macroeconomic perspective – that is, that it imposes the least overall cost or 'drag' to the wider economy:

> any policy that internalizes the carbon price without raising revenue (such as emissions trading with free allocation) suffers these tax-interaction effects without the benefit of the revenue-recycling effect. Because auctioning allowances does benefit from the revenue-recycling effect, it is almost certainly more efficient than free allocation, within the constraints of competitiveness effects. Thus, in practice, given that there is an emissions trading system in place, it is obvious that auctioning has the potential to improve the macroeconomic efficiency of the system.[19]

A further question is that of the perverse incentives created by grandfathering:

> An additional problem with free allocation is that it can lead to rather perverse dynamic incentives. For instance, if future allowances are allocated as a function of present emission levels, firms have an incentive to emit more now in order to extract a larger allocation in the future. Similarly, if free allocation to existing installations is relatively generous, while allocations to new installations are more restrictive (as it is in many Member States) incentives are created for plant lifetime extension rather than plant modernization or replacement. [...] such problems do not arise if allowances are auctioned.[20]

There is also an important equity consideration. Most of the economic rents from the grandfathering of permits in the EUETS 'ultimately accrue to shareholders of the profiting firms, who tend to be wealthier than the general population. As such, in aggregate the current arrangements transfer resources from the poor to the rich.'[21] We therefore conclude that greenhouse gas permits should indeed be sold on the grounds of effectiveness, economic efficiency and equity, rather than grandfathered.

The authors quoted above also settle with unanimity on sale by auction – a proposition examined below.

How should permits be sold?

The choices It is clear that permits should be sold rather than grandfathered, and in much of the discussion above economists favour auctioning as their preferred means of sale. But what are the choices available?

- Permits to be sold at a fixed price without numerical constraint, effectively creating a 'carbon tax' or what economists know as a 'price instrument'.
- Permits to be sold up to a quantity limit by way of auction, in what economists know as a 'quantity instrument'.
- A combination of the two approaches above, creating what economists know as a 'hybrid instrument'.

Another question is whether to have a single global market, or a number of segmented markets for separate countries or industrial sectors. Nicholas Stern is clear on this issue. 'Establishing a carbon price, through tax, trading or regulation, is an essential foundation for climate-change policy,' he writes. 'Economic efficiency points to the advantages of a common global carbon price: emissions reductions will then take place wherever they are cheapest.'[22] But what is the best way to establish this all-important carbon price?

A carbon tax? A fixed-price 'carbon tax' or 'greenhouse gas tax' approach has the advantage of predictability and certainty.

Investors contemplating the building of a nuclear power station or wind farm, which would avoid the carbon tax, can therefore readily assess the value of the effective subsidy they would receive (relative to fossil-fuel generation) over the lifetime of their investment. Furthermore, politicians know that the greenhouse gas tax is not going to spiral unpredictably to very high levels, causing sudden inflationary pressure and economic hardship.

Conversely a greenhouse gas tax is a poor mechanism for controlling the quantity of a pollutant that is emitted. We have already accepted the need for a cap on greenhouse gas emissions (whether imposed on an annual or cumulative basis). This is something that a greenhouse gas tax cannot reliably deliver. One way of increasing the predictability of greenhouse gas output associated with a 'carbon tax' would be to accompany it with stronger direct regulation (see Chapter 5). This might include standards for the energy efficiency of appliances, cars, homes and other equipment, and regulations to prevent the building of new coal power stations if not fitted with 'carbon capture and storage' (CCS).

We have some idea of the costs of various emerging technologies on which to base a carbon price that would bring about particular technology shifts, and hence emissions cuts. See, for example, the McKinsey report *Reducing US Greenhouse Gas Emissions: How much at what cost.*[23] There is little doubt that such an approach could be broadly effective. Problems could emerge over time, however:

- The falling costs of new technology, for example in renewable power generation, might bring about faster initial emissions reductions than anticipated. This would be a good thing, but might impose greater economic costs than necessary to achieve the desired objective.
- Over a longer period, some sectors might stubbornly resist the anticipated cuts in emissions (aviation is one likely example). This might lead to additional direct regulation to compensate.

- Too much direct regulation could force economically sub-optimal technology choices.
- We have no idea of the world's economic trajectory over the period to 2050. High growth would imply greater greenhouse gas emissions, and thus the need for a higher carbon tax, than a lower-growth future.
- Discoveries of substantial new reserves of high-quality crude oil would probably lead to the complete exploitation of the resource, leading to greater than anticipated emissions. The development of technologies to safely produce methane from submarine methane hydrate would have a similar effect.

These factors would imply the need to be able to modulate the carbon tax over time in order for emissions to conform to a planned trajectory. But we then lose the key advantage of a carbon tax: its predictability.

Auction of permits under a cap An auction up to a firm cap is good way to limit the quantity of the pollutant to be emitted. Auction – provided the mechanism is well designed and the auction is open to many bidders – is also the optimal system for securing the full market price for the permits. This is desirable because consumers will end up paying the full market price anyway – just as European electricity consumers have ended up paying the market price for EUETS allowances (EUAs) even though the EUAs were given to generators at no cost (see above).

There is a problem, however, with the use of greenhouse gas permits to an absolutely fixed cap, which is that the price (whether auctioned or grandfathered) tends to fluctuate wildly. Phase 1 of the EUETS is a case in point. In late 2007 Phase 1 EUAs (valid from 2001 to 2007) were trading in the region of 7–8 euro cents, compared to their peak of around €30 in April 2006.

The reason is clear. Permits to pollute become a 'raw material' essential to production just as much as, for example, coal and iron ore are to a steel works – but with the difference that the permits have no intrinsic value, only a scarcity value. Thus if it appears that a given cap will not be reached, permits become effectively worthless – the situation pertaining at the end of EUETS Phase 1. If it appears that a cap may be breached, the value of permits tends towards the short-term cost of abatement – for example, by shifting from lignite to hard coal, or from coal- to gas-fired power generation, or, even more drastic, by closing down industrial plant.

As the Kyoto Protocol approaches its conclusion, therefore, similar price swings may well occur in the global carbon market – with prices fluctuating wildly based on the latest piece of price-sensitive information, such as how one or other industrial country is likely to perform against its emissions targets.

The price swings in a cap-and-trade market can be smoothed to an extent. Part of the reason for the collapse in the price of Phase 1 EUAs is that they could not be carried over, if unused, into Phase 2, which runs from 2008 to 2012. It has now been agreed that unused Phase 2 EUAs will be transferable to a Phase 3 to operate from 2013 to 2020, and this has served to underpin the Phase 2 EUA market.

As to the opposite problem, that prices may spiral to economically damaging levels, one solution is to allow permits to be 'borrowed' – at a cost – from future years' allocations. The main problem here is to design a rigorous system within which borrowing can take place without running the risk of eventual default. We also need to bear in mind that all emissions trajectories are not alike, even if they lead to the same final concentrations of greenhouse gases, as shown by Brian C. O'Neill and Michael Oppenheimer:

> Analysis of policies to achieve the long-term objective of the United Nations Framework Convention on Climate Change, stabilizing concentrations of greenhouse gases at levels that avoid 'dangerous' climate changes, must discriminate among the infinite number of emission and concentration trajectories that yield the same final concentration. [...] Based on the limited available information, some physical and ecological systems

> appear to be quite sensitive to the details of the approach to stabilization. The likelihood of occurrence of impacts that might be considered dangerous increases under trajectories that delay emissions reduction or overshoot the final concentration.[24]

A hybrid instrument The idea of combining aspects of both price and quantity instruments was developed in the 1970s by a distinguished trio of Harvard economists: Martin Weitzman, Marc Roberts and Michael Spence, winner of a Nobel Prize in Economics in 2001. In 1974 Weitzman published his theory of applying a 'mixed price-quantity mode'.[25] This was followed by Roberts and Spence's 1976 paper proposing a 'mixed system'. They argue that when a regulator is uncertain what the actual costs of pollution control will be (a condition that applies abundantly in the case of greenhouse gas abatement):

> a mixed system, involving effluent charges and restrictions on the total quantity of emissions via marketable licenses, is preferable to either effluent fees or the licenses used separately. This follows because a mixed system permits the implicit penalty function imposed upon the private sector to more closely approximate the expected damage function for pollution at each level of total waste output.[26]

In the ensuing discussion, the term 'license' refers to the use of a quantity instrument in which permits are issued up to a cap, and the term 'effluent charges' to a flat-rate tax or charge:

> Effluent charges and marketable licenses have the virtue of inducing the private sector to minimize the costs of cleanup. But in the presence of uncertainty, they differ in the manner in which the *ex post* achieved results differ from the socially optimal outcome. Effluent charges bring about too little cleanup when cleanup costs turn out to be higher than expected, and they induce excessive cleanup when the costs of cleanup turn out to be low. Licenses have the opposite failing. Since the level of cleanup is predetermined, it will be too high when cleanup costs are high and too low when costs are low.

> Given that effluent charges and license outcomes deviate from the optimum in opposite ways, which kind of imperfection is preferable? It turns out, plausibly enough, that the answer depends upon the curvature of the damage function. When the expected damage function is linear, an effluent charge equal to the slope of the damage function always leads to optimal results, regardless of what costs turn out to be, while licenses do not. On the other hand, if marginal damages increase sharply with effluents, licenses are relatively more attractive and yield lower expected total costs than the fee system.
>
> Licenses and effluent charges can be used together further to reduce expected total costs. Each can protect against the failings of the other. Licenses can be used to guard against extremely high levels of pollution while, simultaneously, effluent charges can provide a residual incentive to clean up more than the licenses required, should costs be low.[27]

Note that in the above discussion, the idea that 'excessive cleanup' would arise if the costs turn out to be lower than expected does not apply: if cleaning up greenhouse gas emissions is cheaper than expected we should be glad of it, and take all the low-cost emissions reductions we can. This consideration favours the use of an 'effluent charge'. Conversely, we are in a position with greenhouse gas emissions where 'marginal damages increase sharply with effluents', which points towards the use of licences.

Combining these two considerations suggests the need for a hybrid instrument which simultaneously serves the following two purposes:

1 to act as a flat-rate Pigouvian tax (the effluent charge component) to reflect the social cost of carbon for the level of greenhouse gas emissions defined by the cap that will encourage private investment to reduce future production of greenhouse gases and, under Kyoto2, fund adaptation and mitigation expenditures to limit climate change and the severity of its impacts;

2 to attract a scarcity premium rising with the level of demand for the permits (or licences), which will further promote private investment to reduce future production of greenhouse gases and, under Kyoto2, fund additional investments to further abate greenhouse gas emissions in years to come (see below).

One possible criticism of using a hybrid instrument is that its very complexity would defeat its purpose. Cameron Hepburn argues the opposing case, however:

> The only reason for the focus on pure price and quantity instruments is their simplicity, and for some problems, the benefits of simplicity may be outweighed by the costs of inefficiency. A hybrid instrument – a tailored combination of price and quantity instruments – is a step up in complexity. One important hybrid instrument is a trading scheme with a price ceiling or price floor. The government can implement a price ceiling by committing to sell licences at the ceiling price, and a price floor can be implemented by a commitment to buy licences at the floor price.[28]

To return to our purposes, the first is best achieved by a flat-rate tax, which can be implemented as a 'reserve' price. This will also serve as a long-term price signal to investors that the greenhouse gas permit price will always be at this level or higher, so encouraging investments in long-lived greenhouse-gas-abating plant – whether wind turbines or nuclear power stations – by reducing the risk premium demanded by investors.

The second purpose requires an auction process in which the cost of permits rises according to the balance between supply and demand. However, a pure auction process runs the risk that where supply is fixed and demand inelastic, prices may rise to socially and economically damaging levels.

Fortunately this is unnecessary as well as undesirable. Given that the main greenhouse gas, CO_2, is a 'stock pollutant' (that is, durable in the atmosphere over a multi-century timescale), we should be prepared to 'borrow' permits scheduled for future years to satisfy immediate demand, provided that we can 'pay back' those permits (with 'interest' to allow for O'Neill and Oppenheimer's findings) by withdrawing them from future sale. This avoids the problem described by Peter Barnes:[29] 'The trouble with a safety valve is that it defeats the purpose of a carbon cap. The issuance of additional Permits means, by definition, that the cap will be exceeded.'

In order to reduce the volume of permits in those future years without a recurrence of the problem, we need to invest now in measures that will bring about equivalent or greater reduction in future demand for permits. This can be achieved by, for example, building renewable electricity generation capacity on a scale sufficient to substantially reduce demand for coal-fired electricity.

Provided that we sell the 'borrowed' permits at a price high enough to directly fund these investments, we are secure in the knowledge that the more permits we sell now, the weaker future demand for permits will become. This price we therefore take as our 'ceiling' or 'safety valve', to borrow the phrase of Jacoby and Ellerman.[30]

In conclusion Kyoto2 therefore proposes the following hybrid mechanism:

- greenhouse gas permits to be sold at auction;
- subject to a reserve price representing the 'social cost' of carbon based on our target emissions trajectory – that is, at a level approximating to the Pigouvian optimum;
- subject to a ceiling price or 'safety valve' – at which additional permits would be released into the market to satisfy demand – which must be high enough to accommodate the social cost of carbon plus the cost of investments (for example, in renewable energy) that would reduce demand for permits in future years by a volume at least that of the additional permits released;
- following Hepburn,[31] the 'banker' would at any time be prepared to buy permits at the floor price and sell at the ceiling price to relieve short-term market pressures.

The remaining question is which auction mechanism would be most suitable. This is discussed in Box 4.4, where the discussion leads to the choice of a 'uniform price sealed bid' auction. The auction reserve and ceiling prices would operate as follows:

- if there are bids for a smaller number of permits than are offered at the reserve price, the supply is reduced to the number bid for at the reserve price;
- if there are bids for a greater number of permits than are offered at the ceiling price, the supply is increased to the number bid for at the ceiling price.

A final question is what currency or currencies should be used, so as not to distort the money supply in any particular currency – in the way, for example, that demand for the US dollar is artificially boosted by its role as the dominant currency used for oil transactions. One possible answer is to use SDRs – the 'special drawing rights' invented by the International Monetary Fund (IMF) in 1969, which represent a weighted basket of the US dollar, the euro, the Japanese yen and the pound sterling, according to the role of each currency in international trade and finance.

What should we do with the money?

> 'Mitigation – taking strong action to reduce emissions – must be viewed as an investment, a cost incurred now and in the coming few decades to avoid the risks of very severe consequences in the future. If these investments are made wisely, the costs will be manageable, and there will be a wide range of opportunities for growth and development along the way. For this to work well, policy must promote sound market signals, overcome market failures and have equity and risk mitigation at its core.' Nicholas Stern[32]

Applying theory There is a considerable body of economic theory relating to the raising by government of taxes relating to 'external costs', or in Pigou's phrase 'uncharged losses' (see Box 4.1) – such as environmental costs and public nuisance arising from the operation of a smoky factory – and how the raising of such taxes corrects an economic distortion. Such taxes are considered to be at the 'Pigouvian optimum' when they accurately reflect the extent of damage and nuisance caused by the offending activity.

The raising of 'Pigouvian' environmental taxes has two results:

1 It penalizes the nuisance by attaching a cost to it. This tends to abate the nuisance, in so far as it can be reduced at a cost lower than that of paying the tax.
2 It acquires funds for the government which may then be used for general expenditures and/or to reduce other taxes (see Box 4.2 on the 'double dividend' hypothesis), or to address impacts of the nuisance.

The literature is, however, sparse in its discussion of how environmental tax revenues should be spent. In practice, the first option – to apply the funds to general expenditure, and thus the reduction of other taxes – is invariably chosen. There is no firm reason, however, why this should be the case, and this approach has its problems:

1 where the tax is raised at a level lower than the cost of abatement it will not induce a reduction in the social impact;
2 where the tax induces a partial abatement, there will be residual social impacts;
3 in general, the benefits of reduced taxation and/or increased government expenditure will not reach the specific groups that are suffering the social costs, creating undeserving 'winners' and 'losers'.

A case for compensating climate change victims? Consider taxes on cars and fuel. The driving of cars creates a host of external costs, such as the emission of greenhouse gases and other pollutants, including carbon monoxide, partially combusted hydrocarbons and particulates; noise nuisance; wear on roads and bridges; the creation of congestion affecting other road users; pressure on housing in rural areas; and the danger of injury to other road users. Car taxes clearly reduce these externalities; in relative terms, such is the 'added value' derived from driving cars, however, that in spite of the high level of tax driving none the less creates huge social costs, and greenhouse gas emissions from driving are on a rapidly rising curve even in the EU, where high taxes apply.

Many of the social costs are caused to society in general, so the application of fuel tax revenues to general expenditure could be considered fair. Certain people suffer disproportionately, however – for example, those living next to busy roads, farm workers who cannot afford to live in the countryside (owing to the influx of commuting town workers), and people in other countries who will suffer from climate change. People who live close to busy roads and farm workers are generally relatively poor, and so will benefit less from reductions in other taxation – for example, on income – than people who are rich. And those suffering the impacts of global warming in other countries will receive no benefit at all. This creates classes of undeserving 'winners' and 'losers' in which the winners are generally rich people, and the losers are generally poor people.

This gives rise to the argument that a proportion of fuel tax revenue should be recycled into benefiting people who live near busy roads. This could be achieved, for example, by financing the installation of soundproof double glazing and air-conditioning in their homes, or as a targeted tax reduction. Note that there is a counter-argument by Ronald Coase (see Box 4.3) – that people who live next to busy roads enjoy a corresponding discount in house price or rent and so deserve no additional benefit.

When we apply these considerations to the class of 'climate change victims', however, a different picture emerges, in that:

- the argument for their compensation is stronger, since (as a class) they receive no benefit from either tax recycling or government expenditures;

- the counter-argument that applies to people who have chosen to live by a busy road does not apply to our climate change victims, since they have not generally chosen to live in places vulnerable to its adverse impacts; they may never even have heard of climate change, and have no idea as to the probable impacts they will suffer; and most of the victims will come from as yet unborn future generations.

There is therefore a strong argument for the application of the tax revenues arising from a carbon tax at the Pigouvian optimum (that is, reflecting the damage caused on a chosen emissions trajectory) to benefit climate change 'losers'. The best way to do this is not by way of direct cash compensation, since it would be impossible to target the cash at the right people and at the right times. Instead, the best way to help climate change victims is to reduce the scale of their losses by minimizing the scale of climate change, to assist adaptation and to deal with immediate problems attributable to climate change. This would include, for example, expenditures:

- in water infrastructure to mitigate the effects of drought and the loss of glacial meltwaters;
- to protect or replace cities or major infrastructure subject to sea inundation, such as ports, railway lines, roads, power stations;
- to relocate agricultural or pastoral populations away from areas subject to drought or flood;
- to develop and deploy alternative agricultural technologies to increase resilience against climate change;
- to provide humanitarian relief following catastrophes caused by extreme weather events attributable in whole or in part to climate change;
- to finance additional public health costs to control illness and disease linked to climate change.

This approach is also supported by the economics of Kaldor-Hicks and Pareto efficiency (see Box 4.5). The latter specifically provides for the payment of compensation to those suffering the consequences of a reallocation of income, resources or property rights that is to the general benefit, in order for it to be considered to be a 'Pareto improvement' in economic efficiency.

An idea of the scale of compensation due comes from U. Thara Srinivasan, who finds that rich countries have inflicted environmental damage on poor countries of $47 billion over the last forty years from climate change, stratospheric ozone depletion, agricultural development, deforestation, overfishing and mangrove conversion; indeed, 'through disproportionate emissions of greenhouse gases alone, the rich group may have imposed climate damages on the poor group greater than the latter's current foreign debt'.[33] And as climate change advances, the scale of impacts is likely only to increase.

Low-carbon development There is also a need for an additional impetus to low-carbon technologies. As Nicholas Stern observed, 'pricing carbon, by itself, will not be sufficient to bring forth all the necessary innovation, particularly in the early years', yet 'the development and deployment of a wide range of low-carbon technologies is essential in achieving the deep cuts in emissions that are needed'. Policy should therefore 'foster the development of technology that can drive down the average costs of abatement'.[34]

The IPCC made a similar observation in 2007, showing that 'induced technological change' would reduce by $15 per tonne the carbon price required to stabilize at 550ppm CO_2 eq by 2100.[35]

In the Kyoto2 system, this approach is in fact an essential part of minimizing the pain and hardship that might otherwise be associated with the transition to a low-carbon economy. If the transition were to be entirely motivated by free-market permit prices under a cap, then prices could rise very steeply indeed in order to have the desired result. Under Kyoto2, it is envisaged that permit prices would begin at a relatively affordable level, similar to the current allowance price under the EUETS, but still raising significant funds to finance the transition and so reduce future demand, rising only once the global economy and human welfare had become far less dependent on fossil fuels.

The principle of 'recycling' funds raised in this way now has a powerful proponent: the European Commision is encouraging member states to use the funds they raise from the auction sale of EU allowances in Phases 2 and 3 of the EUETS to transform Europe into a low-carbon economy. It may not have the power, however, to force member states to do this. As reported by the BBC's Roger Harrabin, the UK quickly signalled its opposition to the Commission proposal, arguing that the funds so raised should instead be treated as general taxation.[36]

Deforestation, soils, agriculture Deforestation and agriculture, including the oxidation of fragile soils, are a major source of emissions, amounting to over 30 per cent of human greenhouse gas emissions[37] – more than the entire energy supply sector. These emissions are hard to regulate either directly or by way of market mechanisms (see Chapter 6); they can, however, be addressed cost-effectively through incentives to governments, and by way of direct project funding. It therefore makes sense to apply funds from the sale of permits to reduce these emissions and enhance the role of soils and ecosystems as carbon sinks.

In the process there are significant gains to be won in:

- conserving ecosystems and the biodiversity they embody (also compensating for extinctions expected to result from climate change);
- raising soil fertility and its ability to retain moisture and nutrients (so raising agricultural productivity and reducing vulnerability to climate change);
- improving the livelihoods and security of farmers and forest-dwelling peoples (people who are in general vulnerable to climate change impacts).

Broad areas of spending Accordingly Kyoto2 proposes that the funds raised from the auction should be applied to the following general purposes:

- adaptation to the climate change to which we are already committed as a result of historic greenhouse gas emissions, and of future greenhouse gas emissions that will be inevitable even on the 'best case' trajectory which we hope to achieve, with particular emphasis on the needs of the world's poorest people and countries;
- bringing about a shift to an equitable low-carbon global economy, in which existing energy use based on the combustion of fossil fuels is increasingly replaced by energy from renewable and non-polluting sources and used with greater efficiency, and in which the legitimate aspirations of the 'energy poor' to enjoy the benefits of energy and energy services are met from such sources;
- rewarding countries whose forestry, agriculture and other land management policies lead to the retention of carbon in soils and biomass and reductions in emissions of other greenhouse gases such as nitrous oxide and methane, with attendant benefits for people's livelihoods, food production and the conservation of biodiversity; and financing specific projects to further these same objectives.

All countries should benefit from spending – but especially the poor Funds should also be apportioned to the particular though not exclusive benefit of poor people, poor countries and rapidly developing countries, because:

- Rich countries already enjoy unfettered access to a vast pool of capital through highly developed financial markets. This means that the 'free market' responds efficiently to the greenhouse gas price signal arising from the sale of permits, by raising loan and investment capital to invest in measures to reduce future demand for permits. The ability of market mechanisms to deliver capital for such purposes in rich countries is already amply demonstrated by, for example: the breakneck growth of global biofuel production in response to tax breaks and performance standards in the USA and the EU; and the rapid emergence of the Kyoto Protocol compliance market and the EUETS.

- Poor countries by contrast do not enjoy the same access to loan and equity finance, and this leads to a need to provide capital (whether on commercial or on concessionary terms) to overcome this deficit. In this sense the rationale is the same as that for the World Bank and the various regional development banks, whose main purpose is to advance loans to the governments of developing countries both on commercial and concessionary terms to assist the 'development' process.
- Most of the current increase in demand for fossil fuels and greenhouse gas production is coming from rapidly developing countries, among them China, India, Brazil, Mexico, South Africa and Indonesia.[38] These countries are in the process of building *de novo* entire industrial infrastructures including power stations that will have lifetimes of many decades. In providing additional capital to these countries, over and above what is already being invested, to pay for greater energy efficiency and substantial renewable electricity capacity, these countries can be guided to a more sustainable, low-greenhouse-gas development path.
- This can be done at relatively low cost since there is no need to 'write off' existing investments in, for example, coal-fired power stations, simply to pay the additional cost of providing the required amount of power using renewable or other clean technologies relative to that of building fossil-fuel-powered plant.
- Historical equity suggests that it is the industrialized nations in Annex 1 of the Kyoto Protocol (and their wealthiest inhabitants) that have contributed most to climate change to date which should assume the main responsibility for financing the shift to a low-greenhouse-gas global economy. Since 1850, North America and Europe have produced around 70 per cent of all the CO_2 emissions due to energy production, while developing countries have accounted for less than one-quarter.[39] This is reflected in Climate Convention Principle 1,

which states that 'the developed country Parties should take the lead in combating climate change and the adverse effects thereof'.

- Poor people are more likely to suffer the consequences of global heating in that they are more likely to live in already marginal environments that are vulnerable to climate swings; and faced with adverse change, they lack the resources to adapt, move or otherwise buy their way out of trouble.

It is still important, however, to spend some money in the developed countries, whose economies will bear the principal cost of greenhouse gas regulation through their consumption of fossil fuels. As seen in the USA, where weather-related disasters have recently afflicted Florida, Louisiana and California, and following the UK's floods in summer 2007, the victims of climate change are not and will not all be poor people in poor countries, but also include both rich and poor people in rich countries. The use of adaptation funds in countries such as the USA is important in terms of fairness, and perception of fairness.

In addition, while larger numbers of people are at risk in developing countries, a greater value of assets is at risk in developed countries, as described in the OECD report *Ranking port cities with high exposure and vulnerability to climate extremes: exposure estimates*,[40] a comprehensive assessment of 136 port cities with populations of over 1 million. Applying a risk threshold of a flood once every 100 years, the OECD finds that the top ten cities for asset exposure in 2005 are Miami, Greater New York, New Orleans, Osaka-Kobe, Tokyo, Amsterdam, Rotterdam, Nagoya, Tampa-St Petersburg and Virginia Beach. The situation changes by 2070, however.

> By the 2070s, the Top 10 cities in terms of population exposure (including all environmental and socioeconomic factors) are Kolkata, Mumbai, Dhaka, Guangzhou, Ho Chi Minh City, Shanghai, Bangkok, Rangoon, Miami and Hai Phòng. All the cities, except Miami, are in Asian developing countries. The top 10 cities in terms of assets exposed are Miami, Guangdong, Greater New

York, Kolkata, Shanghai, Mumbai, Tianjin, Tokyo, Hong Kong, and Bangkok. Hence, cities in Asia, particularly those in China, India and Thailand, become even more dominant in terms of population and asset exposure, as a result of the rapid urbanisation and economic growth expected in these countries.[41]

Specific areas of expenditure that will be important in rich countries include:

- Forest and other ecosystem-related payments, since many developed countries also possess substantial forest estates (notably the USA, Canada, the Russian Federation, Finland, Sweden and Norway) and will receive considerable payments to reflect their role in maintaining stocks of biological carbon. The UK and Ireland could also benefit from such payments thanks to their extensive peatlands, including heather moorland, raised bog and blanket bog. The UK's peatlands are estimated to contain some 20Gt of carbon (see Chapter 6).
- Energy efficiency in buildings, which accounts for 20 per cent of greenhouse gas emissions, for the reason that the biggest savings are to be had in the developed countries where most energy is being used (see Chapter 6).
- Energy research, an area in which funding has been sadly lacking over recent decades. Global energy research currently stands at some $10.9 billion per year[42] – a tiny fraction of global energy expenditure, with some $1.5 trillion per year currently being spent on oil alone (see Chapter 6).

The practical detail of how much money might be raised, and how to spend it, is the subject of Chapter 7.

Box 4.1 Arthur Pigou and 'Pigouvian' taxes

The case for environmental taxes or charges was first set out in the early twentieth century by the British economist Arthur Cecil Pigou in *The Economics of Welfare*;[43] Pigou points out that many activities impose 'uncharged losses' or 'incidental uncharged disservices' which have the effect of diminishing overall welfare (the 'national dividend'). This occurs where there is a divergence between 'private net product' and 'social net product':

> In general industrialists are interested, not in the social, but only in the private, net product of their operations. [...] When there is a divergence between these two sorts of marginal net products, self-interest will not, therefore, tend to make the national dividend a maximum; and, consequently, certain specific acts of interference with normal economic processes may be expected, not to diminish, but to increase the dividend.[44]

The situation described is the antithesis of Adam Smith's idealized scenario in which the private and public interests, through the benign operation of free and perfect markets, coincide: 'By pursuing his own interest he frequently promotes that of the society more effectually than when he really intends to promote it.'[45] This may be explained as a 'market failure' – the result in this instance of non-appearance of the 'external costs' on industrialists' balance sheets.

One of Pigou's examples is the operation of a factory in a residential area, producing noise and smoke: 'for this smoke in large towns inflicts a heavy uncharged loss on the community, in injury to buildings and vegetables, expenses for washing clothes and cleaning rooms, expenses for the provision of extra artificial light, and in many other ways'. He continues:

> It is plain that divergences between private and social net product of the kinds we have so far been considering cannot, like divergences due to tenancy laws, be

> mitigated by a modification of the contractual relation between any two contracting parties, because the divergence arises out of a service or disservice rendered to persons other than the contracting parties. It is, however, possible for the State, if it so chooses, to remove the divergence in any field by 'extraordinary encouragements' or 'extraordinary restraints' upon investments in that field. The most obvious forms which these encouragements and restraints may assume are, of course, those of bounties and taxes.[46]

What has become known as a 'Pigouvian' tax would be one raised on the factory owner which reflects the extent of the damage caused by the factory's noise and smoke. The tax is considered to be at the 'Pigouvian optimum level' when it reflects the marginal environmental damage caused by the nuisance. And as environmental economist David Pearce argued in the *Economic Journal* in 1991, 'While most taxes distort incentives, an environmental tax corrects a distortion, namely the externalities arising from the excessive use of environmental services.'[47]

The raising of 'Pigouvian' environmental taxes has two practical outcomes:

1 It penalizes the nuisance by attaching a cost to it. This reduces the nuisance, in so far as it can be reduced at a cost lower than that of paying the tax.
2 It acquires funds for the government which may then be used:
- for general expenditures and/or to reduce other taxes (see Box 4.2 on the 'double dividend' hypothesis);
- to mitigate the social and environmental impacts.

But as Peter Barnes explains in *Capitalism 3*, the extent to which pollution is reduced is unpredictable: 'It's not higher pollution prices we want; what we actually want is less pollution. Taxes are at best a roundabout way to get there. We assume that if we raise pollution prices, pollution will come down. But not even the smartest economist can know how quickly it will come down, or by how much. We can only proceed by trial and error.'[48]

So while Pigouvian taxes represent an improvement they are not a complete solution and will fail to satisfy everyone, in that:

1 where the tax is raised at a level lower than the marginal cost of abatement it will not bring about a reduction in the nuisance or 'social impact';
2 even where the tax does induce a partial abatement of the nuisance, there will still be residual social costs, and these are likely to remain uncompensated – creating undeserving 'winners' and 'losers';
3 the benefits of the tax – both in reduced pollution and in government revenues – are uncertain.

The economic literature is surprisingly sparse in its discussion of how the funds raised from Pigouvian taxes should be used – including Pigou's own writings. In practice governments normally apply the funds to general expenditure rather than 'hypothecating' the tax to deal with or compensate for the impacts of the taxable activity. This may result in either the reduction of other taxes, or increased spending.

This is the case, for example, with a range of 'green taxes' (taxes justified all or in part on environmental grounds) raised in the UK, including fuel taxes, Vehicle Excise Duty, the Climate Change Levy and Air Passenger Tax. The UK government has refused to allocate revenues from the auction of allowances under the EU-ETS to tackle global warming (see Chapter 2).

But despite Pigou's inattention to important detail the Pigouvian theme has been highly influential, and underlies much modern cost–benefit analysis. The 'Pigou Club', an elite group of top-flight economists, writers, politicians and business people who have publicly supported a Pigouvian approach, includes such global notables as Alan Greenspan, Al Gore, Nicholas Stern, Paul Volcker, George Shultz and Nobel Prize-winners Gary Becker and Joe Stiglitz.

Box 4.2 The 'double dividend hypothesis'

We have already seen (Box 4.1) that 'Pigouvian' taxes help to correct the economic distortions of unpaid environmental costs simply in being raised. They can also be 'recycled', however, to reduce the levels of other taxes – for example, taxes on labour, income, capital gains and capital transfer – and so reduce the economic distortions they create. These distortions typically mean that taxes designed purely for revenue generation 'cost' the economy 20 to 50 per cent more than the sums raised. This gives rise to the so-called 'double dividend hypothesis' – that Pigouvian taxes may serve to simultaneously remove two sets of economic distortions and thus doubly enhance the efficiency of an economy.

The existence of the double dividend has been challenged by neoliberal economists, notably Bovenberg and DeMooij,[49] Bovenberg and Goulder[50] and Ian Parry,[51] who argue that Pigouvian taxes aggravate the existing tax distortions and impose a higher economic burden than income taxes. This parodoxical finding is based on the counter-intuitive theory that price rises caused by Pigouvian taxes discourage labour more than direct taxes on labour itself.

Such attacks on Pigouvian taxes are themselves challenged, however – for example, by Jesse Schwartz and Robert Repetto, who demonstrate that:

> this critique rests on narrow and unrealistic assumptions [...] Common to these critical analyses of the double dividend hypothesis is the assumption that the utility function of the representative consumer is separable in environmental quality. This is a peculiar assumption in environmental economics, since it implies that a change in environmental quality has no effect on the marginal rates of substitution between goods and leisure and that consumers' valuation of changes in environmental quality cannot be estimated from market data. Thirty years of empirical research in environmental economics [...] rest on the opposite assumption of nonseparability. Why would analysts make the special and unrealistic assumption of separability? The simplification allows them to ignore the effects of a change in environmental quality on labor supply and to focus attention only on the effect of higher commodity prices on labor supply. [...] When the effects of environmental quality improvements on labor supply are considered, criticisms of the double dividend hypothesis become inconclusive.[52]

In the Kyoto2 analysis we take a view that:

- the classical double dividend hypothesis as set out above is broadly speaking correct, and the neoliberal attacks, which form part of a wider attack on Pigouvian economics, have little merit;
- a Pigouvian tax recycled into reducing other taxes

represents a gain in economic efficiency when judged against Kaldor-Hicks criteria (see Box 4.5);

- a Pigouvian tax recycled into compensating or mitigating the losses of those suffering the consequences of the damage penalized by the tax additionally represents a stronger gain in economic efficiency, judged against the more stringent Pareto criteria (see Box 4.5).

Box 4.3 Ronald Coase and the Coase Theorem

In 1960 the Chicago University economist Ronald Coase published a revolutionary paper, 'The problem of social cost',[53] which led to his winning the 1991 Nobel Prize for economics. He argues that 'Pigouvian' responses to environmental damage 'are inappropriate, in that they lead to results which are not necessarily, or even usually, desirable'. In his analysis there is no perpetrator and victim, but rather activities taking place in a morally neutral space in which we should aim only for the greater economic good:

> The question is commonly thought of as one in which A inflicts harm on B and what has to be decided is: how should we restrain A? But this is wrong. We are dealing with a problem of a reciprocal nature. To avoid the harm to B would inflict harm on A. The real question that has to be decided is: should A be allowed to harm B or should B be allowed to harm A? The problem is to avoid the more serious harm.[54]

In the case of a factory polluting a stream, therefore: 'If we assume that the harmful effect of the pollution is that it kills the fish, the question to be decided is: is the value of the fish lost greater or less than the value of the product which the contamination of the stream makes possible.'[55]

So according to the relative economic advantage deriving from the stream's value as a pollution sink, and as a source of fish, the factory and the angler can strike a deal – or a 'Coaseian pact' – in which either the angler pays the factory to stop polluting, or the factory carries on polluting and compensates the angler for his loss of fishing. As to Pigou's smoky factory:

> Pigou is, of course, quite right to describe such actions as 'uncharged disservices'. But he is wrong when he describes these actions as 'anti-social'. They may or may not be. It is necessary to weigh the harm against the good that will result. Nothing could be more anti-social than to oppose any action which causes any harm to anyone.[56]

More generally the greater economic good, believes Coase, can always be resolved by negotiation among the parties – provided property rights are well defined and the 'transaction costs' of the negotiation are insignificant. Regardless of the particular property rights that apply in any situation, Coase argues, the outcome will be the same economically optimum solution. This in summary is the Coase Theorem – so named not by Coase himself but by George Stigler (who went on to win a Nobel Prize in economics in 1982) in 1966.

So what are the implications of the Coase Theorem to climate change and greenhouse gas emissions? In principle, we would have to conclude, it tells us that it would make no difference if the victims of climate change – Bangladeshi farmers, for example – were to pay polluters (fossil fuel companies or electricity generators, for example) to reduce their production, or if the polluters were to compensate the farmers for the losses incurred from drought and flooding. It is simply up to the two parties to sort it out and reach their Coaseian pact.

For this to take place, however, clear 'property rights' must first be defined. These would specify, for example, what rights the farmers enjoy to equable climate and not to have their land drowned under the sea, and what rights the oil companies have to dispose of their gaseous wastes into the atmosphere – rights that, notwithstanding the existence of the Climate Convention and the Kyoto Protocol, remain undefined today. Moreover, the transaction costs would need to be nil (or at most insignificant) – which is clearly not the case.

A central objective of Kyoto2 is to express the as yet undefined property rights clearly through a comprehensive financial mechanism which allows appropriate mitigation and compensation to be undertaken, with low transaction costs. We can do this without regard to natural justice or morality, which are not instrinsic to the Coaseian analysis. Instead we can simply look to what is possible – since the impossible can be understood as having an infinitely high 'transaction cost'.

This means constructing a mechanism that takes the money from where it is, rather than from where it is not, and from where it is reachable, rather than from where it is unreachable. Those who are suffering and who are expected to suffer most from climate change are:

- generally poor and thus unable to pay on the scale required;
- in many instances not yet born, and thus unable to pay at all.

Thus we are pointed towards raising the required funds from the greenhouse gas producers and the broader class of those benefiting from them. Another guide as to the desirability of a regulatory approach is whether it represents an improvement in economic efficiency as judged according to Kaldor-Hicks and Pareto criteria (see Box 4.5).

Box 4.4 Which auction?

The choice of auction mechanism to be employed for the sale of greenhouse gas permits is critical. Fortunately there is considerable experience of how to structure auctions for the case in question: the sale of many identical items. The main choices are:

- First price or 'pay your bid' (or 'discriminatory price') sealed-bid auction. Each bidder submits one or more sealed bids for bundles of permits at specified prices, and the highest bidders buy them at the prices bid until the permits run out. For bids at the lowest winning price, permits are rationed among bidders.
- Uniform price sealed-bid auction. Each bidder submits one or more sealed bids for bundles of permits at specified maximum prices, and the highest bidders all buy the permits won at the lowest winning price or 'clearance price'. For bids at the clearance price, permits are rationed among bidders.
- Ascending demand schedule auction – in effect, a multiple-round uniform price sealed-bid auction which continues until no bidder is willing to improve their price.
- Ascending clock auction or 'English clock' auction – a multiple-round uniform price auction in which the current price is shown (on the 'clock') at each round,

and buyers signal the number of permits they want to buy at that price, until the volume bid for is less than the volume available, at which point the permits are sold at the price of the preceding round and rationed for those bidders who dropped the volume bid for in the final round. Bidders may be forbidden to increase the volume bid for as the clock ascends.

- A hybrid approach combining elements of the above.

For a consideration of optimal auction design see 'What really matters in auction design', by Paul Klemperer, Professor of Economics at Oxford University.[57] The key aim is to sell the assets in question at their full value to buyers, and this means we must:

- frustrate any attempts by buyers to collude in their bidding to keep prices low;
- attract many bidders, by resisting both formal and perceived barriers to entry;
- apply a realistic reserve price, since 'a stronger bidder in an ascending auction has a choice between either tacitly colluding to end the auction quickly at a low price, or forcing the price up to drive out weaker bidders. The lower the reserve price at which the auction can be concluded, the more attractive is the first option.'[58]

Most of the cases he considers that have been subject to manipulation involve auctions of a single or small number of assets, to a resticted range of possible buyers. In the case of a global auction of greenhouse gas emission permits it is hard to imagine that any bidder, or even any combination of bidders, would be able to 'corner the market'. Even a very large global energy company such as BP will present a demand only of the order of 1 per cent of the total permits available for sale, making collusion and abuse of market power very difficult. And as Klemperer notes, 'The fact that collusion and entry deterrence and, more generally, buyer market power is the key to auction problems suggests that auction design may not matter very much when there is a large number of potential bidders for whom entry to the auction is easy.'[59]

Speculators also have an important role to play, and their participation should be welcomed. As argued in a paper for the Regional Greenhouse Gas Initiative, which considers possible auction types for the sale of allowances from 2009 in the ten participating states of the northeastern USA:

> What if a speculator believes that firms are not buying enough allowances because they have underestimated their need? Then, there is a chance of profiting from the mistakes of others by buying now when prices are low and then selling later when generators have realized their mistake. This effort to profit from the mistakes of others by buying things now that will sell for much more later is exactly what you want speculators to do. This type of speculation is socially productive for two reasons. First, it gives people incentive to make better forecasts of future outcomes as doing so will result in lower risk for society. This risk reduction is a welfare-improving investment. Second, when the speculator enters the market, in purchasing the allowances when other people mistakenly believe that they have little value, the speculator will raise the price of allowances and broadcast to the entire market the assessment that the allowances were undervalued at the old price. [...] Eliminating speculative activity of this type would have the likely effect of increasing volatility rather than reducing it.[60]

Our aims are therefore to:

- keep the entry qualification to the auction low – one way to do this would be to allow smaller bidders to pre-register a credit or debit card, guaranteed by their bank for a certain maximum sum, while larger bidders would need to pay a refundable deposit;
- not to restrict access to the auction to any particular class or classes of buyers – in particular the ability of investors, speculators and private individuals to enter the auction as well as energy and other companies will tend to frustrate any anti-competitive intentions of major bidders;
- create a simple, easily understood auction design that will not deter potential bidders, will keep down costs of operating the auction and mimimize the risk of technical mishaps.

Of the sealed-bid auction types, the uniform price sealed bid is preferable for its simplicity and its ability to attract small buyers. As Peter Cramton and Suzi Kerr argue, uniform pricing

> encourages participation by small bidders, since it is strategically simple and the small bidders benefit from the demand reduction (bid shading) by the large bidders. In contrast, pay-your-bid pricing exposes small bidders to strategic risk, since they may be less able to gauge where the clearing price is apt to be. Hence, among the sealed-bid auctions, a uniform-price auction probably is best for the case of carbon usage permits.[61]

They prefer ascending auction mechanisms, however (note, below, that 'winner's curse' is a bidder's fear that, in winning, they may have paid too high a price):

> Ascending auctions have many advantages over sealed-

> bid formats. A reliable process of price discovery is a primary advantage. Both price and allocation are determined through a process of open competition. Each bidder has every opportunity to improve (raise) its bids, changing losing bids into winning bids. In the end, those willing to pay the most win the permits. Bidders get to choose exactly how many permits they want based on good information about price. An ascending process is especially desirable when bidders' valuations depend on information held by others. Then the bidding process reveals information, which refines the bidders' valuation estimates, enabling them to bid more aggressively without fear of the winner's curse.[62]

And they argue for an ascending clock auction over an ascending auction with demand schedules since:

> it is easier to implement for both seller and buyers, since a buyer only bids a single quantity in each round, rather than a schedule; there is no possibility of undesirable bid signalling, since only the total quantity bid is reported; rapid convergence is guaranteed, since the price increases by one bid increment with each round of bidding.[63]

Others support a uniform price sealed-bid auction on grounds of simplicity and proven efficacy, including the RGGI,[64] reflecting their fear that 'multiple-round auctions can be more conducive to collusion, as they provide participants with opportunities for signaling and detecting when someone has reneged on a collusive agreement'. However, this would not apply to a global auction with many participants. The RGGI paper also notes that in uniform price sealed-bid auctions 'bidders may attempt to manipulate the clearing price by bidding low on "marginal" units in the hopes of bringing down the market-clearing price'. A a similar consideration applies to ascending clock auctions, however.

With little to choose between these two auction formats, uniform price sealed-bid emerges as the Kyoto2 favourite owing to its simplicity, ease of implementation, low cost of operation and participation, and because it is less demanding in terms of communication links – an important consideration in a global auction that may take place largely over the Internet.

Box 4.5 Pareto and Kaldor-Hicks efficiency

'Pareto efficiency' is named after the Italian economist Vilfredo Pareto, who introduced the concept in *Manuale di economia politica* while chair of political economy at the University of Lausanne.[65] In an economic system, a reallocation of goods, resources, income or property rights that can make at least one person better off, without making anyone worse off, is a 'Pareto improvement'. This definition includes the possibility that compensation may need to be paid in return for making a given change. The economic system is 'Pareto efficient' when no Pareto improvement can be made.

By way of example, if abolishing a company's monopoly rights to sell sugar would create an additional £2 million of national product, at a cost to the company of £1 million, and the company was compensated for its loss of monopoly with £1 million, then the change would be a Pareto improvement.

The criterion for a 'Kaldor-Hicks improvement' and 'Kaldor-Hicks efficiency' is the same but does not require that compensation be paid, merely that it could be paid in principle. In our example, the abolition of the sugar monopoly would be a Kaldor-Hicks improvement even without the payment of compensation.

Both Pareto and Kaldor-Hicks criteria are considered to be valuable measures of the efficiency of an economy, and 'improvements' against these criteria to the general benefit. In the Kyoto2 discussion we apply the Kaldor-Hicks criterion as a first test of efficiency, and the more stringent Pareto criterion as a second test.

In practice the Kaldor-Hicks criterion is that most often used. This is the case, for example, with standard cost–benefit analysis, used to analyse the outcomes of possible actions. For example, when cost–benefit analysis is applied to the building of a new bypass, the applicable costs and benefits are aggregated to produce a figure representing the net resulting benefit (or cost). There is no expectation that the consequential 'winners' (for example, those who will be able to drive to work faster) will actually compensate the 'losers' (for example, those who will have to put up with additional noise and pollution from traffic).

To apply these tests of economic efficiency to climate change policy, we first need to decide which potential 'reallocation of resources' is the proper one to consider. There are two main choices:

- the establishment of a financial mechanism to charge greenhouse gas producers for their greenhouse gas production; or
- the production and atmospheric emission of greenhouse gases, with consequent changes in climate, sea level, etc.

To decide which choice is the correct one, consider the atmospheric pollution from a smoky factory – an example used in the discussions by Pigou (see Box 4.1) and Coase (see Box 4.3). There are two separate classes of pollution involved:

1 Soot, ash, other particulates and sulphur, which have an acute but short-term local or regional effect. Once such pollution ceases or is abated by pollution control equipment, the damage arising rapidly ceases. This transient pollution is the kind considered in the literature of Pigou, Coase and others. In 'The problem of social cost',[66] for example, Coase considers a variety of examples of cross-boundary damage or nuisance from the straying of cattle into crops, to the operation of a smoky factory and the pollution of a stream. In every case he implicitly treats the damage as transient and subject to rapid remediation once the immediate cause of the damage has ceased.
2 Carbon dioxide and other greenhouse gases, which have no effect on the local environment but have serious, cumulative, long-term and possibly irreparable effects on the global environment. Once such pollution ceases, its consequences persist for hundreds or indeed tens of thousands of years: greenhouse gases remain in the atmosphere for long periods, ranging from decades in the case of methane to centuries in the case of CO_2, while the consequent disturbance to the climate system may persist for considerably longer. Other examples of long-term, cumulative pollutants include:

- ozone-depeleting gases such as CFCs;
- persistent and bioaccumulative organic chemicals such as PCBs, DDT and other pesticides;
- long-lived radioisotopes from nuclear bomb tests, nuclear accidents, etc.;
- heavy metal pollution, for example involving lead, mercury and cadmium;

- asbestos fibres, especially those incorporated in buildings and factories.

There can reasonably be considered to exist an established right of use, amounting to a property right, to emit transient pollution. The establishment of a pattern of transient pollution presupposes an allocation or reallocation of property rights, income and resources, but once established the continuance of such transient pollution merely perpetuates a status quo.

To require an established factory to reduce its output of smoke to the benefit of neighbours who have over time become quite used to the smoke, or to impose more general clean air legislation, may therefore be considered to be a reallocation of property rights, income and resources. Therefore such a move could justifiably be subject to Kaldor-Hicks or Pareto tests in order to assess its economic efficiency.

Pollution that is cumulative, however, whose impact is long term or permanent, and broad or global in scale, needs to be treated differently, first from a purely practical point of view:

- The pollution is caused by a wide number of parties, most of which cannot be clearly identified, and suffered by a broad number of parties, most of which cannot be clearly identified.
- Even if they could be identified, owing to the time lag separating the act of pollution and its results, which will ensue over a timescale of centuries and millennia, the parties to a negotiation as to the abatement of the pollution are unable to negotiate their 'Coaseian pact' (see Box 4.3) – the economically optimal outcome.
- The usual legal remedies are inapplicable: those who in the year 2100 might seek legal redress against today's

greenhouse gas producers will find that the individuals are all dead, and that the companies are wound up or untraceable, and even if identified unable to pay reparations on the necessary scale (as has been the case with asbestos companies facing claims for mesothelioma from former workers and neighbours). So the legal liabilities for tort or nuisance that would normally apply, and the possibility of which would place limits on behaviour, are void.

- The pollution causes permanent or long-term damage to the income, resources and property rights of others, who consequently suffer permanent as opposed to temporary loss – amounting to an uncompensated 'taking' of their rightful property.

This means that other measures to deal with the problems of such pollution are needed. This has already been the case in some instances:

- PCBs and pesticides produced and used many decades ago are still causing severe damage to human health and damaging wildlife populations, and will continue to do so long into the future, and especially so in the Arctic, where these pollutants are 'distilled' by atmospheric processes. Recognition of the damage caused has led to the increasingly tight regulation of these pollutants in many though not all countries.
- CFCs and other 'ozone-eater' chemicals are still causing the destruction of stratospheric ozone and will continue to do so for some decades to come. International recognition of the severe hazard of ozone depletion, and its long-term and global nature, led to the agreement of the Montreal Protocol on Substances that Deplete the Ozone Layer, which came into force in 1989.
- Concern about long-lived, carcinogenic and mutagenic

radioisotopes from atmospheric nuclear bomb tests in the 1950s and early 1960s led to the 1963 Partial Test Ban Treaty and the Comprehensive Nuclear Test Ban Treaty (agreed in 1996 but not yet in force).

- The use of lead-based paints, and lead-based petrol additives, is now forbidden in all developed countries.
- The use of asbestos is now stringently controlled in all developed countries.

One way to apply economic thinking to the problem of such long-term and broad-scale pollution is to recognize it as bringing about a permanent and irreversible reallocation of resources, property rights and income:

- producers of greenhouse gases and other beneficiaries acquire income and well-being from greenhouse gas production, while those suffering the impacts of climate change lose income, property rights and well-being;
- this process, while mediated by way of complex interactions, represents a transfer of resources from those suffering from climate change, to those causing it by their production of greenhouse gases, and other beneficiaries;
- the transfer taking place is not temporary but long-term or permanent;
- the transfer is progressive, not 'one-off': the more greenhouse gases are produced, the greater the scale of transfer;
- this transfer is taking place not just over distance and across international boundaries, but across time and generations.

The proper treatment of greenhouse gas emissions in the discussion of 'economic efficiency' is therefore to consider the act of pollution itself, rather than the regulation of greenhouse gas emissions, as the 'reallocation' of goods, income, resources and property rights that should be subject to the criteria of economic efficiency.

Under Kaldor-Hicks criteria, we presume an overall economic benefit to society provided the economic benefit to the greenhouse gas producers and other beneficiaries is greater than the consequential costs, as best as we can assess them. One way to ensure that this is the case is to apply a charge for the production of greenhouse gases at least equivalent to their cost, aggregated over space and time – in effect, a Pigouvian tax (see Box 4.1). If the economic benefit of a given production of greenhouse gases is smaller than the charge, that production will then not take place – and economic efficiency will be raised.

Applying the stricter Pareto criterion, some form of compensation would need to be paid, or mitigatory measures funded, by the greenhouse gas producers and other beneficiaries to those bearing the consequential costs, either directly or through projects to ameliorate their situation. This is proposed under Kyoto2.

Box 4.6 Costing the future

How are we to value the future? The question is an important one in considering the economics of climate change, as we have to balance the optimum balance of inter-generational transfers of wealth and of costs. Should we assess the wealth and economic well-being of future generations on a par with our own? Or should we apply a 'discount' to the future so as to value it less?

To discount the future is normal practice, often by a

fixed annual rate, which might typically be several per cent – effectively valuing the future of our great-grandchildren a century hence at about a tenth of our own present. One reason for this is that people alive now are not going to be too bothered about people in a century or more's time – who will after all (as we may imagine) have all kinds of undreamt-of technologies with which to solve the problems we have left them with. Politicians promising a richer world two centuries hence will not attract many votes – most people want benefits now.

One economic justification arises from comparing the future value of two investments: one in reducing some future damages, and another in the economy. Because an investment in the economy (for example, lending money at interest, or equity investment in companies) will generally rise in value over time, an investment in reducing future damages needs to give a return at least as great as the economic investment in order to be justified. Otherwise the future will be better off putting up with the damages, but with the benefit of the cumulative return on the invested capital.

Discounting may also be justified in economic terms as a reflection of anticipated higher incomes in the future – implying that future generations can better afford reductions in their incomes than we can now. As Oxford economist Paul Klemperer explains in the *Financial Times*,

> The root of the problems is that the costs of preventing climate change start now, while many of the benefits come in a hundred years or more. If growth continues at its recent historical rate, world GDP per capita will be at least five times higher in 100 years. So we should not feel too obliged to make sacrifices that make future generations even richer, any more than our grandparents

> should have given up their only television so that we can have yet one more set in the house.[67]

He is of course right that there is no reason for us to sacrifice our televisions today for our grandchildren's future televisions, which are in any case likely to get cheaper and cheaper, and better and better. But the picture changes when we consider natural resources such as soil, forests and wildlife, which are irreplaceable or regenerate over long periods of time. As environmental economist Michael Jacobs, now a member of the Council of Economic Advisers at HM Treasury, wrote in 1991 in *The Green Economy*,

> The landlord deciding whether to spend money on soil conservation measures will not be so concerned about loss of productivity in, say, the year 2050. But the people who will be living in 2050 will be concerned; they would have wanted the farmer to have taken every measure for conservation to keep the soil at least as productive. Discounting thus means that a market system does not provide fully for the future. This is especially true for resources which regenerate very slowly, such as tropical forests and whales. [...] it pays a timber company or whaler to deplete the resource as fast as possible, making maximum profits while spending the minimum in interest payments on their capital requirements.[68]

Discounting applied to the environment, he explained, rests on a

> mistaken premise, namely that the environment behaves like, and can therefore be compared to, money. This view has no doubt arisen because in their attempts to incorporate environmental criteria into their cost–benefit

analysis – the arena where discounting is actually practised – environmental economists have tried to express the environment in monetary terms. Having done this, they have assumed that '£1 million worth' of environment is just like £1 million of cash.[69]

Klemperer allows that his earlier discussion 'doesn't mean that because most likely climate-change scenarios leave economic growth broadly unchanged, we can stop worrying: it simply means that the outcomes that really matter in cost–benefit calculations about climate change are those that are so disastrous that they wipe out the benefits of economic growth'.[70] In other words, the future can take a few knocks from us that will make it a bit less well off than otherwise, but not full-on catastrophe.

A similar view comes from climatologist Stefan Rahmstorf, who believes that the uncertainties inherent in climatic prediction mean that we need to move to a 'risk assessment' approach.

> In view of the uncertainty, what is needed is a risk assessment rather than predictions of abrupt climate change – rather like assessing the risks of a nuclear accident. Abrupt climate changes could be considered 'accidents' in climate change. In addition to the risk of a sudden change in ocean currents, there are other risks which must be considered – such as the risk of the West Antarctic Ice Sheet disintegrating due to global warming (raising the sea level by several metres), or the monsoon circulation changing, or large areas of rainforest drying out. Although the probability of such 'climate accidents' is fortunately not very high, the risks need to be investigated in more detail.[71]

The question of how to incorporate the risk of future

catastrophe into our costings of climate change has attracted the attention of Harvard's Martin Weitzman, as in his review[72] of the *Stern Review of the Economics of Climate Change*.[73] Here he argues that the main problem we need to address is the possibility of truly extreme and catastrophic change, such as a temperature increase of 10°C or more, which would bring costs of such a scale and nature as to destroy not only the global economy but the planet that we live on, at least as we know it. As such: 'Spending money now to slow global warming should not be conceptualized primarily as being about optimal consumption smoothing so much as an issue about how much insurance to buy to offset the small chance of a ruinous catastrophe that is difficult to compensate by ordinary savings.'[74]

Weitzman went on to undertake a mathematical analysis of the 'bad fat tail' – named after the appearance of the curve representing cost and probability of climate change outcomes, in which major catastrophe has a low probability but essentially infinite cost. His treatment, *On Modeling and Interpreting the Economics of Catastrophic Climate Change*, overturns conventional cost–benefit analysis, which does not adequately account for the risk of low-probability, extreme-impact outcomes, and instead places these at centre-stage. Investing in preventing such extreme outcomes, rather than finding an optimal position on a smooth and predictable cost–benefit curve, therefore becomes the main purpose of climate policy.[75]

The main lesson is that we need to refocus the objectives of climate change policy. Rather than trying to limit warming to some more or less arbitrary number of degrees, we must aim to avoid Weitzman's 'ruinous catastrophe' or Rahmstorf's 'climate accident' with a decent safety margin. This means we must first define, and then achieve, an emissions trajectory to that end, paying particular heed to potential climate tipping points. As an extra insurance policy, we need to research geo-engineering options so as to have the option to forestall catastrophe should it threaten to overwhelm us.

When Nicholas Stern addressed the question of whether to discount the future, he came to the conclusion that in the context of global warming policy there is no justification for discounting, except for a small factor reflecting the possibility that humanity might come to a catastrophic end – for example, as a result of an asteroid strike:

> If your, if that consumption is going to come that period after mine, do I give less value? I think the answer to that question should be no. In other words, basically the first approximation for the pure time discount rate which is in the jargon what I'm talking about, should be zero. Now I'm in good company saying that. Frank Ramsey, Amartya Sen, Bob Solow, Pigou, a lot of people have thought seriously about this issue and suggested that pure time discount rating is, pure time discounting, is not ethically justified.[76]

Indeed, there is a case for applying a negative discount rate – that is, to value the environment more in the future than now:

- as people get richer, and better able to meet their immediate needs, so they will value the quality of the environment more highly;
- progressive depletion of environmental resources will make them scarcer, and so more valuable;
- as populations increase, we must multiply rising individual valuations of the environment by a greater number of people;

- certain environmental damages have consequences which multiply over time; the 'runaway greenhouse effect' (see Chapters 1 and 8) is one powerful example of this.

But for the purpose of Kyoto2, we set aside the discount rate question (in any case a blunt and inadequate instrument) and instead focus on the ethics of what we reasonably may, and may not, do to the future. We may reasonably impose on future generations some reduction in their enjoyment of industrial and technological progress; we may not, however, destroy the irreplaceable essentials of the biosphere – such as healthy soils, water, atmosphere, wildlife, forests and other ecosystems, and equable climate. Thus we should make our main objective the prevention of serious climate accidents and the ruinous catastrophe of runaway global heating, whose essentially limitless costs would overwhelm all the benefits of economic growth and other human progress.

5 | Non-market solutions

> 'Recently, after giving a high school commencement talk in my hometown, Denison, Iowa, I drove from Denison to Dunlap, where my parents are buried. For most of 20 miles there were trains parked, engine to caboose, half of the cars being filled with coal. If we cannot stop the building of more coal-fired power plants, those coal trains will be death trains – no less gruesome than if they were boxcars headed to crematoria, loaded with uncountable irreplaceable species.' Jim Hansen[1]

The market is not all-powerful

> 'However politically unfashionable it may be, and however inimical it is to the business community, there is an urgent need to return to the tried and tested means that do deliver real results in terms of emissions reductions, such as stricter regulation, oversight and penalties for polluters on community, local, national and international levels, as well as support for communities adversely impacted by climate change.' Kevin Smith[2]

The market-based, economics-driven approach to tackling global warming (Chapter 4) is powerful and necessary. It does not, however, represent 100 per cent of the solution. Just as, according to Stern, climate change itself represents 'the greatest market failure the world has seen',[3] so even the most sophisticated market mechanisms we might create will leave gaps and may contain implicit market failures of their own.

Market failures can take many forms. The one Stern was talking about was the simplest, where someone causing damage does not pay the cost of the damage. Other forms of market failure include:

1 Ill-informed decision-making, either because the information is not available or because it is too complicated for the decision-maker to take into account.
2 Over-discounting the future even where the costs are known and understood. The human mind is very prone to discount future costs. Just as we defer financial costs with high-interest credit card finance and end up paying a high price for so doing, so we mentally discount future energy costs, and pay a high price for it.
3 Divided responsibility and cost burden. For example, landlords of rented 'buy to let' properties don't care about their thermal efficiency since they don't pay the bills, and a tenant won't improve the property's insulation because they may not be there long enough to recoup the cost. And electronics manufacturers often choose to save a few pence in manufacturing cost rather than use energy-efficient circuits that will save customers many pounds' worth of electricity.
4 Uncertain price signals. Even where price signals in a market are strong, efficient investments will not take place where the signal is uncertain over the investment lifetime, as investors will seek an additional 'risk premium'. This is one reason why the UK's Renewables Obligation, and the Kyoto Protocol's CDM, deliver carbon savings at high cost (see Chapter 2).
5 A reluctance to write off 'sunk costs' even when it is efficient to do so. Just as this applies to old cars with high maintenance costs, the same thinking may be applied to houses, power stations and entire industries. This is only exacerbated when price signals are uncertain as the written-off investment might (however briefly) turn out to be worth something after all.
6 Activities taking place beyond the scope of any conceivable market mechanism. There is no obvious way to bring the methane emissions of a poor rice farmer in the Mindanao Highlands into the global carbon market, nor the forest clearance of a subsistence farmer in the Amazon, nor the emissions from wildfires in the remote Siberian taiga.
7 Lack of choice. Energy/greenhouse gas emission costs associ-

ated with a product may be overwhelmed by other factors. Thus a green-minded family with four children might end up buying a gas-guzzling SUV purely because it is the only car big enough to hold them all.

8 Lack of access, or inadequate access to credit. Poor people can be locked into a poverty trap of high energy costs, because they never have the money to spend on making their homes more efficient. And so on. Even where they have access to credit it may be on exorbitant terms which would exceed the return on an intrinsically profitable energy-saving investment.
9 Price signals that are weak when aggregated with other costs.
10 The power of established incumbents to exclude competition, for example in power generation (see below).

With regard to the final point, it is interesting to consider the strength of carbon price signals at €20/tCO_2 or 2€c/KgCO_2 (roughly the 2007 price of Phase 2 EUETS allowances), and at €100/tCO_2 or 10€c/Kg. These translate into the following additional energy costs:

Fuel	unit	KgCO_2	extra cost at 2€c/KgCO_2	extra cost at 10€c/KgCO_2
Oil	barrel	400	€8.00 (£5.60)	€40 (£56)
Petrol/diesel/fuel oil	litre	2.5	5€c (3.5p)	50€c (35p)
Petrol/diesel/fuel oil	KWh	0.25	0.5€c (0.35p)	2.5€c (17.5p)
UK electricity	KWh	0.43	0.86€c (0.6p)	4.3€c (3p)
Natural gas	KWh	0.19	0.38€c (0.27p)	1.9€c (£1.3p)
Coal	KWh	0.30	0.6€c (0.56p)	3€c (2.1p)

In most of these cases, the price signal would certainly be enough to influence the behaviour of energy companies and the business sector, but many consumers and especially better-off consumers would hardly notice the difference.

In any case, it is clear we can achieve additional benefits in the form of reduced demand for fossil fuels by adopting complementary non-market approaches even after the main Kyoto2 mechanism is in place. In general such measures can best be justified from an economic standpoint where the measures taken overcome market failures such as those listed above. McKinsey's report *Reducing US Greenhouse Gas Emissions: How Much at What Cost?*[4] indicates that there are 1.2–1.8 Gt CO_2 emissions reductions to be had in the USA (17–25 per cent of 2006 emissions of 7.2 Gt) at negative cost. The main reason why these free gains have not been taken already is because of market failures:

> Unlocking the negative cost options would require overcoming persistent barriers to market efficiency, such as mismatches between who pays the cost of an option and who gains the benefit (eg, the homebuilder versus homeowner), lack of information about the impact of individual decisions, and consumer desire for rapid payback (typically 2 to 3 years) when incremental upfront investment is required.

Many of these market failures are best addressed by direct regulation. Other potential benefits of regulation include increased clarity and reduced costs of compliance and oversight. And the world should act urgently, argues McKinsey's report:

> Many of the most economically attractive abatement options we analysed are 'time perishable': every year we delay in producing energy efficient commercial buildings, houses, motor vehicles and so forth, the more negative-cost options we lose. The cost of building energy efficiency into an asset when it is created is typically a fraction of the cost of retrofitting it later, or retiring it before its useful life is over.[5]

An earlier McKinsey Global Institute (MGI) report, *Curbing Global Energy Demand Growth: The energy productivity opportunity*,[6] considers the potential for energy savings worldwide by raising energy efficiency, and finds that energy demand growth to 2020 could be more than halved by taking on only projects that deliver an internal rate of return (IRR) of 10 per cent or more. Instead of a projected 2.2 per cent energy demand growth, these projects would deliver energy demand growth of under 1 per cent – saving

135 quadrillion BTUs (40 trillion KWh) of energy per year, equivalent to 150 per cent of the US's energy consumption today. This would reduce global energy demand in 2020 by between a fifth and a quarter.

But 'Market forces alone will not capture the substantial potential for higher energy productivity and lower energy demand growth,' MGI reports. Targeted policies are needed to 'overcome the price distortions and market imperfections that are currently acting against higher energy productivity'.[7]

Efficiency standards on goods

In Chapter 2 we examined the role of regulation through standards in restraining greenhouse gas emissions. These include:

- clear energy labelling (now mandatory for many goods in the EU), which overcomes type (1) market failures;
- minimum energy standards (as required for some goods in the EU and increasingly in other countries), which overcome type (2) market failures;
- a combination of the two – clearly better than either on its own.

A standards-based approach is often a highly efficient way of reducing greenhouse gas emissions. For example, a $40 million programme under the Montreal Protocol to move away from CFC refrigerants in China, and simultaneously raise the efficiency of refrigerators, is estimated to be preventing the emission of 100 million tonnes of CO_2 – an effective carbon price of $0.40/t$CO_2$. Carried out via the Kyoto Protocol's CDM it would have cost, at $20/t$CO_2$, $2 billion.

A number of countries have also announced restrictions on inefficient incandescent light bulbs, most recently China, which announced its intention to phase out incandescents over ten years at the Climate Convention meeting in Bali in December 2007. This move is expected to result in a 0.5Gt CO_2 reduction per year in greenhouse gas emissions, and is being supported by a grant from the Global Environment Facility (GEF) of $25 million. Taking the first decade's benefit at 2.5Gt, this works at a cost of 1\$c/tCO_2. If financed through the CDM at \$20/tCO_2, it would have cost \$50 billion.

This standards-based approach should be extended more widely – not only to a wider range of products including buildings, computers, home entertainment systems and vehicles, but to all countries. This is most important in the most rapidly developing countries, where many people are buying cars, fridges, TVs and other appliances for the first time. Any purchase of an inefficient model will cause increased greenhouse gas emissions persisting over a decadal timescale. The extra technology costs incurred in developing countries should be financed by means of a multilateral fund in the manner of the Montreal Protocol, funded from the proceeds of the permit auction.

Efficiency standards in buildings

If we include upstream emissions associated with electricity and heat, some 20 per cent of greenhouse gas emissions arise from buildings, both residential and commercial.[8] This includes 3.3Gt CO_2 from direct combustion of fossil fuels, 5.4Gt of indirect CO_2 emissions from the power sector, and contributions from burning biomass.

Direct and upstream emissions from buildings are also expected to rise sharply on 'business as usual' trends, by 70 per cent in 2030 and by 140 per cent in 2050 respectively, emphasizing the importance of targeting this sector. The transmission of market forces (such as energy price rises) into investment decisions, however (to insulate walls and lofts, for example), is weak and subject to a number of market failures. For example:

- The landlord of a rented property will tend not to be very concerned about its thermal efficiency since they will not be paying the bills (see above).
- Builders will skimp on insulation to reduce building costs, leaving the residents to pay higher fuel bills.
- Owner-occupiers are often unaware of the level of their energy expenditures, and ignorant of the potential to cut them, but

will be acutely conscious of the cost of one-off expenditures on energy efficiency measures such as installing double-glazed windows.

- People dread having builders in owing to the mess, dirt, noise, disruption, security risk, fear of being ripped off, uncertainty that the outcome will be as desired, and the difficulty of finding good and reliable builders, plumbers and other craftsmen – quite aside from the cost. Accordingly a lot of work that people would like to have done remains undone, including work to improve thermal performance and wider energy efficiency.
- Poor people living hand to mouth do not have the money to invest in reducing energy bills, and lack access to credit other than at punitive rates of interest.
- Few consumers are aware of the energy implications of appliances at the time of purchase, and consequently make ill-informed choices based on small, short-term price advantages which may be overwhelmed by cumulative energy costs over the appliance lifetime.

McKinsey's report,[9] which identifies 1.2–1.8 Gt CO_2 of emissions reductions to be had in the USA at negative cost, notes that achieving these gains will involve overcoming persistent market failures. Some 700–900 Mt of these gains are to be had from improving the efficiency of buildings and appliances, including: 'lighting retrofits, improved heating, ventilation, air-conditioning systems, building envelopes, and building control systems; higher performance for consumer and office electronics and appliances, among other options'.

The result is that even as energy costs rise, people are stuck paying higher bills rather than making (in principle) economically advantageous investments that would reduce those bills. This situation can be overcome by a combination of regulation and grants to incentivize improvements in the energy performance of buildings. Initially the regulations could be applied to buildings at the time of sale, requiring a tailored package of improvements to be made within a reasonable time of purchase, say two years, supported by grants that would cover much of the cost.

Unlike investments in clean energy infrastructure, where the need for supplementary investment is in developing countries, the market failures described here are taking place in all countries, and the greatest energy savings are to be had in the rich countries, which consume most energy.

Funds should also be targeted at developing countries such as China and India that are in midst of a building boom and where standards are both lax and often evaded, since it is far cheaper to build energy efficiency into new build rather than retro-fit at a later date. A multilateral fund could be used to help developing countries draw up building codes, to fund technology transfer, and to train and employ the additional buildings inspectors that would be needed to make the regulations effective.

The transport sector – particular considerations

> 'Nobody needs a car which does 10 or 15 miles to the gallon. In my view it simply should not be allowed. I think government should introduce progressively increasing levels of efficiency for cars which would prevent the manufacture of huge polluting cars [...] For social things we do not say the wealthy can avoid doing what is correct and needed by society. When we eliminated open fires in London we did not say that if you live in Kensington and Chelsea you can toast your crumpets in front of an open fire, we said nobody but nobody can have an open fire.' Sir Mark Moody Stuart, chairman, Anglo American, former chairman, Shell[10]

According to the IPCC the global transport sector is responsible for about 13 per cent of greenhouse gas emissions.[11] Given the policy and media emphasis on transport-related emissions in the UK this is a surprisingly small figure – all the more so when you consider that it takes in all the cars, motorbikes, trucks, trains, boats, ships and aircraft in the world.

But these emissions are fast growing. Even in the EU road

vehicle emissions are set to rise by a third from 1990 to 2010.[12] The situation is more acute in Asia, where CO_2 emissions from vehicles are projected to rise 3.4 times for China and 5.8 times for India[13] from 2006 to 2036.

What makes transport emissions especially hard to constrain is the extremely high 'added value' perceived to result from transport. This makes for a highly inelastic market, in which people's travel habits are only weakly influenced even by strong price signals. Thus the more than quadrupling of oil prices over the last few years from around $30 to $140 per barrel has had little perceptible effect on demand.

As we have seen already (Chapter 2), taxes on petrol in the UK come to about 64p/litre. An extra 3.5p carbon price (equivalent to €20/tCO_2) would do little to change driving habits. Indeed, since the present high price of oil is the result of demand rather than production cost, the effect on the end price would in all probability be less than this. Another consideration is that even with high fuel prices, fuel is only a small part of the overall cost of motoring, with many drivers spending far more each year on road tax, parking permits, insurance, asset depreciation and maintenance/MOT costs – further masking the fuel price signal.

The person buying a new car experiences a particularly muted fuel price signal. The fuel it will use during the few years they own it is a small fraction of the overall cost of ownership, the greatest part by far being depreciation. By the time the car has changed owners a few times, fuel will represent a higher fraction of the cost of ownership. The used car buyer, however, is limited in their choice of purchase to what was originally bought new.

Accordingly, to leave this whole job of restraining growth in vehicle emissions to the carbon price alone would involve painful increases in other energy costs such as domestic heating. Hence the need for energy efficiency standards on vehicles and other incentives – all the more so as there are no significant technical challenges in achieving considerable improvements. It is rather a question of realigning manufacturers' priorities towards energy efficiency, relative to style, comfort and power. There have recently been several notable moves to this end:

- the fuel efficiency standards of the State of California, which greatly exceed the unambitious federal US standards, and have been challenged in the federal courts by US automakers (see Chapter 2);
- the standard the European Commission is seeking to apply within the EU, that new cars sold should on average achieve 130 grams of CO_2 per kilometre (g/km) (opposed by a powerful coalition of European car makers);
- the UK government's higher rate of Vehicle Excise Duty on high-emitting cars (see Chapter 2) and reduced rate for efficient vehicles;
- the punitive level of 'congestion charge' raised by London on high-emitting cars entering the congestion zone, of £25 per day for vehicles emitting more than 225 g/km, and the 100 per cent discount for vehicles emitting less than 120g/km (subject to a legal challenge by Porsche).

Developed countries certainly do have the capacity to cut their vehicle emissions, through a combination of measures including:

- increased vehicle efficiency;
- the adoption of alternative automotive technologies as in electric, hydrogen and hybrid cars;
- the adoption of clean fuels originating from renewable or other clean energy sources, including electricity, hydrogen and 'good' biofuels (but not the current 'bad' biofuels; see Chapter 2);
- improved public transport;
- including the designation of bus lanes;
- prioritizing road space for pedestrians and cyclists;
- while reducing the road space available for private cars;
- a shift towards freight on rail and water;
- urban and suburban redesign to reduce the need for travel;
- increased and better-targeted taxation.

But however effective such measures may be in developed countries, global emissions from vehicles appear certain to continue to rise over coming decades – regardless of efficiency improvements, however desirable – as a result of projected increases in vehicle numbers. The recent launch of the Tata Nano in India is surely a sign of things to come: this small, no-frills car is priced at about $2,500, and is expected to sell at over 1 million units per year, while the Indian car market is projected to be worth $145 billion a year by 2016.[14]

Of course, it would be possible to prevent this by means of the measures listed above, and restrictions on car use and ownership. Governments are unlikely, however, to resort to unpopular coercive measures, or risk restraining economic growth. Technological improvements will surely come, but over a decadal timescale.

Likewise, aviation emissions are rising at 3 per cent per year, and the permit price would need to reach very high levels to significantly deter flying – even allowing for the 'aviation multiplier' which would double or treble (or more – see below) the price relating to CO_2 emissions alone. Prospects for improving the fuel efficiency of aircraft are also far more limited than in the case of cars. George Monbiot's aviative 'love miles'[15] (not to mention fun miles, business miles and freight miles) will be with us for a long time to come.

One peculiar characteristic of aviation emissions is that they have a very strong short-term warming impact owing to non-CO_2 greenhouse gases (see Chapter 2). In the year following an aircraft journey, the warming impact is thirty-six times more than that of the CO_2 alone, and still 3.7 times more over twenty years. So one effective way to stave off an immediate 'runaway warming' crisis would be to drastically curtail aviation, either through direct regulation or through a price mechanism that would make the cost of flying prohibitive for most journeys. But the wider economic and social consequences would be considerable – a more acceptable alternative would be for the aircraft to emit reflective high-altitude aerosols (see Chapter 6).

The continuing growth of world trade is also projected to involve by 2020 a 75 per cent increase in emissions from shipping, which transports 90 per cent of inter-country trade by tonnage (see Chapter 2). Here again there are limited prospects for efficiency gains, because ships are already highly efficient relative to any other transport mode; indeed, 1 litre of fuel on a modern VLCC (Very Large Crude Carrier) is claimed by the industry to move 1 tonne of cargo more than 2,800 kilometres.[16] The very efficiency of the shipping sector makes its continued growth largely immune to oil price increases – the 'Khazzoom-Brookes postulate' in action (see Chapter 4).

This all suggests that global transport emissions will not be reduced in the short term. Indeed, they will increase, and the best we can achieve is to restrain that increase. But does this matter? Our concern is to reduce total global greenhouse gas emissions, not the emissions of each sector in its own right. The biggest and cheapest gains are to be had in energy supply, responsible for 25.9 per cent of emissions, and in industry, with its 19.4 per cent share, by avoiding deforestation, which causes 18 per cent of emissions, and by improving the energy performance of buildings – so these are the areas where the main policy and investment focus should be.

Under Kyoto2 we can therefore (at least in the short term) envision the growing emissions from transport as a source of funds through the greenhouse permit auction, to be recycled into achieving low-cost cuts in emissions elsewhere – for example, by fitting coal power stations with 'carbon capture and storage' (CCS), financing the accelerated development of renewable power generation, improving end-user energy efficiency and re-engineering industrial processes.

Only in the longer term can we expect to see a widespread shift to non-fossil fuels in the transport sector, as the emissions cap tightens, permit prices rise, fossil fuels become scarcer and more expensive, alternative technologies mature, and low-carbon fuels from renewable or other clean sources come to market.

The Montreal Protocol

> 'The success of the Montreal Protocol shows us that there are global instruments that can help curb the impact of human activities on the global environment. We should draw lessons from this experience, and strive to replicate it.' Ban Ki-moon, United Nations Secretary-General[17]

We have already seen how the Montreal Protocol (see Chapter 2) has proved highly effective not only in protecting the stratospheric ozone layer, but also in controlling emissions of some 'potent industrial greenhouse gases' (PIGGs). In September 2007 revisions to the Montreal Protocol were implemented in which the phase-out of one class of PIGG, the weakly ozone-depleting HCFCs, was accelerated, at a stroke reducing future emissions by 18–38Gt CO_2 eq. Interestingly the move was mainly motivated by a desire to curb global warming – not the Montreal Protocol's original purpose.

We have also seen how the Kyoto Protocol's Clean Development Mechanism (CDM) has achieved meagre gains in reducing emissions of another class of PIGG, HFC-23, at enormous public cost (see Chapter 2).

The technologies already exist to suppress or replace these PIGGs. For example, PFCs arise from the use of a consumable carbon anode in the Hall-Héroult process for smelting aluminium. The industry halved its perfluorocarbon (PFC) emissions between 1990 and 2000; new technologies exist, however, which eliminate PFC production altogether. The 'inert anode' system developed by Energy Research Company in the USA not only eliminates PFC production but reduces electricity consumption by 25 per cent.

This suggests that the Montreal Protocol approach could be extended to other PIGGs, including HFC-23, sulphur hexafluoride (SF6), 22,200 times stronger than CO_2, used in magnesium casting, and the PFCs produced during aluminium smelting – such as hexafluoroethane, 11,900 times more powerful than CO_2. As Michael Wara argues,

> An alternative mechanism for reducing HFC-23 would require a

> separate protocol to the United Nations Framework Convention on Climate Change, but would be administratively tractable because of the small number of installations involved. Indeed, a similar mechanism has proven successful in compensating developing nations for the cost of switching from ozone-depleting substances under the Montreal Protocol.[18]

It is certainly the case that the main Kyoto2 mechanism (Chapter 4) or another rigorous greenhouse gas pricing system would drive out the use and release of HFCs, PFCs and other PIGGs over time. Direct regulation with targeted financial support, however – either under the Montreal Protocol, or emulating its modus operandi in a new protocol to the Climate Convention – could achieve the same result more quickly, and with a lighter burden of regulation and oversight. Moreover, it may be possible to get this single move approved in a relatively short time.

Emissions from deforestation

> 'Halting the loss of the earth's forests is one of the most cost-effective steps we can take to cut carbon dioxide emissions.' President George Bush Senior[19]

> 'We must start to pay for the services that these great forests provide to us [...] In the simplest of terms, we have to find a way to make the forests worth more alive than dead [...] Unbelievable as it might seem, we are destroying our planet's air-conditioning system.' Prince Charles[20]

Greenhouse gas emissions from the destruction of forests, peatlands and swamps contribute about 17.5 per cent of the annual increment,[21] through emissions of CO_2, methane and nitrous oxide. In the tropics alone deforestation is producing emissions of over 1Gt per year.[22] There are particular problems, however, in controlling these emissions owing to their dispersed nature, the difficulty in distinguishing emissions from natural sources and those caused by human intervention, and the impossibility of accurate measurement. To control these emissions in the same way as those from fossil fuels and other industrial sources is not a practical proposition. Yet, as Stern argues,

> Curbing deforestation is a highly cost-effective way of reducing greenhouse gas emissions. Emissions from deforestation are very significant – they are estimated to represent more than 18% of global emissions, a share greater than is produced by the global transport sector [...] Action to preserve the remaining areas of natural forest is needed urgently. Large scale pilot schemes are required to explore effective approaches to combining national action and international support.
>
> Policies on deforestation should be shaped and led by the nation where the particular forest stands. But those countries should receive strong help from the international community, which benefits from their actions to reduce deforestation. At a national level, defining property rights to forestland, and determining the rights and responsibilities of landowners, communities and loggers, is key to effective forest management. This should involve local communities, respect informal rights and social structures, work with development goals and reinforce the process of protecting the forests. [...]
>
> Compensation from the international community should take account of the opportunity costs of alternative uses of the land, the costs of administering and enforcing protection, and the challenges of managing the political transition as established interests are displaced.[23]

The question of how to reward forest conservation has been a hot topic in Climate Convention meetings, not least at the December 2007 meeting in Bali, under the generic heading of 'Reducing Emissions from Deforestation and Degradation' (REDD). The discussions are complex, but boil down to two main approaches:

- to pay countries for reducing deforestation relative to a baseline of past deforestation rates, and/or future projections of deforestation;

- to pay countries according to a fixed formula based on forest area and/or the carbon stock represented.

Both have problems:

- the first rewards most the countries who have historically deforested most, or who project the grandest plans for future deforestation;
- the second means that in order to prevent deforestation where it is most profitable (where there is existing transport infrastructure, fertile soil, water and access to markets for logs and agricultural commodities) payments would need to be set at a very high level, far in excess of that needed to conserve remote forests that are under no threat.

The Kyoto2 response is therefore to reward countries that preserve these critical ecosystems with payments for adherence to country-specific Forest Agreements. The destruction of forests takes place, in general, because forest countries can make more money by using the land for agriculture, as they capture the value of standing timber, then of annual harvests of soyabeans, palm oil, beef and other produce. Reward payments would therefore have to be sufficient to protect forests from these competing land uses. Countries would be rewarded based on maintaining agreed areas:

- for pure conservation, with no exploitation save that of indigenous or long-established peoples;
- for limited, sustainable exploitation focused on non-timber products;
- for more intensive exploitation, including for timber but subject to certification for sound management;
- of plantation, but including measures to protect soils, water and biodiversity;
- of degraded/destroyed forest undergoing restoration/re-establishment to one of the above categories.

The level of recompense would be made based on such factors as:

- area of forest land conserved/under restoration;
- carbon stocks held in the national forest estate;
- achievement of specific biodiversity objectives;
- achievement of forest restoration/re-establishment targets;
- adherence to social standards for local, traditional and indigenous peoples;
- specific, actual costs arising as a result of specific problems – for example, specific funding might be needed to pay for forest wardens, to establish sustainable agro-forestry projects, to buy farmland for the settlement of shifting/shifted agriculturalists, institutional support and capacity building, to buy out existing interests in forests (such as logging rights), to close off roads, to remove invasive exotic species.

Agriculture

Agriculture is of key importance in climate change policy:

- Agriculture is responsible for about 15 per cent[24] of greenhouse gas emissions, from its use of fossil energy; fertilizer manufacture; conversion of excess nitrate fertilizer to nitrous oxide; and direct emissions of CO_2, methane and nitrous oxide from soils, manures and livestock, from the decay of organic material in soils and from the burning of waste biomass.
- The world's soils hold far more carbon (2,300Gt in the top 3 metres) than all terrestrial ecosystems combined (650Gt).[25] This makes it essential to both conserve carbon in soils, and to enhance the role of soils as carbon sinks, especially since this tends to enhance soil fertility, resilience and the retention of moisture and nutrients.
- Agriculture faces the prospect of considerable disruption from climate change, including higher temperatures and increased risk of drought and flood.[26] Areas already under water stress are expected to become more arid. Farmers all over the world will need to adapt to these changes, for example by growing different crops, or different crop varieties adapted to higher temperatures and the risk of both drought and flood. About

one billion rural people worldwide are also poor, subsisting on $1 or less per day,[27] and they overwhelmingly depend on farming for their survival. These poor people have no resources to fall back on when afflicted by extreme weather events associated with climate change. It is therefore essential to boost the resiliency of their farming systems in the face of changing climate, including soil and water management, and the crop varieties available to them.

- Agriculture is the source of the world's food and many other goods. With projected human population rising to 9 billion by 2050 and rising per capita demand for agricultural commodities, leading to a projected doubling in demand for food by 2050, the continued productivity of global agriculture will be essential to human welfare. There is already widespread evidence of reduced grain yields from cereal crops, including rice and wheat, as temperatures rise, problems that will mainly affect production in tropical countries where population increases are adding most strongly to demand.

A major programme of agricultural reform is therefore needed to address these vital issues. See, for example, the FAO's *Adaptation to climate change in agriculture, forestry and fisheries*.[28]

As with emissions from deforestation (part of which are essentially agricultural where the driver is conversion to farmland) agricultural emissions are diffuse and hard to measure. It is therefore very difficult, and would also be politically contentious, to regulate such emissions or incorporate them into a market mechanism. Also, Kyoto2 already proposes to regulate nitrate fertilizer to reflect its conversion by soil bacteria into nitrous oxide, and fossil fuels and other energy inputs would already have been regulated at source.

Kyoto2 therefore looks to the model of the Montreal Protocol. Standards and guidelines would be established on best practice to minimize greenhouse gas emissions from farming. In OECD countries and others where subsidies are paid to farmers, payments would be conditional on adherence to these guidelines. A substantial new programme of research into raising the resilience and productivity of farming under climate change is also needed. In developing countries, agricultural extension programmes funded through a multilateral fund would bring appropriate technologies to farmers and inform and educate them on how to minimize their greenhouse gas emissions.

As the *World Development Report 2008* points out, a post-2012 climate settlement should create incentives

> for sequestration of carbon in soils (for example, through conservation tillage) and for agroforestry in agricultural landscapes. Incentives are also needed for investment in science and technology for low-emission technologies, such as cattle breeds that emit less methane. Many GHG mitigation measures can have win-win outcomes for poverty and the environment. Other promising approaches are changes in agricultural land management (conservation tillage, agroforestry, and rehabilitation of degraded crop and pasture land); overall improvement of nutrition and genetics of ruminant livestock; storage and capture technologies for manure; and conversions of emissions into biogas. Many of those approaches have win-win outcomes in higher productivity, better management of natural resources, or the production of valuable by-products, such as bioenergy. Others require substantial investment at the global level, such as the development of low-emission rice varieties and livestock breeds. The 'public good' nature of research in this area warrants international support for innovative, cost-effective solutions that will reduce emissions from livestock and rice paddy fields through advances in breeding and through the use of advanced biotechnologies.[29]

Redirecting capital investment

Enormous capital investments are currently being made in power generation capacity in China, India and other developing countries. China alone is currently commissioning about 100GW of centralized coal-fired power capacity every year to satisfy burgeoning demand for electricity in industry, commerce and homes. Each such plant is likely to be kept running for fifty to seventy-five years. As the International Energy Agency (IEA) observes,

> The emergence of China and India as major players in global energy markets makes it all the more important that all countries take decisive and urgent action to curb runaway energy demand. [...] Investment now being made in energy-supply infrastructure will lock in technology for decades, especially in power generation. The next ten years will be crucial, as the pace of expansion in energy-supply infrastructure is expected to be particularly rapid.[30]

According to the IEA, China and India will respectively (under the business-as-usual scenario) invest $3.7 trillion and $1.25 trillion in energy supply infrastructure over the twenty-four years from 2006 to 2030, 75 per cent of the sums going into the power sector. Much of this investment is going into coal-fired generation – the cheapest present-day option – and this factor underlies the sharp increases in global greenhouse gas emissions of recent years.

Once this coal-fired electricity supply infrastructure is in place, it will be hard to change as the countries involved will have no desire to scrap this expensively built plant, and even retro-fitting 'carbon capture and storage' (CCS) would be a major cost. The finance that is already available for these coal-fired stations could, however, with additional finance, either be diverted into building renewable generators such as wind farms and concentrated solar power stations, or be used to build more efficient plants, including decentralized combined heat and power (CHP) (see below), with the capacity for the future fitting of CSS. As Nicholas Stern points out,

> Countries such as India and China are expected to increase their capital infrastructure substantially over coming decades, with China alone accounting for around 15% of total global energy investment. If they use low-emission technologies, emission savings can be 'locked in' for the lifetime of the asset. It is much

cheaper to build a new piece of capital equipment using low-emission technology than to retro-fit dirty capital stock.[31]

Supplementary finance from the permit auction proceeds should therefore be applied to this purpose, as set out in more detail in Chapter 7. Note that in many instances savings will result from such redirection of investment, as described below.

Only clean coal

One corollary of the argument presented above is that all new coal-fired power stations should be 'clean' – that is, fitted with 'carbon capture and storage' (CCS). The argument for this form of regulation has been powerfully made by Jim Hansen:

> Coal reserves contain much more carbon than do oil and natural gas reserves, and it is impractical to capture CO_2 emissions from the tailpipes of vehicles. Nor is there any prospect that Saudi Arabia, Russia, the United States and other major oil-producers will decide to leave their oil in the ground. Thus unavoidable CO_2 emissions in the next few decades will take atmospheric CO_2 amounts close to, if not beyond, the level needed to cause dangerous climate change. The only practical way to prevent CO_2 levels from going far into the dangerous range, with disastrous effects for humanity and other inhabitants of the planet, is to phase out use of coal except at power plants where the CO_2 is captured and sequestered.[32]

It is most essential to act swiftly in the case of new power stations anywhere in the world since it is far cheaper to incorporate CCS during construction than as a 'retro-fit' (see above). In developing countries the extra cost of CCS (or switching to other clean energy sources) could be sustained by a multilateral fund, while industrialized countries reflect the requirement in their domestic law. Already California (see Chapter 2) has applied greenhouse gas emissions standards to its electricity, requiring all new power generation in the state to be at least as efficient as a new combined cycle gas turbine (CCGT) station – which would require a coal-fired station to incorporate at least an element of CCS.

Hansen now advocates an initial 350ppm CO_2 eq target, achievement of which would require that we halt construction of any new coal plants not equipped with CCS.

> Present policies, with continued construction of coal-fired power plants without CO_2 capture, suggest that decision-makers do not appreciate the gravity of the situation. Continued growth of greenhouse gas emissions, for even another decade, practically eliminates the possibility of near-term return of atmospheric composition beneath the tipping level for catastrophic effects. The most difficult task, phase-out over the next 20–25 years of coal use that does not capture CO_2, is Herculean, yet feasible when compared with the efforts that went into World War II. The stakes, for all life on the planet, surpass those of any previous crisis. The greatest danger is continued ignorance and denial, which could make tragic consequences unavoidable.[33]

Another essential part of this approach is to halt the development of unconventional carbon-rich fossil fuels such as oil- or tar-bearing sands and shales, or develop them only in conjunction with CCS. This position now forms part of the Kyoto2 proposals.

Reducing cement emissions

Portland cement manufacture is a major source of CO_2, representing over 5 per cent of global CO_2 emissions. Production, which reached around 1.8 billion tonnes per year (Gt/y) in 2007, has also been projected to 3.8Gt/y by 2020, and to reach over 5Gt/y by 2050. Almost half of world production is in China, thanks to its phenomenal economic growth and accompanying building boom.

The CO_2 emissions arise in two ways: from burning fossil fuels to heat lime and other ingredients to 1,400–1,500°C, which produces 0.4–0.6t CO_2/t cement (depending on the fuel used); and the CO_2 produced by calcinating lime – that is, driving the

CO_2 out of calcium carbonate to make calcium oxide, which produces 0.5–0.6t CO_2/t cement (depending on the balance of ingredients). Thus making 1 tonne of cement produces about 1 tonne of CO_2.

Under Kyoto2 permits would be needed to cover both types of emissions, creating an incentive to minimize them: at a CO_2 price of €20/t, the CO_2 cost would be €0.50 for a 25Kg bag retailing at about €5, adding 10 per cent to the cost, or closer to 20 per cent at wholesale prices. The scope for incremental reductions is, however, limited. Cement manufacturers in Europe have already reduced their emissions by switching to lower-carbon fuels, by adopting more efficient kiln designs, and by raising the proportion of waste materials such as fly ash and powdered slag. Meanwhile 'emerging economies have some of the cleanest cement plants, due to newly built facilities'.[34] The greatest scope for savings is in North America, home to the 'older, least efficient plants'. All but very deep emissions cuts are, however, liable to be overwhelmed by the pace of increased production.

One way to cut deeply into CO_2 emissions from cement is 'carbon capture and storage' (CCS) – the CO_2 emissions from calcinating lime are highly concentrated, and thus more suitable for CCS than the more diffuse emissions from burning fossil fuels. Another approach, under development by the Australian Sustainable Energy Research Centre and India's Energy Resources Institute, is to use the CO_2 emissions to fertilize the growth of algae, which can then be dried and converted into fuel.

But a more elegant solution is to find substitutes for conventional Portland cement. Geopolymer concretes made from a mixture of water-soluble alkali metal silicates and powdered aluminosilicate minerals such as fly ash, pozzolanic sands or lava have great potential: the geopolymer cement mix can be made at much lower temperature than Portland cement, and overall CO_2 emissions are 80 per cent lower.[35] They also harden faster than Portland cement and are highly resistant to fire and chemical attack.

Further alternative cements are based on ground-granulated

blast furnace slag, which may account for 70–80 per cent of weight, together with admixtures of gypsum (calcium sulphate) and lime or Portland clinker. Depending on the precise formulation, these may be known as 'Portland blast furnace cement', 'slag-lime cement' or 'super-sulphated cement'. The end product is typically as strong as Portland cement, but it is weaker in its early stages. All these slag-based cements are highly resistant to sulphate and other pollutants – a major advantage in polluted urban and industrial environments. Again, CO_2 emissions are low relative to Portland cement.

The main factors inhibiting the more widespread acceptance of geopolymers and other alternative cements are the lack of experience of working with them, the potentially catastrophic consequences of materials failure, and the conservative nature of the building industry. Modern Portland cements have been in use since 1842 and so enjoy a huge head-start advantage. In order to promote wider acceptance of 'eco-cements' (unconventional cements with reduced CO_2 emissions) a major research effort is needed that will provide precise, long-term data to the building industry of optimal formulations and strength.

Once this information is available, the market signal from CO_2 pricing will help to push the industry towards the use of eco-cements. An additional push could, however, be delivered by a regulatory approach, for example through building standards aimed at reducing the CO_2 embodied within buildings. Regulations should be drawn up that would ensure that, for a given application, the lowest-CO_2 cement would be used. By way of example, Portland cement might still be considered safest for pre-stressed steel–concrete roof beams, but a geopolymer cement might be entirely satisfactory for laying a concrete floor slab or manufacturing concrete blocks.

Ending energy subsidies

McKinsey's report *Curbing Global Energy Demand Growth: The energy productivity opportunity*[36] identifies fuel subsidies as a major cause of high energy consumption, and their removal would reduce the consumption of transport fuels by 3 million barrels of oil a day. Transport fuel subsidies are highest in the Middle East, for example in Iran, where they take up 16 per cent of GDP. As a result vehicles in the Middle East have an average fuel consumption twice those in countries where such fuel subsidies do not apply. In total 11 per cent of the world's petrol is subsidized, and 27 per cent of the world's diesel.

Similar considerations apply to electricity subsidies in China and Russia, kerosene subsidies in China and India, and heat/natural gas subsidies in Russia. An end to the latter could create a 43 per cent reduction in consumption.

In the EU, there are also many energy subsidies, both direct and indirect, as recorded by the European Commission.[37] For example, state aid to aviation in 2006 and 2007 amounted to €121 million for airport infrastructure, and €163 million for start-up aid for new routes, a total of €284 million, while subsidies of €1.5 billion per year were granted to the maritime transport sector during 2004–06. Subsidies to the EU coal industry, through a combination of investment aid, operating aid and aid for inherited liabilities, amounted to some €2.7 billion in 2007. This figure is due to fall, but only to the still-substantial sum of €2.2 billion in 2010.[38]

With an aggregated global fossil fuel subsidy estimated at $235–300 billion per year by the New Economics Foundation in 2004,[39] there is a strong case for a rapid phase-out of all subsidies to fossil fuels, ideally with the savings being invested in improved energy efficiency and support to non-fossil energy production in order to prevent hardship. The rapid termination of fossil fuel subsidies accordingly forms a core part of the Kyoto2 proposals.

Energy market reform

Currently 68 per cent of fossil fuel emissions arise from the generation of heat and power. As reported by Thomas Casten, chairman of Recycled Energy Development LLC of Westmont, Illinois, these emissions can be drastically reduced by recycling what is now treated as 'waste' energy. 'Opportunities for additional efficiency abound, particularly by recycling waste energy within the industrial sector,' he writes. 'Recycled energy's unused potential may be society's best-kept secret.'[40]

The 'waste' energy to be exploited falls into two categories:

- Waste heat from electricity generation, which can provide useful thermal energy for heating, cooling and industrial processes. The waste heat can be used via 'combined heat and power' plants sited near thermal energy demand. If an easily achievable 50 per cent of the waste heat from US power generation were recycled in this way, US fossil energy consumption would be reduced by 13 per cent.
- Diverse waste energy streams from industrial processes, which may take the form of hot exhaust, low-grade fuel, high-pressure steam and gas. All of these are energy sources that can be tapped for either power or heat, or both. Around 1GW of industrial energy is currently recycled in the USA, but this is only about 10 per cent of the available resource. Fully exploited, waste industrial energy could provide about 20 per cent of the US electricity supply.

Taken together, this recycling of waste energy from industry and power generation could cut the US fossil fuel burn by one-third, while also returning a positive (in some cases very positive) return on investment. Similar figures apply to other developed countries, and indeed developing countries. This would of course require a substantial re-engineering of energy systems, with a widespread decentralization of power generation.

At present some 92 per cent of the world's power is generated at large, remote generation plants, while 7.5 per cent comes from CHP plants close to thermal demand. This last figure belies considerable national variation – the USA and the UK both come in below the global average, while Denmark achieves over 50 per cent. The generally low figure for CHP generation may be attributed to the higher capital cost of CHP of $1,380/KW, compared to $890/KW for centralized generation.

But once the capital cost of transmission and distribution is included the position is reversed. Take into account the reduced transmission losses from locally embedded generation and the discrepancy becomes astonishing. Adding a new KW of end-user load costs $3,269 when the electricity comes from a large central generator, but only $1,432 from local CHP. A generation infrastructure based on many small CHP plants confers greater stability to the grid and reduces the need for back-up generation capacity.

So why is CHP the exception and not the norm (except in Denmark)? Casten's answer is simple: 'the current market for heat and power is not free'. Established utilities are able to block new entrants to the power game by way of legal monopolies, ownership of the distribution system, grid connection charges, the non-compensation of environmental damages (see Chapter 2), the 'grandfathering' (give-away) of valuable pollution permits to established power generators but not to new entrants, and regulatory oversight that rewards high capital investment and thus penalizes efficiency. Casten's answer to this is simple: radical market, legal and regulatory reform to remove existing barriers and perverse incentives.

His own experience shows what is possible even under existing regimes:

> Over the past 25 years, I have led companies that invested more than US$2 billion in 250 local generation plants in 22 states, Canada and Mexico. The worst of these facilities uses less than half the fuel and emits less than half the CO_2 of the average central generation plant. These energy-recycling plants contribute more than 10,000 megawatts of thermal and electric generating capacity. Every one of the plants saves money for its host and yields an acceptable rate of return to its investors.

There are other systemic distortions to energy markets that are calling out for reform. In particular, consumers are rarely exposed to the true marginal cost of the energy they consume, and so are not incentivized to modulate their consumption in line with supply and demand. As McKinsey's report *Curbing Global Energy Demand Growth: The energy productivity opportunity* points out,

> Global energy markets are rife with market inefficiencies and distortions. Consumers lack the information and capital needed to improve energy productivity and, in the real world, tend to put considerations of convenience, comfort and safety above cost. And many of them are shielded from the true cost of energy they use because of subsidies and non-marginal pricing, which further mutes any potential price response.[41]

One example of this is one most of us are familiar with: the price we pay for electricity. Although marginal wholesale electricity prices fluctuate wildly according to the instantaneous state of supply and demand, with sharp spikes at peak times, most of us pay a fixed unit price. In order for the lights to stay on, electricity production has to match demand at all times, an exercise demanding considerable skill, cost and no little waste of energy in maintaining a contingency of 'spinning reserve'.

An alternative approach would see demand responding to supply by means of real-time price signals sent out on the electricity supply wires. When supplies were stretched high prices would dampen demand, and at times of excess supply prices would fall and stimulate demand. Smart meters would record the amount of power consumed (as now) but also the price to apply to each unit, based on marginal market costs at the time of use.

Of course, consumers would not run around their houses all the time turning appliances on and off. Instead appliances would incorporate circuits that would respond to price signals by turning the appliance on and off automatically. Thus a freezer would 'stock up' on cold using cheap night-time electricity, and gradually warm up while prices were high. A washing machine would wait until electricity prices were low before running, subject of course to manual override. An iron or electric kettle would warn the consumer – maybe by way of an alarm light or audible signal – if the price rose beyond a pre-set threshold. Electric cars plugged in on charge would wait for prices to drop before drawing current.

The immediate result of this 'real-time pricing' and 'responsive demand' would be that the grid and the underlying power generation system would operate more cheaply and efficiently, and consumers would on average pay less for their electricity – a win-win scenario for consumers and for emissions. A longer-term benefit would be that grids would be able to accommodate a higher fraction of intermittent renewables, for example from wind, wave and solar photovoltaic (PV), without the need for expensive fossil-powered back-up generators to step in when the wind dropped.

But we should ideally go a stage farther to make the electricity grid a genuine network (like the Internet), in which there is no longer a clear distinction between 'supplier' and 'consumer'. High connection charges and anti-competitive conditions surrounding small-scale electricity supply (as in the UK today) should be dropped, encouraging small-scale embedded generation whether from wind turbines, rooftop solar PV panels, fuel cell boilers (which simultaneously generate both heat and power) or exercise bicycles doubling up as generators. Likewise electric cars left on charge might switch into reverse if prices went high enough – discharging energy back into the system, and making money for their owners in the process. Again, this would benefit all concerned: reducing emissions and costs, and enhancing grid stability through the decentralized actions of many independent agents responding to real-time market conditions.

The key need in the cases discussed here is to remove existing market barriers and distortions, and to create genuinely free markets that work for all participants and produce environmental benefits. It may appear paradoxical that new laws and regulations will be needed to achieve this. Perhaps we need to recognize that free markets rarely if ever arise spontaneously, as the powerful will always seek ways to distort, restrict or corner markets for their benefit. Effective regulation is an essential prerequisite of freedom, in markets as in society.

Box 5.1 Ronald Coase on direct regulation

'It is my belief that economists, and policy-makers generally, have tended to over-estimate the advantages which come from governmental regulation. But this belief, even if justified, does not do more than suggest that government regulation should be curtailed. It does not tell us where the boundary line should be drawn. This, it seems to me, has to come from a detailed investigation of the actual results of handling the problem in different ways. [...] direct governmental regulation will not necessarily give better results than leaving the problem to be solved by the market or the firm. But equally there is no reason why, on occasion, such governmental administrative regulation should not lead to an improvement in economic efficiency. This would seem particularly likely when, as is normally the case with the smoke nuisance, a large number of people are involved and in which therefore the costs of handling the problem through the market or the firm may be high. [...] In the standard case of a smoke nuisance, which may affect a vast number of people engaged in a wide variety of activities, the administrative costs might well be so high as to make any attempt to deal with the problem within the confines of a single firm impossible. An alternative solution is direct Government regulation. Instead of instituting a legal system of rights which can be modified by transactions on the market, the government may impose regulations which state what people must or must not do and which have to be obeyed.'[42]

6 | Allocating resources

> 'The problem with action on climate change is that politically plausible programmes have a tendency to sound too small for the size of the challenge, whereas plans that match the challenge in their scope tend not to sound politically plausible.' *Nature* editorial[1]

> 'Up to now, the polar bear has been the poster child for climate change. We need to use every politically correct and scientifically sound trick in the book to convince the world that humanity really is the most important species endangered by climate change.' Dr Margaret Chan, Director-General of the World Health Organization[2]

How much?

First, an order of magnitude estimate of how much money could be raised in the Kyoto2 auction of greenhouse gas production permits. Current emissions are around 50Gt CO_2 eq per year, acording to the IPCC.[3] Of this approximately two-thirds (33Gt) are amenable to 'at source' control, including emissions from fossil fuels, other industrial gases and fertilizer-related N_2O, and excluding other land-use-based emissions. Apply the approximate current price of allowances under the world's largest carbon market, the EUETS (see Chapter 2), of around €20, and we reach a sum of €660 billion, or $1 trillion. The precise sum raised will of course depend on the stringency of the cap and the strength of demand for permits.

As the cap bites, initial abatement of emissions will come in the areas where they are most cost-effectively achieved and the price of permits will tend towards the abatement cost. There remain significant opportunities for low- or even negative-cost emissions reductions in the USA, a McKinsey study reveals,[4] with cuts of 3–4.5Gt/y achievable at under \$50/t CO_2 eq, of which 40 per cent is already profitable at a zero-carbon price. Similar considerations will apply in other OECD countries.

Most of the low- and negative-cost reductions identified by McKinsey, however – for example in energy-efficient building and lighting – have not been made only as a result of existing market failures and will not therefore respond well to a carbon price signal. Instead we look to emissions reductions that will respond well to a carbon price signal, for example in energy supply. Substantial opportunities exist in power generation, of which the lowest-cost options include fuel switching (coal to natural gas), 'carbon capture and storage' (CCS) systems to remove CO_2 from power station exhaust and store it in secure undergound reservoirs, and developing new renewable capacity, such as concentrated solar power (CSP) or wind.

As regards CCS, the Department of Trade and Industry (now the Department for Business, Enterprise and Regulatory Reform) estimated in 2007[5] that retro-fitting coal power stations can be achieved for about £22 (€31, \$44)/t CO_2, and £30–35 (€43–50, \$60–70) for retro-fitting CCGT gas-fired stations. Building new power stations with CCS produces results at slightly lower cost. Of course, additional opportunities will also exist at similar cost – whether nuclear, wind, wave, new hydroelectric, concentrated solar power (CSP) or other technologies.

This indicates that even as a greenhouse gas emissions cap bites, and produces real emissions reductions, permit prices are likely to rise to €30–40 and remain there for some years until the scope for these technologies is exhausted. Meanwhile substantial additional energy R&D spending (both in the public and private sectors) should be producing further reductions in clean energy costs, moderating the scarcity premium on permits as the volume sold diminishes. The combination of reduced sales volume and higher prices indicates that the sum raised is likely to remain in the region of €1 trillion per year for some years.

With current world GDP of about \$66 trillion[6] this would represent about 1.5 per cent of world product. This is greater than Nicholas Stern's estimate[7] that 1 per cent of world product would be sufficient to meet the costs of climate change adaptation and mitigation, with stabilization at 550ppm. Our aim, however, is to fund a more rapid transition to a low-carbon economy, a carbon-neutral world and stabilization at the much lower level of 350ppm CO_2 eq.

Of course, €1 trillion is a large sum of money, but it is of a scale comparable with existing expenditures of less obvious benefit:

- Oil consumption in 2006[8] was 84 million barrels per day, and prices are currently around $100 per barrel. This implies a world expenditure of $8.4 billion per day, or $3 trillion per year. Oil prices have risen in the last few years from around $30 per barrel, so of the $3 trillion per year, $2 trillion per year represents the effect of recent price increases alone. In other words the entire Kyoto2 programme would cost around half as much as recent price increases in oil alone.
- The US presence in Iraq, as of 2007, costs $120 billion per year. Note that this is probably an underestimate. In their article 'Iraq War will cost more than $2 trillion'[9] Linda Bilmes and Joseph E. Stiglitz consider not only direct budgetary costs, but also the wider economic impact of lost lives, medical care, jobs disrupted and oil price repercussions, and reach an estimate of $2.267 trillion, in the USA only. See also the Joint Economic Committee Majority Staff report, 'War at any price',[10] which estimates $1.3 trillion for 2002–08.
- Global military expenditure of $1.2 trillion in 2006.[11]
- OECD agricultural subsidies (2002/03) of $324 billion per year.
- Fossil fuel subsidies of at least $235 billion per year and perhaps as much as $300 billion per year.[12]
- Total perverse subsidies by governments of some $2 trillion per year (as published in 2001), in terms of both direct costs and uncompensated external costs, in fossil fuel, nuclear

power, forestry, fisheries, water, agriculture and road transport sectors.[13]

- The exposure of UK taxpayers arising from the government's rescue of the failing Northern Rock bank of about £100 billion.
- Biofuel subsidies that are currently more than $10 billion per year in the EU and the USA, which would reach $100 billion per year in order to supply 30 per cent of automotive fuels (see Chapter 2), and which result in greater greenhouse gas emissions than burning mineral oil.
- €30 billion worth of emissions allowances handed out at no charge to Europe's power companies under the EUETS, every year, which they then sell on to their customers at the full market price.
- Losses by US banks during the sub-prime mortgage crisis in 2007 of approximately $100 billion, which did not stop the top five US banks alone paying out $39 billion in bonuses to employees.[14]
- Nicholas Stern[15] estimates the the net present value of adopting a path towards stabilization at 550ppm of CO_2 eq relative to a 'business-as-usual' emissions trajectory at $2.5 trillion for each year for which the 550ppm trajectory is followed.

We shall examine, below, how the need for funding compares with the sum available.

Who?

What bodies would be in charge of the auction and police compliance, and would supervise the spending of the funds? Given that the fund would have an income of some $1 trillion a year, the question is an important one.

Ultimate accountability must of course rest with the treaty organization, the Climate Convention. There is no need, however, for it to actually do everything itself. Central banks already have considerable experience of running multiple-item auctions, as this is how government bonds are generally sold into financial markets. The auction itself might therefore be best operated by a coalition of the world's central banks, and the largest such banks, the US Federal Reserve and the European Central Bank, would play pivotal roles.

As to the disbursements, several funds already exist and their role could be expanded: the Multilateral Fund of the Montreal Protocol, and the three adaptation funds of the Kyoto Protocol itself. A number of international organizations exist with appropriate experience and expertise to manage the funds. These include the World Bank, the UN Environment Programme, the UN Development Programme, the Food and Agriculture Organization of the United Nations, the Global Environment Facility and the International Energy Agency. It might also be desirable to create a new United Nations Environment Organization which would draw together existing UN environment treaty bodies and agencies.

While some of these organizations (the FAO in particular) have faced criticism in recent years for poor performance, there is no particular reason to suppose than any new organizations would perform any better. In any case, their role would be that of agencies, and accountability would remain with the Climate Convention.

It is also proposed that national governments should be responsible for the supervision and regulation of the production of fossil fuels and of other greenhouse gases within their territories, this role being subject to oversight by Climate Convention officials. In return for performing this role, to encourage diligent performance, and to partially compensate for loss in royalty and other revenues arising from fossil fuels, governments satisfactorily performing their duties receive a small percentage of the value of the permits surrendered for operations taking place within their jurisdictions. At 5 per cent this would imply an expenditure of €50 billion.

A role for the private sector? The Kyoto Protocol's Clean Development Mechanism (CDM) has overall proved to be an inefficient mechanism for abating greenhouse gas emissions (see Chapter 2). It has succeeded in mobilizing considerable private capital, however, and in stimulating the creativity of entrepreneurs, and some excellent projects have come out of it. It would be a shame to bring all this to an end under a new climate protocol and lose the expertise and commitment of the better companies in the sector.

Much of the inefficiency of the CDM arises from:

- the uncertainties inherent in the market for Certified Emission Reductions (CERs) – so investors demand a risk premium;
- its short-term nature, arising from the effective closing date of 2012 – so that only 'quick buck' projects can be funded rather than those bringing longer-term benefits;
- the fixed price of CERs across sectors – even though CERs may be generated at far lower cost in some sectors, and in some countries, than in others.

If these sources of inefficiency were addressed, there could be a role for a reformed CDM under Kyoto2, in which the Climate Convention or national governments would (using monies from the Climate Change Fund) offer to buy in CERs from specific sectors, regions and countries at appropriate fixed prices. This would remove much of the uncertainty now afflicting carbon markets, allow longer-term projects, provide funding more precisely attuned to the costs involved, and encourage investors to develop projects in specific countries that might otherwise be left out (much as most of Africa is left out of the current CDM). The same companies now designing and implementing CDM projects would therefore enjoy a continued and very likely expanded role.

One major difference is that these CDM projects would no longer be expected to bring about absolute reductions in emissions relative to a theoretical 'business-as-usual' baseline, as at present, but rather to relieve pressure on the caps on greenhouse gas emissions, and so moderate demand for, and the economic burden of, permits. Such projects would be of particular value in tackling emissions relating to agriculture or other land use, and so outside the core Kyoto2 mechanism, especially where large capital investments were needed.

Involving communities There is a danger that the spending of the Climate Change Fund would be seen as a top-down process that pays insufficient attention to the needs and wishes of local communities. It is essential that communities should be involved in how money is spent on projects that affect them, and should be able to influence how they are run through democratic processes. For small-scale projects, for example to introduce renewable power generation into rural villages, or increase local resilience against flooding, community councils and other local organizations should be in charge, while taking advice from appropriate specialists.

Adaptation Fund

> 'Our actions over the coming few decades could create risks of major disruption to economic and social activity, later in this century and in the next, on a scale similar to those associated with the great wars and the economic depression of the first half of the 20th century.' Nicholas Stern[16]

Even if the world were to stop emitting greenhouse gases immediately, the global temperature would rise by about 1°C over the next century thanks to time lags in the climate system, while the thermal expansion of the oceans alone would cause some tens of centimetres of sea level rise over a multi-century timescale. And that's not about to happen: greenhouse gas emissions are rising and will inevitably carry on doing so before even the most effective measures can force them down. Even with policies aimed at limiting temperature rises to 1.5°C, such are the uncertainties that we should be prepared for 2°C. As noted by Stern,

> Adaptation is the only response available for the impacts that will occur over the next several decades before mitigation measures can have an effect [...] The additional costs of making new

> infrastructure and buildings resilient to climate change in OECD countries could be $15–150 billion each year (0.05–0.5% of GDP).
>
> The challenge of adaptation will be particularly acute in developing countries, where greater vulnerability and poverty will limit the capacity to act. As in developed countries, the costs are hard to estimate, but are likely to run into tens of billions of dollars [...] Adaptation efforts in developing countries must be accelerated and supported, including through international development assistance [...]
>
> The poorest developing countries will be hit earliest and hardest by climate change, even though they have contributed little to causing the problem. Their low incomes make it difficult to finance adaptation. The international community has an obligation to support them in adapting to climate change. Without such support there is a serious risk that development progress will be undermined.[17]

This will be neither a small nor a cheap job, as the IPCC warned in April 2007.[18] Disappearing glaciers will create freshwater shortages for about one-sixth of the world's population. By 2020, between 75 and 250 million Africans will 'be exposed to an increase of water stress due to climate change', while 'In some countries, yields from rain-fed agriculture could be reduced by up to 50%.' In Central, South, East and South-East Asia more than a billion people will be short of fresh water by the 2050s, while 'densely populated coastal areas will face severe flood risk from both sea and river flooding'.

As described by Mark Lynas in *Six Degrees*,[19] even 2°C would be enough to melt almost all the glaciers in the Alps, the Andes and the Sierra Nevada in the western USA. The average European summer would be like the most extreme summer now, and a hot summer would be like the climate of the Middle East and cause tens of thousands of excess deaths. Places that are wet will get wetter, dry places will get drier, and rain will be concentrated into intense storms. Drought will become more frequent and severe in Australia and the western USA, while the Kalahari Desert will expand across southern Africa and extend northwards to the Congo Basin. Sea levels could rise by more than a metre by 2100, and then continue to rise for centuries as the Greenland and West Antarctic ice sheets melt away.

Cities in particular will be vulnerable to climate change, especially in countries such as India, China, Bangladesh and Vietnam with large populations in coastal zones. Hazards include sea level rise, storms, high water tables undermining foundations, groundwater salinization and loss of beaches. Inland cities too will be at risk of storm flooding, mudslides, water shortages caused by glacial retreat, heatwaves, increased risk of disease and loss of food supply from agricultural hinterlands. As David Satterthwaite writes,

> Well-governed cities can reduce these risks, but in most African and Asian cities 33–50 percent of people live in illegal settlements which lack good water and sanitation provision, paved roads and storm drains. Many settlements are on risky sites such as floodplains, coastal areas or unstable hillsides. Their inhabitants have limited capacity to invest and city governments often refuse to work with them.[20]

Port cities will be at particular risk, as shown in an OECD assessment[21] of 136 port cities with populations of over a million. Considering a 1-in-100-year flood as the risk threshold, the report finds that:

> The total value of assets exposed in 2005 across all cities considered here is estimated to be US$3,000 billion; corresponding to around 5% of global GDP in 2005 (both measured in international USD). By the 2070s, total population exposed could grow more than threefold to around 150 million people due to the combined effects of climate change (sea-level rise and increased storminess), subsidence, population growth and urbanization. The asset exposure could grow even more dramatically, reaching US $35,000 billion by the 2070s; more than ten times current levels and rising to roughly 9% of projected global GDP in this period.

> On a global scale, for both types of exposure, population growth, socio-economic growth and urbanization are the most important drivers of the overall increase in exposure. Climate change and subsidence significantly exacerbate this effect although the relative importance of these factors varies by location. Exposure rises most rapidly in developing countries, as development moves increasingly into areas of high and rising flood risk.[22]

Addressing these impacts will carry a huge price tag. According to the Oxfam report 'Adapting to climate change – what's needed in poor countries, and who should pay',

> Adaptation will cost at least $50bn each year, and far more if global emissions are not cut rapidly [...] But rich countries have so far pledged a mere $182m to international funds for developing country adaptation – less than 0.5 per cent of the minimum amount that Oxfam believes is needed overall. Funding just the most urgent and immediate adaptation priorities of the least developed countries (LDCs) is likely to cost $1–2bn. Among donors, the mood is anything but urgent: they have so far delivered $48m to the international fund set up for LDCs – less than five per cent of what's needed: enough for Haiti, Samoa, and Kiribati, but no more. Not only is this funding a fraction of what is needed, but it is almost all being counted towards long-standing commitments to provide 0.7 per cent of national income as aid. Only the Netherlands has explicitly committed to provide climate-related finance in addition to this.[23]

Meanwhile the true scale of investment required is illustrated by developing-country expenditures at home:

> Rich countries are investing in their own climate change adaptation, with budgets for individual projects at home outstripping their total contribution to international adaptation funds.
> The UK – the biggest contributor to international funds so far, pledging $38m – is investing £178m ($347m) in cooling systems for the London Underground, partly in preparation for climate change. The Netherlands, pledging $18m to international funds,

is spending at least €2.2bn ($2.9bn) on building new flood dykes at home, in anticipation of climate-change impacts.[24]

The cost of new water infrastructure to replace lost glaciers, of resettling populations, of building flood protection structures around cities, or relocating cities from areas made uninhabitable by drought or flood, of rebuilding factories, oil refineries, roads, bridges, railway lines, ports and power stations threatened by flood or undermined by melting permafrost, will certainly require investment on a scale comparable to that of rebuilding Europe after the Second World War.

But while the Marshall Plan and associated programmes delivered some $25 billion in aid to western Europe from 1947 to 1951, worth around $1 trillion in today's money (5 per cent of the USA's GDP), the international response to climate change has so far been lacking, with the World Bank estimating[25] that the Kyoto Protocol's Adaptation Fund will contain under $500 million by 2012. Donations and pledges to the other two adaptation-related funds, the LDCF and the SCCF, came to $133 million as of May 2006 (see Chapter 2).

Accordingly Kyoto2 adopts the approach recommended by the World Bank in 2007 in its *World Development Report 2008: Agriculture for Development*, designed to address these failures.

> Carbon taxes based on the polluter pays principle could become a major new source of revenues to fund adaptation programs. The international community needs to devise new mechanisms to provide a range of global public goods, including climate information and forecasting, research, conservation and development of crops adapted to new weather patterns, and techniques to reduce land degradation. Because of the long time lag between the development of technologies and information systems and their adoption in the field, investments to support adaptation need to be initiated now.[26]

Kyoto2 proposes to dedicate an initial $200 billion per year to the Adaptation Fund, in order to to deal not only with current problems but to tackle pre-emptively the problems that are expected to arise in the future, taking particular account of the risks of sea level rise.

Clean Energy Fund

> 'We have to figure out how to live without fossil fuels some day anyhow – so why not sooner?' Jim Hansen[27]

In 2005 the G-8 Gleneagles Summit asked the World Bank to produce a roadmap for accelerating investments in clean energy for the developing world. In response it produced its 'Clean Energy Investment Framework' (CEIF), which aims to increase access to energy, especially in sub-Saharan Africa (apparently not from clean sources); accelerate the transition to a low-carbon economy; and adapt to climate variability and change. The CEIF estimates the necessary scale of energy investments at $165 billion per year for a decade, plus numerous extra costs:

> According to the Framework, the power sector needs $165 billion in investments each year this decade. Only about half of that is financed. Tens of billions of US$ per year are also required to cover the incremental costs of transitioning to a low carbon economy. The added costs of climate proofing projects associated with aid and concessionary finance to developing countries will amount to a few billion a year, while the total costs borne by developing country public and private sectors is likely to be some tens of billions per year.[28]

The World Bank also estimates the incremental capital costs of substantially decarbonizing the energy supply in non-OECD countries at $30 billion per year until 2050, relative to a 'business-as-usual' scenario.[29] The figure is echoed by Nicholas Stern:

> Scaling up flows of carbon finance to developing countries to support effective policies and programmes for reducing emissions would accelerate the transition to a low-carbon economy [...] a transformation in the scale of, and institutions for,

> international carbon finance flows will be required to support cost-effective emissions reductions. The incremental costs of low-carbon investments in developing countries are likely to be at least $20–30 billion per year.[30]

To test the figure, we take the IEA's estimate that China and India will respectively (under the business-as-usual scenario) invest $3.7 trillion and $1.25 trillion in energy supply infrastructure over the twenty-four years from 2006 to 2030, 75 per cent of the sums going into the power sector.[31] This is approximately $5 trillion, or $200 billion per year. If a supplementary 25 per cent of that sum can redirect the investment into clean energy sources such as wind power, 'concentrated solar power' (CSP) or equipping the power stations with 'carbon capture and storage' (CCS), that implies a spend of $50 billion per year.

Although a relatively new technology, CSP is approaching price competitiveness with coal[32] and costs are likely to fall as the technology is scaled up. Continued financial support may be required, however, in building long-distance DC power grids to carry power from remote hot deserts to consumers.

We also need to make similar investments in other developing countries, which we assume doubles the cost arising from India and China alone. Then once the boom in new power generation subsides, we need to move to eco-upgrading existing power plants in developing countries. An ongoing requirement for $100 billion per year therefore seems more credible than the World Bank's $30 billion, in order to move developing countries towards entirely clean power production.

We can reasonably assume from this discussion that an annual investment of around $265 billion per year is needed to both increase access to energy, and ensure that the energy is produced from low-carbon sources. The actual scale of investment forthcoming under the CEIF is barely 1 per cent of this figure, however,[33] at $10 billion for the three years 2006–08 (or about $3.3 billion per year).[34]

In 2006 financing for renewables and energy conservation

amounted to just $805 million out of a total energy sector commitment of $4.4 billion, rising to $1.43 billion in 2007 – a worthwhile increase, but still insignificant compared to the $30 billion a year the Bank has identified as necessary.[35]

Noting that half of the $165 billion per year for energy sector investments is already funded, Kyoto2 proposes that additional energy sector funding of the order of $180 billion per year should be placed in a Clean Energy Fund to bring about a decisive move towards clean energy in developing countries by 2050. In this context the announcement on 28 January 2008 by US president George Bush of a $2 billion international Clean Technology Fund to promote clean energy and fight climate change[36] represents a welcome step in the right direction, but is two orders of magnitude too small.

In industrialized countries with good access to investment capital and efficient markets the effect of the carbon cap should be sufficient to drive the necessary investments in developing clean sources of energy without any need for supplementary financing. The areas that will need additional support in developed countries are energy R&D, which is at present underfunded, and energy conservation (see below).

Note that if the 'safety valve' or 'ceiling price' is achieved at the permit auction, this triggers additional investment into the Clean Energy Fund to reduce future demand for fossil fuels.

Energy conservation in buildings

As noted by McKinsey in *Curbing Global Energy Demand Growth: The energy productivity opportunity*,[37] residential buildings consume about a quarter of global energy demand. Using established, accessible technologies like efficient lighting, good insulation and efficient water heating could cut the sector's energy demand growth from 2.4 per cent to 1 per cent, saving almost 10 trillion KWh or 5 per cent of global end-use energy demand in 2020. It follows that more ambitious conservation programmes (as described in Chapter 5) could achieve greater reductions in energy use.

But how great? In her report *Home Truths*, Brenda Boardman, of Oxford's Environmental Change Institute, proposes an energy efficiency programme that would benefit 25 million homes by 2050 through a mix of direct grants, low-interest loans and tax concessions, at an initial cost of £10.5 billion per year from 2008 to 2018, falling to around £8 billion per year.[38] The total public cost to 2050 is £355 billion, equivalent to £14,200 per house, or about $28,000. These measures would initially be directed towards those in greatest need, such as those households identified as suffering from 'fuel poverty', to help them overcome difficulties created by energy price increases.

This suggests that a contribution from the Climate Change Fund of $10,000 per house should prove sufficient to get such programmes in motion in developed countries, with the balance provided by the government. In developing countries with smaller homes, reduced heating requirements and lower building costs, 100 per cent funding would be amply covered by $10,000 per home. To apply our suite of energy efficiency measures to 1 billion homes worldwide would cost $10 trillion. If the programme runs over forty years, this implies an annual global spend of $250 billion, resulting in an 80 per cent cut in residential energy demand by 2050.

This expenditure should be matched by governments adopting stringent standards for energy efficiency in new buildings and appliances. As the IEA reports, 'each dollar invested in more efficient electrical appliances saves $3.50 of investment on the supply side', and thus developing countries facing heavy power sector investment burdens would benefit directly from such measures.[39] The initial technology transfer costs faced by developing countries in imposing and complying with such efficiency standards should be paid out of auction proceeds, but the measures will rapidly become self-financing through reduced demand for energy and supply-side infrastructure investment, so no long-term funding requirement arises.

Also note the great potential to reduce CO_2 production from cement by switching to alternative 'eco-cements' with greatly reduced CO_2 emissions associated with their manufacture relative to Portland cement – 20 per cent in the case of geopolymer cements (see Chapter 5). Current production of about 1.8Gt of Portland cement per year produces a similar tonnage of CO_2 emissions, estimated at 5–8 per cent of the total, and production is estimated to rise to 5Gt by 2050. The main need here is to research the performance of eco-cements and their suitability for specific applications, to publish the results to make them available to the building industry and regulators, and to develop appropriate standards. A 50 per cent reduction in emissions from cement manufacture by 2050 should be achievable, representing a saving of some 2.5Gt of CO_2 emissions per year.

Relative to the $250 billion already allocated these costs will be *de minimis* and do not need to be specifically accounted for.

Clean Energy Research Fund

Government-funded global energy research and development spending is currently running at about $10.9 billion per year, of which about $1.29 billion is spent on energy conservation, $1.34 billion on fossil fuels, $1.18 billion on renewable energy, $4.35 billion on nuclear energy (of which under $1 billion on fusion), $617 million on hydrogen and fuel cell technologies, and $504 million on energy storage, conversion and distribution.[40] A breakdown of these figures is sadly not available as the IEA has yet to receive the necessary data from governments and most particularly from the EU.

This represents 57 per cent of the level of spending in 1980, when global energy R&D spending reached a peak of $19 billion. It is not immediately clear why this should be the case. Of course, the high spending in 1980 was in reaction to the 1978 oil shock, but the world is currently in the midst of a 'global warming' shock, an unprecedented oil price shock with prices of $100 per barrel or more, and impending resource shortages, especially of oil and gas. These add up to very strong reasons to be spending considerably more on energy R&D than in 1980, not 43 per cent less. As Gwyn Prins and Steve Rayner argue in *Nature*,[41]

> We stare at stark divergences of trends. On the one hand, the International Energy Agency predicts a doubling of global energy demand from present levels in the next 25 years. On the other, since 1980 there has been a worldwide reduction of 40 percent in government budgets for energy R&D. Without huge investment in R&D, the technologies upon which a viable emissions reduction strategy depends will not be available in time to disrupt a new cycle of carbon-intensive infrastructure. So investment in energy R&D should be placed on a wartime footing.

The IEA is in full agreement: 'Given the scale of the energy challenge facing the world, a substantial increase is called for in public and private funding for energy technology research, development and demonstration, which remains well below levels reached in the early 1980s.'[42]

The current balance of spending also reflects a misallocation of resources. The sum dedicated to nuclear fission is excessive in that it is (or by now ought to be) a mature and market-ready technology which can compete head to head with other energy sources, having already absorbed some hundreds of billions ($) of government investment since the mid-1970s. This is not to deny a possible role for nuclear fission, even a substantial one in the future if this is how investors choose to allocate their resources, but the time for major government support should by now be over.

Nuclear fusion, by contrast, is underfunded, and all the more so after recent cuts by the USA to the ITER experimental reactor at Cadarache, France.[43] Fusion will certainly not be producing useful quantities of power before 2050; it is in the post-2050 world, however, that global carbon emissions need to reduce to near zero. Much of the lowest-cost coal will by then have been burnt,[44] and the lowest-cost reservoirs suitable for 'carbon capture and storage' (CCS) from coal-fired power stations (see above) will have been filled.

We may hope (and even expect) that renewable technologies will by 2050 have advanced to the point that fusion power is not needed. Nevertheless, it would be unwise to put all our investment eggs into the renewables basket. Consider, for example, the fact that some parts of the world are either poor in renewable energy resources, or their renewable resources may be strongly seasonal. There is a significant potential role for nuclear fusion post-2050, and it would be prudent to ensure that the technology is available at that date. In particular there is a pressing need to develop and test the materials with which to construct fusion reactors. A significant increase in fusion funding is therefore desirable.

Energy storage is clearly underfunded, as any significant move to renewable energy will be greatly assisted by the availability of efficient, large-scale electricity storage technologies. The need arises from the intermittent nature of much renewable electricity supply, such as that arising from wind power, wave power and solar PV, and the variable if more predictable output from other renewable sources such as tidal power and concentrated solar power (in dry desert areas). Renewable energy, energy conservation and hydrogen/fuel cells would also benefit from additional expenditure, and appear to be underfunded relative to nuclear fission in particular.

It is also surprising to see $1.3 billion of government research spending directed towards fossil fuels: the main priority should be to move away from fossil fuels, and the fossil fuel sector is highly profitable in its own right and does not obviously need additional government support. The current spending on fossil fuel research represents, in effect, a subsidy to the fossil fuel sector – just when we should be doing the reverse, and making it pay its full external costs.

The only element of fossil fuel R&D that deserves such funding is that into CCS. It is therefore unfortunate to see that government funding for CCS is not forthcoming, with the USA's withdrawal of $1.3 billion from the FutureGen CCS partnership, a lack of enthusiasm in the UK and the European Commission's announcement in January 2008 that there was 'no possibility of significant funding from the EU budget'.[45]

We also note the proposal by environmental economist Bjorn Lomborg for a treaty that would oblige countries to invest 0.05 per cent of their GDP in 'non-carbon energy technologies', and his alternative proposal for a global $2 carbon tax that would raise $50 billion for R&D.[46] In fact, if applied only to fossil fuels and industrial gases it would raise closer to $60 billion.

Bearing in mind all the above, Kyoto2 proposes to supplement the existing pattern of energy research, trebling the overall spend at its earlier peak in 1980 to $60 billion, and redirecting the focus of spending into renewables, conservation, hydrogen and fuel cells, energy storage and CCS. Governments will remain free to choose their own areas of spending; their choices could be guided, however, by the use of match funding for energy research into the areas favoured by Kyoto2. This will require an initial allocation of $50 billion per year to be placed in a Clean Energy Research Fund.

Forests and other terrestrial sinks

> 'I am the Lorax. I speak for the trees.
> I speak for the trees, for the trees have no tongues.
> And I'm asking you, sir, at the top of my lungs ...'
>
> Dr Seuss, *The Lorax*[47]

Greenhouse gas emissions from deforestation contribute about 17.5 per cent of the annual increment,[48] through emissions of CO_2, methane and nitrous oxide. There are particular problems in controlling these emissions owing to:

- their dispersed nature, making them hard to control, and hard or indeed impossible to measure with accuracy;
- the difficulty of distinguishing with certainty between emissions that are of natural origin, and those that are due to deliberate human interventions;
- issues of national sovereignty: in particular, forest-rich developing countries do not take kindly to other countries telling them what they may and may not do with their forests.

These three factors make it inconceivable (whether or not in principle desirable) that these emissions should be controlled at source in the same way as emissions from fossil fuels and other industrial sources. There are also many problems with the approach currently being developed under the Climate Convention to protect forests, which is to incorporate reduced emissions from deforestation and degradation (REDD) within the carbon trading framework (see Chapter 2). To begin with we need to cut greenhouse gas emissions both from forest destruction and from fossil fuels – not to trade the one off against the other.

Accordingly the Kyoto2 response is to reward countries that preserve these critical ecosystems with payments for adherence to country-specific codes, based on the value of the carbon storage and other climate system roles of their forests, and of the costs (including opportunity costs) involved in their conservation. All payments would be strictly contingent on the achievement of biodiversity as well as carbon objectives, and the respect of the rights of traditional forest owners, users and dwellers.

Global forest area amounts to some 4 billion hectares containing 638Gt of carbon, plus about 1.4 billion hectares of wooded land. Forest destruction is proceeding at about 13 million hectares per year, with a net deforestation rate of 6.3 million hectares per year.[49] Following Chapter 5, our task is to bring this source of emissions, totalling 17.5 per cent of annual emissions, to a halt by paying countries to abide by country-specific Forest Agreements.

The World Bank has estimated that 'to achieve a 10–20 percent reduction in rates of deforestation, the amount of financing required would be in the range of $2–25 billion per year'.[50]

The objective is inadequate: to prevent catastrophic climate change, our objective should be to halt deforestation, and preserve forests, especially the long-established forests that embody most carbon. It is not enough to bring about a net re-creation of forests, if that means replacing carbon-rich old forests with new forests that will not achieve their full carbon storage potential for a century or more: we need to both keep the forests we have, and to establish new forests that will absorb carbon from the atmosphere over their growing period.

The cost range indicated by the World Bank is surprisingly wide – an indication of the difficulty we face in deriving an accurate figure. So let's try another means of calculation. If we suppose that deforestation for agriculture on average produces a financial gain of $400 per hectare per year, then the loss of 13 million hectares of forest can be avoided with targeted payments amounting to about $5 billion per year. In order to stop the focus of deforestation from simply moving elsewhere, however, we also need to reward at a similar level the retention of an additional, larger area of forest that would remain vulnerable to deforestation. Multiply our figure by ten to take in this additional area of vulnerable forest, and we reach a figure of about $50 billion per year.

We also need a broader mechanism to reward countries for maintaining forests and other carbon-rich ecosystems that are safe from the threat of destruction in the longer term. If we apply payments to 5 billion hectares of forest and woodland at an average rate of $10 per year, this would cost a further $50 billion per year.

Other, non-forest ecosystems are also in dismal condition and suffering continuing decline, and these too deserve protection in order to carry out their ecosystem functions and contain their embodied carbon, as reported in the Millennium Ecosystem Assessment 2007:

> First, approximately 60% (15 out of 24) of the ecosystem services examined during the Millennium Ecosystem Assessment are being degraded or used unsustainably, including fresh water, capture fisheries, air and water purification, and the regulation of regional and local climate, natural hazards, and pests. The full costs of the loss and degradation of these ecosystem services are difficult to measure, but the available evidence demonstrates that they are substantial and growing [...] Over the past 50 years, humans have changed ecosystems more rapidly and extensively

> than in any comparable period of time in human history, largely to meet rapidly growing demands for food, fresh water, timber, fiber, and fuel. This has resulted in a substantial and largely irreversible loss in the diversity of life on Earth.[51]

Peatland ecosystems are especially important in this regard due to the huge volumes of biological carbon which they embody. The swamp forests of South-East Asia (including those converted to agriculture) are estimated to contain some 42Gt of biological carbon (equivalent to 155Gt of CO_2). Out of an original 27 million hectares of swamp forest in the region, 12 million hectares are already deforested and mostly drained, and these are responsible for 2Gt of annual CO_2 emissions – 8 per cent of that deriving from fossil fuels as the dried-out peat oxidizes.[52]

Available funds should therefore be aimed most specifically at these swamp forests, to keep the surviving 13 million hectares in good condition, and to begin to restore the degraded area by blocking off drainage channels to raise water levels. Developed countries too need to conserve their peatlands – including the UK with its extensive peatland resources, such as the 4,000-square-kilometre Flow Country in northern Scotland, which could embody as much as 20Gt of carbon (equivalent to 74Gt CO_2). These are currently suffering from widespread burning to attract grouse for shooting, leading to desiccation and decomposition.[53]

We also need to extend our mechanism for forest retention to other biomes that embody less carbon per hectare, but still substantial amounts in aggregate, including in the underlying soils, such as grassland, savannah, steppe, moorland and shrubland. The main principles here are to avoid conversion to agriculture and overgrazing. If such payments are applied to 10 billion hectares (of which about half would be degraded but capable of recovery), this will require a further $100 billion.

There is also the question of restoring badly damaged ecosystems that cannot simply regenerate of their own accord, and especially forest ecosystems where the re-establishment of native tree cover may require considerable effort, especially where soils have been eroded, or new sub-climax vegetation is preventing regrowth of trees. This applies most urgently to the 12 million hectares of drained swamp forest in South-East Asia, where emissions from oxidation and fire amount to 2Gt per year.

Following Stavins and Richards, we assume a typical restoration cost of $2,500 per hectare.[54] On part of this land we will also need to compensate owners, cultivators and commoners, and assume an average cost of $1,500 per hectare. If we aim to restore native forest and woodland on 1 billion hectares, this will cost $4 trillion. If put into effect over forty years, this corresponds to an annual cost of $100 billion.

These figures are of course highly imprecise but convey a sense of the sums required. Add them all up and we reach $300 billion per year for a comprehensive package of: targeted payments to preserve vulnerable forests; general payments to reward the good management and conservation of all forests and other carbon-embodying ecosystems and underlying soils; and the progressive restoration of lost forests.

These measures will also contribute significantly to the preservation of biodiversity in forest and other ecosystems, by restoring large areas of contiguous habitat. Significant biodiversity will none the less be at risk of extinction from global warming and the shift of climate zones, as described in *Nature* in 2004: 'We predict, on the basis of mid-range climate-warming scenarios for 2050, that 15–37% of species in our sample of regions and taxa will be "committed to extinction". [...] minimal climate-warming scenarios produce lower projections of species committed to extinction (approximately 18%) than mid-range (approximately 24%) and maximum-change (approximately 35%) scenarios.'[55] These widespread 'climate extinctions' are expected because:

- Even where suitable 'wildlife corridors' exist which species may use to migrate from areas rendered unsuitable for them by climate change, into more optimal areas, slow-moving species will not be able to move fast enough unassisted.
- Natural barriers may prevent species and ecosystems from

migrating. In South Africa, for example, the rich biodiversity of the Cape cannot migrate farther south because it is limited by the sea. In the mountain areas of Spain[56] butterflies' upward migration into cooler, higher zones is limited by mountain altitude. The same principle applies in other mountain areas, including high-biodiversity cloud forests of Central and South America, where individual mountain peaks often represent unique biodiversity 'islands' – and of course not just to butterflies but to entire ecosystems. Another example is the polar bear, at risk from the loss of summer sea ice in the Arctic, which was consequently listed as 'vulnerable' in the IUCN Red List of endangered species in 2006.

One solution is to assist species migration, as proposed by Jason McLachlan.[57] But for many species and ecosystems – such as polar bears and South Africa's Cape floristic kingdom – there will be nowhere to go. Diverse factors may hinder successful introductions. And as noted by Bob Holmes in 'Assisted migration: helping nature to relocate',

> To complicate things further, climate change will not simply push existing ecosystems towards the poles. Instead, conditions are likely to change in unpredictable ways, creating climate combinations and ecosystems never seen before. For example, much of the south-eastern US is likely to end up with an entirely novel climate during the next 100 years, according to a recent analysis by John Williams and his colleagues at the University of Wisconsin.[58]

For these reasons assisted migration should take a lower priority than limiting the extent of climate change, and broader conservation efforts that will in general bolster ecosystem resilience. An initial assessment suggests that the costs involved in assisted migration will lie within the margin of error inherent in the $350 billion per year already allocated.

These forest and other ecosystem conservation and restoration measures constitute the largest single element of the entire budget, and they deserve to: they are essential – as highlighted by James Lovelock in his Royal Society lecture[59] – not only in maintaining stocks of biological carbon, but in enabling the functioning of our planet's climate system and all the local and regional ecosystem services that are currently being eroded.

These services are unrewarded through any existing market mechanism. They have tentatively been valued, however, at $160 per hectare per year in the case of boreal forest.[60] If we apply this figure to 10 billion hectares of forest, woodland and other ecosystems, we reach a figure of $1.6 trillion per year for the value of their ecosystem services – surely worth paying $300 billion per year to preserve. To put the sum in context, OECD countries spend over $324 billion per year on agricultural subsidies (2001–03 average).

Agricultural reform

> 'We must do everything we can to assure the transformation of our food production system so that it helps us to combat global warming and, at the same time, to feed ourselves, in what will almost certainly be far less favourable conditions.' Edward Goldsmith[61]

Agricultural reform is key to the control of greenhouse gas emissions and to human welfare. An encompassing solution to climate change will involve:

- reducing emissions of greenhouse gases from agriculture;
- increasing carbon retention in soils;
- maintaining genetic diversity in crops and livestock;
- investing in agricultural research and extension work to help farmers adapt to climate change, maintain or increase productivity, and make their farming systems more resilient to climate change and extreme weather events.

Kyoto2 already proposes to regulate some agriculture-related emissions at source, in particular those relating to the use of fossil fuels both directly and indirectly. It is also proposed to regulate nitrate fertilizer to reflect its conversion by soil bacteria into nitrous oxide, a greenhouse gas 300 times as powerful as CO_2. Some half or more of nitrous oxide emissions from agriculture, however, arise from livestock dung, manures and slurry. Agriculture also produces great quantities of methane from livestock, and from wet rice farming.

As with emissions from deforestation, the emissions are diffuse and hard to measure. It is therefore very difficult (and would also be politically contentious) to regulate such emissions or incorporate them into a market mechanism. A better approach would be that of the Montreal Protocol: standards and guidelines would be established on best practice to minimize greenhouse gas emissions from farming. In OECD countries and others where subsidies are paid to farmers, payments would be conditional on adherence to these guidelines. In other countries, agricultural extension programmes, funded through a multilateral fund, would bring appropriate technologies to farmers and inform them of how to minimize their greenhouse gas emissions.

Accordingly, Kyoto2 proposes a major programme of research and development into 'climate-friendly' farming, and to raise the resilience of farming systems under climate change. An essential part of this package will be the maintenance of genetic diversity of both crop varieties and breeds of livestock, including that of wild relatives.

It is hard to derive an exact figure for the costs involved, so one basis of estimation is to look at the costs of existing organizations. Thus the FAO's budget for 2006 and 2007 is $765.7 million, or $383 million per year. And the Consultative Group on International Agricultural Research (CGIAR), which employs 8,500 scientists and back-up staff in 100 countries and whose affiliates run all the major genetic banks, operates on a budget of $458 million (2006). We therefore conclude that an expenditure of the order of $1 billion per year could bring about significant advance in agricultural research capability.

As argued by Goldsmith,

The most obvious method of preventing soil-loss and indeed of increasing the organic matter in the soil, is by the use of manures, compost, mulches and cover crops such as forest bark, straw or other organic materials which can be fed back into the soil. These serve to protect the soil from erosion, desiccation, excessive heat and to promote, in this way, the decomposition and mineralisation of organic matter.[62]

Another valuable technique is 'conservation tillage' to minimize disturbance to the soil. In *Reducing global warming through forestry and agriculture*, Steven R. Schroeder and Kenneth Green argue that conservation tillage practices as already widely practised in the USA (37 per cent of cropland in 1998) have the potential to sequester in soils a significant 1Gt of carbon per year (approximately 3.7Gt of CO_2).[63] They do not include in their paper a cost estimate, but the costs are in all probability negative: that is, the benefits of higher soil fertility and nutrient and water retention capacity, while reducing fossil fuel use in farm machinery, outweigh any additional costs. Indeed, McKinsey estimates a $7/ tCO_2 negative cost from conservation tillage.[64]

Agroforestry – planting of trees and/or woody shrubs in association with crops – can also be hugely beneficial. The trees and shrubs bind soils, protect delicate crops and soils from excessive direct sun (and thus desiccation and oxidization) and produce goods in the own right from fruit and nuts to coffee and cocoa, not to mention leaf fodder for cattle and goats. In addition agroforestry locks up additional biological carbon in wood, roots and soils. While generally labour intensive, multi-species agroforestry is often highly productive, especially in tropical environments. The principal cost is that of introducing agroforestry techniques into areas where farmers are not already familiar with them, but from that point on they bring economic and agronomic benefits as well as the carbon benefits.

A further technology with considerable promise is the use of crop residues, forestry wastes and other organic wastes, such as slaughterhouse waste, to produce 'bio-oil' by rapid pyrolysis of the organic matter in an oxygen-free furnace. The resulting gases are condensed to make the bio-oil – a dark brown fluid with about half the energy density of mineral oil – leaving a residue of fine ash and charcoal or 'bio-char'. The bio-oil may either be used locally to fire boilers and similar plant, or collected in tankers and removed for further processing, for example for conversion into automotive fuels, or as a chemical feedstock.

But in this context our main interest is in the bio-char. While it could be made into briquettes for sale, or milled for incorporation into the bio-oil, an alternative use is as a soil additive (together with the ash). Applied in quantities as low as 2–5 tonnes per hectare, it improves soil structure and moisture and nutrient retention (especially of nitrate and phosphate), so reducing the need for fertilizer. As described by Johannes Lehmann, biogenic carbon was used in this way in the Amazon region in pre-Columbian times, giving rise to the rich '*terra preta*' soils that are still sought after by farmers today, containing over 100 tonnes of charcoal per hectare. Incorporating bio-char into soils also constitutes an excellent long-term carbon sink. Unlike organic matter, which oxidizes in soil to leave only 10–20 per cent after five to ten years, charcoal resists oxidation and survives intact over thousands of years.[65]

According to Lehmann, some 160Mt of of carbon per year (590Mt of CO_2) could be sequestered into soils as bio-char using current waste streams, and this could be increased with rising cellulosic biofuel production to 580Mt of carbon per year (2.15Gt of CO_2), equivalent to about 10 per cent of current emissions from fossil fuels. The benefit could be magnified, however, by another property of bio-char in soil: the suppression of methane and nitrous oxide emissions, by an as yet unknown mechanism. Further research is needed to quantify these benefits in different soils and circumstances; they are, however, potentially highly significant.

The main funding to accelerate the development of bio-oil (and bio-char) would come out of our renewable energy budget. Some additional payments to farmers might be needed to encourage them to incorporate the bio-char into their soils rather than sell it. A a first step, however, would be to thoroughly research the agronomic benefits of bio-char enriching soils of different types and in different climates, to determine whether any additional incentive beyond that of the soil improvement itself is even needed.

Another important development is that of nitrate-efficient crop varieties. Carbon emissions from agriculture contribute about 1 per cent of greenhouse gas emissions, but agricultural nitrous oxide accounts for 6 per cent.[66] Now California-based Arcadia Biosciences has developed a GM technology that enhances the ability of roots to take up nitrogen from the soil. This allows current yields of oilseed rape to be maintained under a 40 per cent cut in nitrate application,[67] while research is under way to develop similarly modified wheat.

Other technologies with a similar effect are likely to be developed, whether using GM or conventional plant-breeding techniques. And they appear certain of widespread deployment owing to a winning combination of cost savings to farmers, local environmental benefits from decreased nitrate pollution to surface waters and seas, and the global environmental benefit of reduced nitrous oxide emissions. The inclusion of synthetic nitrate production under the main Kyoto2 framework would provide an additional incentive.

The use of nitrate-efficient crop varieties should be combined with nitrate-efficient farming practices, such as applying nitrate in slow-release formulations and timing applications to crops' main growing periods, and this is something that should be promoted under Kyoto2. There is also a case for the funding of public research to develop nitrate-efficient crop varieties that would be made freely available to farmers worldwide without the need to pay licence fees, and so achieve a broader reach and more rapid deployment.

We have already estimated a $1 billion cost of agricultural research. As for extension work to bring information about cover crops, conservation tillage, improved crop varieties and other techniques to farmers and farming communities, at a cost of \$5 to reach a farmer (often by way of farmers' organizations), it will cost \$10 billion per year to reach 2 billion farmers once each year.

This suggests a total funding requirement of about \$11 billion per year in order to fund agricultural research and development, transform the effectiveness of outreach to farmers worldwide, and accelerate the adoption of improved farm practices aimed at raising resilience to climate change, reducing greenhouse gas emissions and enhancing carbon sequestration in soils. If this succeeds in sequestering 3.7Gt of CO_2 per year in soils (as set out by Schroeder and Green)[68] then this is being achieved at a distinctly advantageous \$3/tCO_2, together with all the other consequential benefits of improved water and nutrient retention, reduced fertilizer demand and reduced emissions of methane and nitrous oxide.

Geo-engineering

> 'Nature, Mr. Allnut, is what we are put in this world to rise above.' Katharine Hepburn in *The African Queen*, 1951

As set out in Chapter 1, there is a real danger that global warming caused by human activities could give rise to a 'runaway greenhouse' effect in which positive feedback effects overwhelm the direct climate forcing, even if greenhouse gas emissions are severely constrained. If this takes place, even the most extreme reductions in greenhouse gas emissions would be of no avail in safeguarding the climate. In these circumstances the only remaining option would be to 'geo-engineer' a cooler Earth. Thus economist Martin Weitzman writes, in his seminal study of the economics of improbable catastrophe, of

> the desperate need to comprehend much better all of the options for dealing with high-impact climate-change extremes, which should include undertaking well-funded detailed studies and experiments about the feasibility, possible environmental

side effects, and cost-effectiveness of climate-engineering options to slim down the bad fat tail quickly in emergency-runaway cases where things might be beginning to get out of hand.[69]

A number of geo-engineering solutions have been proposed, including:

- Iron (and/or other nutrient) enrichment of ocean waters to stimulate additional growth of plankton, so drawing CO_2 out of the atmosphere and depositing a proportion of this carbon into deep sediments. Experimental results have so far been mixed. See, for example, Alan Watson's 'Minimal effect of iron fertilization on sea-surface carbon dioxide concentrations', which reports that 'our results do not support the idea that iron fertilization would significantly affect atmospheric CO_2 concentrations'.[70]
- The use of tubes in ocean waters, powered by wave action, to pump nutrient-rich deep waters to the ocean surface in order to stimulate additional growth of plankton, some of which would sink to the sea bed.[71] This technology has been proposed by the US company Atmocean, which envisages that '3m diameter by 200m deep pumps spaced 2km apart will be positioned across 80% of the world's oceans' in order to sequester 2Gt carbon per year, or 7.4Gt CO_2. Quite aside from the views of yachtsmen and shippers, building and maintaining these pipes would be a vast and expensive enterprise. A further problem is that one effect of the pumping would be to bring up dissolved CO_2 from deeper waters along with the nutrients. The technology may have a limited role in specific areas of ocean but certainly not on the scale proposed.
- To deploy mirrors in space to reflect sunlight. See, for example, Roger Angel's 'Feasibility of cooling the Earth with a cloud of small spacecraft near the inner Lagrange point', which proposes the placing of 20 trillion metre-sized sunshades in a 100,000km cloud in space at a cost of 'a few trillion dollars' to reflect 1.8 per cent of sunlight.[72]
- To introduce sulphate aerosol into the stratosphere to reflect

sunlight, mimicking the effect of volcanic eruptions. A low-cost way of doing this would be to shift to high-sulphur fuel in aviation – a possibility considered in more detail below. This approach was first proposed by Mikhail Budyko in 1977.[73]

- To create a saline aerosol above the world's oceans, powered by wind, to increase the reflectivity of stratocumulus clouds. The proposal was first made by John Latham in 1990.

There is particular promise in approaches that increase the Earth's reflectivity to incoming solar radiation, as these have an immediate effect on the planet's energy balance. By contrast geo-engineering solutions that reduce atmospheric CO_2, such as the fertilization of surface ocean waters, act only indirectly on the radiation balance and over many years of operation. They may in time have a valuable contribution to make, but they will not act fast enough to arrest runaway heating – for which immediacy of result will be of the essence.

The IPCC reports that in 2005 the total atmospheric concentration of greenhouse gases was 455ppm CO_2 eq, but that this was reduced by the effect of reflective aerosols to 375ppm CO_2 eq.[74] This is a dramatic effect, and its sheer scale suggests that enhancement of reflectivity has the potential to be a highly effective option. We must also give preference to solutions that are inexpensive, reversible and have low secondary environmental impacts. The last two listed above qualify on all counts, and we therefore examine them more closely.

In the current phase, in which further research is required before considering moving on into 'production mode', the costs are insignificant. An initial allocation of $0.5 billion is suggested for geo-engineering research.

Cloud albedo enhancement In 1990 NCAR physicist John Latham proposed[75] that global warming could be neutralized by controlled increase of the reflectivity of low-level, shallow, maritime stratocumulus clouds, which cover about a quarter of the oceanic surface. This would be achieved by introducing into the clouds micrometre-sized saline particles which would create new droplets, thereby increasing cloud albedo.

Engineer Stephen Salter of Manchester University is examining the idea that this could be achieved using a fleet of unmanned wind-powered 'Flettner rotor' yachts guided by GPS systems which would travel the oceans, using submerged propellers to power the production of the saline aerosol. He and Keith Bower examined this global cooling concept further in 2006, concluding that:

> In many situations considered to be within the ambit of the mitigation scheme, the calculated [albedo change] values exceeded those estimated by earlier workers as being necessary to produce a cooling sufficient to compensate, globally, for the warming resulting from a doubling of the atmospheric carbon dioxide concentration. Our calculations provide quantitative support for the physical viability of the mitigation scheme and offer new insights into its technological requirements.[76]

A significant proportion of the saline droplets, each weighing about 10^{-17}Kg, will be transported upwards by turbulence to enter the clouds above, and Latham surmises that this ascent may be electrically assisted – they are naturally charged, so the negative ones will experience an upward pull in the Earth's electric field.[77] Electrostatic atomization may prove the most efficient way to create the droplets, but the technique requires further investigation.

Latham proposes to take his research forward by 'planning and executing a limited-area field experiment in which selected clouds in a field of marine stratocumuli are inoculated with seawater aerosol, as proposed earlier, and airborne and satellite measurements are made to establish, quantitatively, the concomitant microphysical and radiative differences between adulterated and unaffected adjacent clouds'.[78]

And cloud albedo enhancement is a low-risk, ecologically benign and easily reversible option: 'the only raw material needed is seawater, which would largely fall back into the oceans within a few days', and the cloud reflectivity could be measured from satellites and the seawater droplet disseminators switched on or off in response.[79]

Latham's estimate of costs is again *de minimis* as far as the Kyoto2 budget is concerned: $50 million for research and assessment, a capital investment of $50 million to 'tool up' to build the spray vessels, and a further $120 million per year to build sixty spray vessels per year, including replacements, operation and maintenance costs. 'These figures pertain to maintaining the Earth's temperature constant at the values existing at the time of deployment. If it was wished to reduce the temperature to some lower value, a corresponding increase in the number of vessels would be required.'[80]

Sulphate aerosol

> 'One way known to reduce heat input, observed after volcanic eruptions, is to increase aerosol scattering in the stratosphere. Deployment of 3 to 5 million tons per year of sulfur would be needed to mitigate a doubling of CO_2. This amount is not incompatible with a major reduction in the current atmospheric sulfur pollution of 55 million tons per year that goes mostly into the troposphere.' Roger Angel[81]

In 2004 aviation consumed 222Mt of jet fuel,[82] and this is rising at 3 per cent per year,[83] so we assume 250Mt for 2008. Aviation-grade kerosene typically contains about 0.1 per cent sulphur, so our 250Mt annual burn emits about 0.25Mt. The low sulphur content is the consequence of refining – the heavy fuel oil used in shipping typically contains about 2 per cent sulphur, while the limit set by the International Maritime Organization (IMO) is 4.5 per cent. At the 2 per cent level, 250Mt of aviation fuel would emit 5Mt of sulphur – at the top of the target range of 3–5Mt.

Thus our 'back of the envelope' calculation suggests that if the aviation sector switched to high-sulphur kerosene – that is, kerosene from which the native sulphur has not been refined out – while flying at high altitude, enough sulphate aerosol could be emitted to the upper troposphere and lower stratosphere to have a significant cooling effect. Unlike more high-tech options such as space mirrors, this option would be effectively free, subject to the cooperation of fuel refiners, airlines and military air forces. We also know that the risks of introducing sulphate at altitudes of 9–13km would not incur serious risk, since this is precisely what major volcanic eruptions from Krakatoa to Pinatubo do anyway, with no permission from anyone.

There are, of course, complicating factors. Aviation tends to take place at altitudes of 9–13km, and the lower end of this range is in the turbulent troposphere, where sulphur will rapidly mix down and rain out. Emit substantial sulphur into the stratosphere, however, and this will tend to deplete stratospheric ozone. This will have a cooling effect since ozone is a greenhouse gas, but it is clearly undesirable to substantially erode the stratospheric ozone layer as it recovers from the impact of CFCs and other ozone-depleting chemicals.

Another concern is that the deliberate introduction of sulphate to the upper atmosphere would add to the existing acidification of soils and ocean, arising from existing sulphate pollution and the rising carbon dioxide concentration. There is a simple solution to this, however, which is to 'offset' any sulphate introduced into the upper troposphere or stratosphere by a corresponding, additional reduction in the sulphate emitted in the lower troposphere, for example by shipping and power stations, so that there would be no net increase in acidification.

The main present need, however, is for more research, including large-scale practical experiments in cooperation with one or more airlines. As argued by Robert Dickinson over ten years ago:

> Two promising approaches, according to COSEPUP [The Committee on Science, Engineering, and Public Policy, USA] (1992), are the employment of aerosols in the stratosphere, directly as reflectors, or in the troposphere, for the seeding of clouds to increase cloud amounts and brightness. Besides technological

> and economic feasibility, such schemes could be relatively reversible, and describing their impact may be within the reach of future scientific study. The climate system is not yet sufficiently understood for such actions to be warranted. However, there is considerable potential for an increased understanding of what such actions might do through the study of the role of similar aerosols already added to the climate system. In particular, the most intense volcanoes (e.g. Pinatubo) supply the stratosphere with enough aerosol over a period of a year or two to cancel out greenhouse warming from a resulting doubling of carbon dioxide. Furthermore, the addition of sulfate aerosols to the troposphere from the burning of fossil fuel may already be canceling out globally up to half of the greenhouse-gas warming. These comparisons suggest that at least 10 times as much sulfate aerosol would be needed in the troposphere as would be needed in the stratosphere for a comparable climatic effect.[84]

Costs would be low, given that aircraft are flying anyway, and that it actually costs oil refiners money to take the sulphur out of fuel. Once (and if) established that this was a desirable option, airlines might well pursue this geo-engineering option voluntarily in order to present themselves to the public as part of the solution to climate change, rather than as a growing part of the problem. But one cost that would need to be funded is that of offsetting the new high-altitude sulphate with reductions in existing low-altitude emissions. If we take as the abatement cost the current price of advance sulphur emissions permits in the 2007 auction of the US Environmental Protection Agency (EPA) of about $200 per ton of SO_2 (or $400 per ton of sulphur), abating 5Mt of sulphur would cost $2 billion.

In 2006 Paul Crutzen suggested an alternative and more expensive approach:

> burning S_2 or H_2S, carried into the stratosphere on balloons and by artillery guns to produce SO_2. To enhance the residence time of the material in the stratosphere and minimize the required mass, the reactants might be released, distributed over time,

> near the tropical upward branch of the stratospheric circulation system. In the stratosphere, chemical and micro-physical processes convert SO_2 into sub-micrometer sulfate particles. [...] This can be achieved by a continuous deployment of about 1–2 Tg [Mt] S per year for a total price of US $25–50 billion, or about $25–50 per capita in the affluent world, for stratospheric residence times of 2 to 1 year, respectively. The cost should be compared with resulting environmental and societal benefits, such as reduced rates of sea level rise.[85]

Any budgetary allocation at this stage would be to fund research rather than deployment. This would be measured in millions rather than billions and would thus be *de minimis* as far as the Kyoto2 budget is concerned.

Emergency Relief Fund

Natural disasters are expected to increase in frequency and severity under a regime of global heating, as the IPCC warns in its *Climate Change 2007: Impacts, Adaptation and Vulnerability*.[86] More heatwaves and heavy precipitation events are 'very likely', while increased incidence of drought, high sea level flooding and intense tropical cyclone events are 'likely'.

Under Kyoto2, considerable funds (see above) would be spent on adapting to climate change and reducing vulnerabilities. The benefits will be felt over the long term, however, and many more millions of people will meanwhile suffer from extreme weather events. It is therefore reasonable to apply funds from the permit auction to emergency humanitarian relief, and particularly in poor countries, where populations are most vulnerable.

The question is: what level of funding should be provided to account for the role of global heating in contributing to these disasters? Natural disasters happen anyway with or without global warming, and the impacts of such events are exacerbated enormously by human actions, in particular the destruction or degradation of natural ecosystems (a problem which Kyoto2 also proposes to address – see above). For example:

- The widespread loss of coastal mangrove forest leaves coastlines far more vulnerable to flooding from storm-surge events.
- Deforestation and overgrazing in watersheds increases water run-off and increases the severity of flooding downstream under heavy rain.
- The colonization of vulnerable, formerly uninhabited or sparsely inhabited areas by otherwise landless or homeless people puts them at entirely predictable risk of weather-related harm. With rising global populations and skewed distribution of land ownership, increased human suffering from extreme weather events is likely to increase even in the absence of climate change.

We also need to consider the costs of these extreme weather events. No comprehensive assessment has been made, although insurers are keenly aware of the liabilities they face. In *Climate Change and the Financial Sector: An Agenda for Action*, WWF and Allianz Global Investors report that:

> Storms in 1999 and floods in 2002 each cost 13 billion euros, while a heat wave in 2003 cost 10 billion euros. [...] Globally, climate change already results in about 160,000 deaths a year, and this is likely to rise sharply because of increasing shortages of food and water. The extraordinary heat wave in 2003 caused 27,000 deaths in Europe and disrupted agriculture, inland shipping, and electricity production. Huge swathes of forests covering a total of 5 percent of Portugal's surface area were destroyed in a loss put at one billion euros. By the end of this century such a summer could be routine. Mediterranean agriculture might be in a state of collapse. Everywhere in Europe rainfall will be more intense. The number of major floods in Europe has already risen from one per year to 15 in recent decades. In the UK, the annual cost of flooding this century will rise to as much as 30 billion euros.[87]

The major humanitarian need, however, is to compensate

poor victims of extreme weather events who lack insurance and other resources on which they can fall back. Cyclone Sidr, which hit the coast of Bangladesh on 15 November 2007, is estimated to have killed up to ten thousand people, and affected millions: flooding farmland, including rice crops awaiting harvest, with sea water, destroying homes and businesses, felling forests and cutting off essential transport links. Total costs are likely to run into billions of dollars, with immediate emergency relief operations demanding tens of millions of dollars.

China is also highly prone to major flood events owing to the vast watersheds of its major rivers. In November 2003 the Chinese Ministry of Civil Affairs reported economic losses of 188.6 billion yuan (US$22.7 billion) from a range of natural disasters including earthquake, flood, drought, landslide and mud-rock flow, and expenditures of 3 billion yuan ($361 million) for emergency relief.

Under Kyoto2, the main recovery expenditures would be funded by the adaptation budget, and used not just to rebuild but to increase resilience in the face of future climate impacts. Emergency relief requires far smaller sums – on the basis of China's experience in 2003, under 2 per cent of total damage.

Oxfam argues that weather-related crises are already on the increase:

> The total number of natural disasters has quadrupled in the last two decades – most of them floods, cyclones, and storms. Over the same period the number of people affected by disasters has increased from around 174 million to an average of over 250 million a year. [...] The total number of natural disasters worldwide now averages 400–500 a year, up from an average of 125 in the early 1980s. The number of climate-related disasters, particularly floods and storms, is rising far faster than the number of geological disasters, such as earthquakes. Between 1980 and 2006, the number of floods and cyclones quadrupled from 60 to 240 a year while the number of earthquakes remained approximately the same, at around 20 a year.[88]

For an order-of-magnitude estimate of the sums Kyoto2 should devote to emergency relief we assume future annual extreme weather damages of $1 trillion, of which the 'climate change contribution' is typically 50 per cent, and that the emergency relief requirement is 2 per cent. This yields a total of $10 billion as the annual sum to be devoted to emergency relief for extreme weather events related to climate change.

Applying another approach, if we take Oxfam's figure of 250 million people a year affected by natural disasters, and budget $100 per person for emergency relief, then assume that 40 per cent of this cost is attributable to climate change (less than the 50 per cent assumed earlier to exclude non-weather disasters), we reach the same figure of $10 billion. This suggests that the figure is a reasonable one to adopt as a first approximation.

Limiting population increase

The population question is ever contentious, but to omit from this book any discussion of the role of population numbers in global warming would be intellectually dishonest. As John Bongaarts noted in 1992, 'Existing scientific assessments of the potential for climate change resulting from a manmade "greenhouse effect" have devoted relatively little attention to the role of demographic change.'[89]

This remains the case today. Yet achieving cuts in greenhouse gas emissions on the scale indicated as necessary by climate science, of as much as 90 per cent of levels in 2000, by 2050 (see Chapter 1) will be difficult enough as it is, without doing so against a background of rising human numbers.

Simply put, if our numbers increase, then the cuts in per capita emissions must be even greater in order to meet any given emissions target. The world's population has doubled to approximately 6.6 billion since 1960, and is expected to reach 9 billion by 2050. If this further increase takes place, then to achieve a 90 per cent cut in total emissions, per capita emissions would have to be cut by 93 per cent. And if we fail to respond and continue on a 'business-as-usual' path, the resulting emissions trajectory will be all the higher in approximate proportion to population increase.

A further problem with increasing population, especially in the developing world, is that more people will be forced into marginal locations that are at risk from extreme weather events, especially flood, such as riverine flood plains, lake beds and low-lying coastal lands, often in or near cities. Protecting these people from climate risk therefore requires increased expenditure in adaptation, or relocation to less risky areas.

But how should we respond? There are an estimated 137 million women[90] who would like to be able to limit their own fertility but who are unable to do so because they lack access to family planning advice and contraceptive technologies, and a further 64 million using less effective contraceptive methods.[91] This is leading to 52 million unwanted pregnancies per year, of which roughly half result in births. The United Nations Population Fund (UNFPA) expects demand for reproductive health services to increase by 40 per cent in the next fifteen years. There is therefore a case for considering extending such provision where it is presently limited or denied, in line with the UNFPA objective (one of several) to provide 'universal access to reproductive health services by 2015'.

Substantial provision has already been made through UNFPA, and through other programmes funded by private foundations and intergovernmental aid. There remain gaps in coverage, however, and funding shortfalls relative to commitments made at UNFPA's 1994 International Conference on Population and Development, currently amounting to over $7 billion.

In 2006 UNFPA received a total income of $605 million, of which $360 million represented donations by member states – the USA being conspicuously absent from the list of donors. An allocation of funds under Kyoto2 to support UNFPA reproductive health programmes would clearly be of assistance. This should be done in such a way, however, as to ensure that these funds are additional and allow UNFPA to expand its work, instead of displacing contributions from other sources and making up shortfalls in national contributions.

But how effective a means of abating greenhouse gas emissions would this be? As Tom Dyson notes, 'By itself an increase in the world's population of roughly one half (i.e. 47 percent) will not lead to a similar proportional rise in CO_2 emissions from the burning of fossil fuels. The reason is that most of the coming demographic growth will occur in poor countries, which – almost by definition – burn relatively small amounts of coal, oil and natural gas.'[92]

Birth control provision appears, however, to be justifiable in terms of the carbon price, even in the poorest countries. If $500 million per year (almost a doubling of its current spending) would enable UNFPA to provide universal access to reproductive health services, in the process avoiding 25 million unwanted births, that would represent $20 per unwanted birth avoided. In the poorest countries such as Niger, per capita annual emissions are around 0.1 tCO_2, or say 5t over a fifty-year lifetime, indicating an abatement cost of just $4/$tCO_2$. This is far lower than current carbon prices and thus represents a cost-effective means of achieving emissions reductions. Moreover, in many developing countries per capita emissions are far higher, and increasing.

In rich countries with higher emissions the cost is far lower. For example, in the USA, where population is projected to rise from 300 million to over 400 million by mid-century, per capita annual emissions are around 20 tCO_2. Each avoided unwanted birth in the USA therefore reduces emissions by 1,500 tCO_2 over a seventy-five-year lifetime. Even assuming a far higher reproductive healthcare cost of $150, this yields an abatement cost of only $0.10/$tCO_2$.

A provisional allocation of $500 million is accordingly proposed to help UNFPA achieve universal access to reproductive health services. This could easily be increased if it did not prove sufficient.

Financing additional healthcare costs caused by climate change

'I believe that climate change will ride across this landscape as the fifth horseman. It will increase the power of the four

> horsemen that rule over war, famine, pestilence, and death – those ancient adversaries that have affected health and human progress since the beginning of recorded history. [...] Concerning pestilence, abundant evidence links the distribution and behaviour of infectious diseases to climate and weather. As the scientists say, climate defines the geographical distribution of infectious diseases. Weather influences the timing and severity of epidemics.' Dr Margaret Chan, Director-General of the World Health Organization[93]

Climate-sensitive risk factors and illnesses are among the most important contributors to the global disease burden, and higher temperatures will increase their prevalence. For example, infectious diseases limited by low temperatures will increase their range, among them diseases carried by mosquitoes and other biting insects. As Margaret Chan points out, 'diseases transmitted by mosquitoes are particularly sensitive to variations in climate. Warmth accelerates the biting rate of mosquitoes and speeds up maturation of the parasites they carry.'[94]

Prime among the mosquito-borne diseases is malaria, which already kills about one million people every year. As temperatures rise so the range of the *anopheles* mosquitoes which carry the disease is expanding north, south and upwards into presently malaria-free uplands, for example in the East African highlands.[95] Lymphatic filariasis or elephantiasis is another ancient mosquito-borne scourge, currently affecting some 120 million people, whose spread would be assisted by higher temperatures.

Well-targeted interventions offer some hope: Egypt and China have eliminated lymphatic filariasis using chemotherapy, and in so doing they have increased their resilience to climate change. But if these efforts are not replicated in other countries, and matched for other diseases, the deteriorating conditions associated with climate change will anchor even more people in disease and poverty.

Warming also brings an increased risk of other little-known or entirely novel tropical diseases, such as hantavirus pulmonary syndrome, and the Nipah virus, which surfaced in Malaysia in 1999, having emerged from its original reservoir among wild bats. We need to develop new strategies for their rapid identification, treatment and control.

Other more commonplace diseases whose prevalence will increase under climate change include malnutrition caused by food shortages, estimated to kill 3.7 million people every year, and diarrhoea, which kills some 1.9 million people every year. 'Such conditions and other health outcomes will be increasingly affected by accelerating climate change through its adverse effects on food production, water availability and the population dynamics of vectors and pathogens,' reports WHO in its 2008 *Climate Change and Health* report.[96]

General adaptation measures such as those proposed above will help to combat the extra disease burden of climate change. Actions taken in response to climate change, in particular reduced fossil fuel burning, will also bring substantial health benefits from reduced air pollution. And there will also be a health benefit from warmer winters in temperate zones, although this benefit will be offset by the adverse impacts of higher summer temperatures. In aggregate there will be a cost, and specific measures will need to be taken to address the new climate-related health impacts.

In response WHO proposes three 'overarching goals for the international response to protect health from climate change':

- to ensure that concerns about public health security are placed at the centre of the response to climate change;
- to implement adaptive strategies at local, national and regional levels in order to minimize the impacts of climate change on the health of human populations;
- to support strong actions to mitigate climate change and to avoid further dramatic and potentially disastrous impacts on health.

These goals, says WHO, can be achieved by working through existing public health frameworks with the following objectives:

- Raise awareness of the need to ensure public health security by acting on climate change.
- Strengthen public health systems to cope with the threats posed by climate change.
- Enhance capacity to deal with public health emergencies.
- Promote health development.
- Enhance applied research on health protection from climate change.
- Monitor and evaluate delivery.
- Foster cross-disciplinary partnerships.

WHO does not provide any overall costing; its proposed budget, however, stands at $4,227 million for the biennium 2008/09, or about $2 billion per year. This expenditure is of course supplemented by national government, international development, charitable and private expenditures in the countries in which WHO operates. It seems safe to suppose, however, that a doubling of the existing WHO budget should, for the foreseeable future, be of an order sufficient to address the health impacts of climate change, given that other adaptive, agricultural and emergency related expenditures are already proposed (see above). Accordingly $2 billion per year is allocated for this purpose.

Totals

Our very approximate estimates of the level of annual spending required above amount to:

- $50 billion (returned to governments for enforcement);
- $200 billion (Adaptation Fund);
- $120 billion (Clean Energy Fund for the deployment of clean energy technologies);
- $250 billion (domestic energy conservation);
- $50 billion (Clean Energy Research Fund);
- $300 billion (forest and other ecosystem maintenance);
- $11 billion (agricultural reform);
- $0.5 billion (geo-engineering);

- $10 billion (Emergency Relief Fund for extreme weather events related to climate change);
- $0.5 billion (assistance to the United Nations Population Fund);
- $2 billion (assistance to the WHO for health-related expenditures).

This comes to a total of $994 billion per year – very close to the $1 trillion that we expect to have available. This demonstrates that proceeds of the Kyoto2 auction would produce funds of an adequate scale to tackle the problems of climate change, both causes and consequences, decisively and effectively, while at the same time producing enormous ancillary benefits to the environment and the wider quality of life.

7 | The Great Dying

> 'Remember that as Ronald Reagan used to say, you ain't seen nothing yet. You've got 0.7 degrees above 1850 now. I've been talking about the possibility, if we're unwise and let business as usual go on, of five degrees centigrade and above. And remember that these damages are not just linear, they don't just rise step by step, they're highly nonlinear. [...] Five degrees centigrade is a very large increase. The difference between where we are now and where we were in the last Ice Age, 10–12,000 years ago, is five degrees centigrade. Five degrees centigrade transforms the physical geography of the world and thus the human geography of the world, how we live and [...] where we live our lives and how we live our lives. And this is the kind of thing you have to contemplate.' Nicholas Stern[1]

> 'Microbial mats covered much of the sea floor. A scarce infauna of small, deposit-feeding vermiform animals burrowed feebly just below the sediment surface. This lasted for maybe a million years. [...] On land, for millions of years, virtually the only tetrapod was the plant-eating *Lystrosaurus*, subsisting on the few surviving herbaceous plants. Forest communities were absent until the Middle Triassic.' Michael J. Benton and Richard J. Twitchett[2]

The Permian-Triassic (P-Tr) extinction 250 million years ago was 'the most extensive loss of species of any known event of the past 550 million years', writes Robert Berner[3] – so severe that it is widely known as 'the Great Dying'. An estimated 95 per cent of the Earth's species were wiped out, including 70 per cent of terrestrial vertebrates and over 90 per cent of marine species.[4]

On land the extensive coniferous forests, swamps and woodlands of the Permian were eliminated, with entire floral realms and ecologically complex animal communities vanishing from the fossil record. The loss of plant cover in turn led to massive soil erosion. For some 4–5 million years subsequently, land vegetation consisted almost entirely of low-growing ferns, and it was not until the middle Triassic that forest ecosystems returned,[5] leading to the so-called 'coal gap' – an 8-million-year interruption in coal deposition:

> Throughout Europe, plant megafossil information indicates that ecosystem recovery to precrisis levels of structure and function did not occur before the transition between the Early and Middle Triassic. [...] The recovery of equatorial, semi-arid conifer forest in Europe is approximately coeval with the delayed recovery of humid peat forest in higher latitudes, as evidenced by the Early Triassic 'coal gap'.[6]

The situation was replicated in the oceans.

> The P-Tr crisis appears to be in harmony with the situation in the marine biosphere. Diversity analysis and paleoecologic study of benthic invertebrate faunas has for some time indicated, most notably by the interruption of reef building, that shallow marine ecosystems too did not fully recover before the Middle Triassic. Records of radiolarians suggest a similar delay in the return to precrisis levels of zooplankton productivity. Curiously, in comparison to all other major ecologic crises in Earth history, repopulation after the P-Tr crisis proceeded exceptionally slowly.[7]

Benton and Twitchett concur, citing investigations at sites in northern Italy and the western USA:

> Initial benthic low-diversity communities were composed of small-sized, epifaunal suspension-feeding opportunists, which were living under suboptimal environmental conditions of low oxygen and low food supply.[8]

A scientific consensus has recently emerged that the probable immediate cause was a 600,000-year period of intense volcanism that created the Siberian Traps – a vast deposit of flood basalt that flowed out of giant openings in the Earth's crust, with a volume of 2–4 million cubic kilometres, extending over 1.6 million square kilometres and to a depth of 400–3,000 metres.

Isotopic analysis of zircons in ash deposits at the P-Tr boundary in China indicates that the main pulse of the extinction was 'synchronous with the Siberian flood volcanism'.[9] Likewise Sandra Kamo, who applied similar techniques on ash from six sites in China and Russia, reports:

> The coincidence of ages that bracket the volcanic event with those that bracket the age of the Permian-Triassic boundary ash strongly supports arguments that Siberian Flood volcanism was a major cause of the biological extinction that defines the end of the Permian period. [...] Extrusion of 2–4 million km^3 of volcanic material in such a brief geologic time interval (0.6 Myr [million years]) would have released suffciently large quantities of CO_2, SO_2, fluorine, and chlorine rapidly enough to wreak destruction on atmospheric and biospheric systems.[10]

An alternative theory from Luann Becker attributes the extinction to bolide impact involving a large asteroid or comet.[11] The two interpretations are not mutually exclusive, however, in that a bolide impact could have triggered the major volcanic events that clearly did take place.

In any case the Permian-Triassic exinction was not a single event, but rather an unfolding process of events taking place over tens of thousands of years. As described by Richard Twitchett, based on contemporaneous marine and terrestrial samples from the boundary layer in Greenland, 'Collapse of the marine and terrestrial ecosystems took between 10 and 60 k.y. [thousand years]. It took a further few hundred thousand years for the final disappearance of Permian floral elements.'[12]

At the outset the volcanic eruptions thrust large volumes of ash and sulphate aerosol into the atmosphere, the scale of which was amplified by site-specific geological peculiarities, including an unusually large pyroclastic fraction, writes Kamo: 'atypically, the volcanic sequence contains 20% by volume of pyroclastic material, eruption of which would have been accompanied by almost complete release of contained gases'.[13] This caused acute global darkening, cooling and acidification, with terrestrial ecosystems the first to suffer. This is reflected in the geological record: the dead vegetation led to a fungal explosion, followed by massive soil erosion once the earth's protective vegetation was gone.

Then a second set of climatic drivers came into play whose effect was powerfully heating. As well as ash and sulphate, the volcanic eruptions emitted vast volumes of CO_2, which mostly remained in the atmosphere as all the biological carbon sinks had been destroyed. Indeed, this volcanic CO_2 was augmented by the decomposition of dead biomass, and by the burning of the enormous coal and peat deposits of the Permo-Carboniferous Tunguskaya sequences – the world's largest coal basin – over which the molten basalt had flooded.

This CO_2-induced heating of about 5°C then triggered large releases of methane, mainly submarine deposits of methane hydrate laid down during the late Permian – leaving a geological marker in the form of an abrupt shift in carbon isotope abundance towards 'light' 12C carbon and away from 'heavy' 13C. As Benton and Twitchett explain,

> The assumption is that initial global warming at the P-Tr boundary, triggered by the huge Siberian eruptions, melted frozen gas hydrate bodies, and massive volumes of methane rich in 12C rose to the surface of the oceans in huge bubbles. This vast input of methane into the atmosphere caused more warming, which could have melted further gas hydrate reservoirs. The process continued in a positive feedback spiral that has been termed the 'runaway greenhouse' phenomenon. Some sort of threshold was probably reached, which was beyond where the natural systems that normally reduce carbon dioxide levels could operate effectively. The system spiralled out of control, leading to the biggest crash in the history of life.[14]

Temperatures rose globally and temperature differentials between high and low latitudes reduced, so diminishing the forces driving oceanic and atmospheric currents. As the oceans stagnated they became anoxic, and bacterial action converted the abundant sulphate into sulphide, in particular the toxic gas hydrogen sulphide (H_2S) – as revealed by the chemical biomarkers of *Chlorobiaceae* – purple and green sulphur bacteria, photosynthesizers that respire H_2S and live only in anoxic, H_2S-rich environments, according to Kliti Grice:[15] 'Biomarkers diagnostic for anoxygenic photosynthesis by Chlorobiaceae are particularly abundant at the boundary and into the Early Triassic. Similar conditions prevailed in the contemporaneous seas off South China. Our evidence for widespread photiczone euxinic conditions suggests that sulfide toxicity was a driver of the extinction and a factor in the protracted recovery.'[16]

The H_2S permeated throughout the oceans and the atmosphere, where, as Lee Kump argues, it caused the total destruction of the ozone layer that protects the Earth from ultraviolet solar radiation.[17] Kump's atmospheric photochemical modelling indicates massive fluxes of H_2S to the atmosphere more than two thousand times greater than current fluxes from volcanoes, leading to 'toxic levels of H_2S in the atmosphere' and methane levels above 100ppm, compared to 1.8ppm in 2007. The H_2S thus provided a powerful additional 'kill mechanism during the end-Permian'.

This second phase of methane-induced heating could have added another 5°C to average global temperatures, producing a total temperature rise of about 10°C. We cannot be certain, however, of the precise sequence of events. Multiple releases of methane and CO_2 probably took place over an extended period, as described by Evelyn S. Krull and Gregory J. Retallack:

> An explanation for such a long-term release of methane has to involve an efficient trigger mechanism as well as a positive feedback system. The marine regression during the Changxingian [very late Permian] stage would have substantially lowered hydrostatic pressure in shelf environments and could have led to

> initial clathrate destabilization and methane release. This would have led to the first pulse of 13C-depleted methane and the onset of an increase in greenhouse gases (CH_4 and CO_2). Additional greenhouse gases such as CO_2 and H_2O from the eruption of the Siberian Traps during the latest Changxingian stage (250 +− 0.2 Ma [million years]) may have furthered paleoclimatic warming. In response to this warming trend, clathrates in the polar regions could have become increasingly unstable, resulting in a second pulse of 13C-depleted methane. This additional release of methane and CO_2 would further add to greenhouse warming and generate a positive feedback cycle of clathrate destabilization and global warming.[18]

In his 2007 Royal Society lecture, James Lovelock looked at another more recent period of extreme warming, which he believes is directly comparable with the position today.

> The best known hothouse happened 55 million years ago at the beginning of the Eocene period. In that event between one and two teratonnes of carbon dioxide were released into the air by a geological accident. [...] Putting this much CO_2 in the air caused the temperature of the temperate and Arctic regions to rise 8°C and of the tropics 5°C and it took about 200,000 years for conditions to return to their previous state. In the 20th century we injected about half that amount of CO_2 and we and the Earth itself are soon likely to release more than a teratonne [1,000 Gt] of CO_2.[19]

The 'Paleocene-Eocene Thermal Maximum' (PETM) described by Lovelock caused a series of extinctions of its own (notably in deep oceans rendered anoxic by higher temperatures and stagnation), accompanied by major ecological changes on land and sea as oceans warmed and forests spread to the polar regions. As at the Permian–Triassic boundary, the transition was accompanied by a major shift in the isotopic balance of carbon, which again suggests major releases of methane from submarine deposits. Given the 10,000-year timescale of these emissions, the main radiative forcing would have been from the methane's oxidation product, CO_2. Climatologists are mystified, however, about the scale of the temperature rise, since according to Sluijs[20] 'the radiative forcing of the CO_2 resulting from the injection of 2,000 Gt of biogenic methane is not enough to explain the magnitude of PETM climate warming'.

One response is to attribute the carbon isotope signal to a 'global conflagration' of forests, peatlands and possibly coal. John A. Higgins and Daniel P. Schrag find that 'the oxidation of at least 5000 Gt C of organic carbon is the most likely explanation for the observed geochemical and climatic changes during the PETM, for which there are several potential mechanisms'.[21]

Another explanation is a mutually reinforcing combination of methane eruptions and carbon dioxide emissions from fires, in which every temperature rise both leads to additional methane emissions from seabed or permafrost reservoirs, and dries out vegetation and peaty soils to make them more susceptible to burning. The particular significance of methane in this scenario is that large, sudden methane emissions create a powerful radiative forcing acting on a decadal timescale, during which CO_2 levels could increase as a result of fires, and lead in turn to long-term radiative forcing acting over a millennial timescale.

As Euan Nisbet explains,

> Large-scale releases of methane from geological reservoirs are, it is postulated, capable of delivering such a thermal shock to the global climate that a permanent change is initiated. In this hypothesis the initial greenhouse warming that results from the addition of methane elicits so strong a response from other parts of the climate system (e.g. change of albedo by ice melting, reorganization of ocean circulation, carbon dioxide degassing from warming seas) that a step-change in climate takes place. In consequence, even when the source of the methane fades, the climate has made a long-term shift.[22]

This sounds distinctly similar to the Permian-Triassic heating which was also based on a synergy of carbon dioxide – in this case principally volcanic in origin – and eruptions of methane, followed by massive production of H_2S. Similar mechanisms are known to be operational today, with methane pivotal in ending recent ice ages. As Nisbet writes,

> Methane emissions from geological reservoirs may have played a major role in the sudden events terminating glaciation, both at the start of the Bølling/Allerød and also at the end of the Younger Dryas. These reservoirs include Arctic methane hydrates and also methane hydrate stored in offshore marine sediments in tropical and temperate latitudes. Emissions from hydrate stores may have resonated with tropical wetland emissions, each reinforcing the other. Because methane is such a powerful greenhouse gas, much smaller emissions of methane, compared with carbon dioxide, are required in order to have the same short-term impact by climate forcing. The methane-linked hypothesis has much geological support from sea-floor evidence of emission. [...] There are large remaining hydrate reservoirs in the Arctic and in shelf sediments globally, and there is substantial risk of further emissions.[23]

We also need to remember that the climate system includes long delay mechanisms, such as the time lag of hundreds or thousands of years between a warming at the Arctic surface and the transmission of the resulting warm pulse to a depth of hundreds of metres, where the main methane reservoirs reside: 'the thermal shock penetrating the permafrost is inexorable, even if the methane abundance in the air has fallen and the surface is cooling again. More bursts will occur, from the deeper, larger reservoirs, which the heat shock may take thousands of years to reach.'[24]

This all suggests that humankind should adopt a policy of extreme caution as we unwittingly experiment with the climate system. Otherwise the consequences are all too likely to be long term and irreversible. We can of course hope that the resulting wave of extinction – if we fail to act, that is – will be of the more modest order of the Palaeocene-Eocene Thermal Maximum than a full-blown Permian-Triassic-scale crisis with 95 per cent of life propelled into extinction.

Yet we cannot be sure. A 5°C temperature increase caused by human emissions could, as did a similar temperature rise caused by volcanic emissions 250 million years ago, trigger a methane-mediated 'runaway greenhouse' leading to a full 10°C temperature rise and the extinction of most life on Earth – and without so much as an asteroid to blame for it. But whether it would take the Earth 8 million years to recover from the human onslaught, or merely a few hundred thousand years, is surely irrelevant as far as our species is concerned. Either way, it is unlikely to witness the result.

8 | Questions and answers

> 'Heads of state, meeting today on the tropical island of Switzerland, have reached consensus. Predictions of global warming have no foundation in science.' Dr Margaret Chan, Director-General of the World Health Organization, quoting an unnamed British journalist[1]

What is Kyoto2?

Kyoto2 is a global system intended to forestall the 'runaway greenhouse' effect (see Chapter 1), stabilize the global climate and make sure this planet remains a safe and pleasant home for humanity and other species for the foreseeable future, in a way that is equitable, economically efficient and brings about other significant environmental and development gains – and so delivers the objective of the 1992 Climate Convention: the 'stabilization of greenhouse gas concentrations in the atmosphere at a level that would prevent dangerous anthropogenic interference with the climate system [...] within a time frame sufficient to allow ecosystems to adapt naturally to climate change, to ensure that food production is not threatened and to enable economic development to proceed in a sustainable manner'.

How long should Kyoto2 run for?

In order to provide the necessary incentives for long-term investment, and to deliver its objective, Kyoto2 should run at least until 2050 – by which time it should also have achieved its objective of making the world climate neutral in terms of greenhouse gas emissions. It would, of course, need to be subject to periodic revisions in the light of any problems emerging, experience of which measures have been more or less successful, and the real-world outcome of climate change.

Who might the winners and losers be at the national level, and who is therefore most likely to support or oppose it?

Kyoto2 is about more than just 'dividing up the cake' in a zero-sum game in which every winner creates a corresponding loser. Clearly there will be some economic players that lose, relatively speaking, and this category includes the coal industry. But in the wider picture it aims to make us all winners, in that we are all losers if catastrophic climate change takes place – and that is what Kyoto2 would prevent. It will also moderate the impacts of such climate change as is unavoidable through adaptation expenditures, and by retaining and rebuilding ecosystems to enhance the wider global life-support system. So instead of being a zero-sum game it is a positive-sum game, in which all of us are winners, even though some bear more of the cost than others.

Certain countries will pay more than others, and the costs will end up being carried by fossil fuel energy users (in so far as the producers are able to pass on the cost of the permits they will need through the market) and by the producers when they have to cut their margins or scale back production that is rendered unprofitable.

Coal producers will typically suffer as coal is a particularly high-carbon fuel; 'carbon capture and storage' (CCS) technology will ensure, however, that the coal industry continues to play a big role in global energy supply. Countries such as Venezuela and Canada with large tar reserves will also find these resources devalued somewhat owing to their high carbon content, but as conventional oil reserves dwindle, continuing demand for oil fuels in the transport sector will ensure a continuing demand and high prices.

Oil and gas producers will suffer reduced margins, since the price of these fuels is determined more by the balance of supply and demand in the marketplace than production cost. Consequently the price of permits will raise effective production cost, without necessarily raising market prices, and so reduce producers' income. Accordingly the main opposition will come from major fossil-fuel-producing countries. Saudi Arabia comes to mind. But even Saudi Arabia might receive significant benefit from renewable energy expenditure: its plentiful sunshine and established energy infrastructure would make it a prime candidate for large-scale solar energy development, perhaps producing hydrogen for export.

As a general point, all countries will pay, and all countries will benefit from spending. Poor countries will benefit especially from adaptation expenditures, forest/ecosystem payments and clean energy development. Rich countries will benefit from energy research funding, and then even more so from the worldwide deployment of the resulting clean energy technologies. Much energy conservation and efficiency spending will be directed to rich countries – because that's where most energy is being used. Some rich countries will also do well out of ecosystem payments, including the USA, Canada, Russia, Sweden, Finland and New Zealand.

What would the effect be on energy prices?

Fossil energy prices are inherently unpredictable. One problem is that demand is highly inelastic in the short term – that is to say that it takes a really big price increase to reduce demand, and a really big price drop to increase demand. So, as long as supply and demand are in balance, prices remain roughly level. But as soon as supply begins to exceed demand, prices drop sharply, and as soon as supply falls short of demand, prices soar. These effects are often accentuated by speculative trading.

One result of this price instability is to discourage long-term investment in high-priced energy assets, even when it appears favourable at current prices. You may have a price of $100 per barrel now, but to develop a large, expensive new resource (such as an oil shale or tar sand deposit) that is profitable at $50 per barrel you will be looking to the price in five to twenty-five years' time, with no guarantee that it may not have fallen to $45 per barrel by the time the resource is in production, putting you into loss. Such factors make for time lags in supply response to demand pressures. As a result energy markets are prone to swing between oversupply and undersupply.

If we look at the variablity of the oil price over the last few years, with oil trading in the region of $30–140 per barrel, the effect of Kyoto2 will be small in comparison – at €20 ($30)/t$CO_2$ (the current EUETS price), the per-barrel cost of permits is about $11. At the fuel pump, that's about 3.5p/litre. Likewise, on gas and electricity, the cost would be about 0.27p and 0.6p/KWh respectively – rather less than recent variability in fuel costs (see Chapter 5).

But in fact the effect would probably be smaller. Oil and gas prices in particular are mainly determined by the balance of supply and demand and the growing scarcity of these fuels, rather than production cost. Greenhouse gas production permits are a production cost, and their cost may therefore be only weakly reflected in consumer prices during this time of scarcity.

This may be the case with coal also. Historically coal has been abundant, and its price therefore tied to production cost. The price has, however, risen from around $30 per tonne over the period 1998–2003 to over $120 in early 2008, suggesting that coal is not so abundant after all: if it was, mines would have increased production.[2] Accordingly the same principle may apply to coal as to oil, and the effect on market prices may be muted.

The long-term market incentives created by Kyoto2 towards clean and lower-carbon energy production, however, combined with direct spending on clean energy research and deployment and energy efficiency and conservation, will abate and ultimately reduce demand for fossil fuels. This will reduce the scarcity premium and so push the price down – to an extent that could even exceed price increases resulting from the cost of permits.

Energy research will also result in the development of low-cost renewable and other clean energy sources, which will be increasingly competitive with, and ultimately cheaper than, fossil fuels – especially as the low-cost fossil resources are exhausted. So in the long term the effect of Kyoto2 will be to simultaneously increase energy supply and reduce energy prices and energy-related pollution.

These effects will be slowest to take place in the transport sector, owing to the highly desirable characteristics of oil fuels in cars, trucks, ships and aircraft. But in the medium term this too will change, with the development of electric vehicles and the emerging fuel cell economy based on hydrogen from renewable generation and (longer term) from high-temperature nuclear fusion. The last redoubt of oil will probably be in aviation – but provided we have cut fossil fuels out pretty much everywhere else, the world can probably live with that.

What about the effect of higher fuel prices? Won't poor people be hardest hit?

Higher fuel prices are something people are already learning to live with following significant price increases in oil, gas and electricity costs over the last few years. Any further price increases caused by Kyoto2 would be minor compared to fluctuations that have recently taken place. And under the EUETS European customers are already paying a carbon price for their electricity amounting to some £31 per household per year – the money, however, is going to the electricity generators (see Chapter 2), and their shareholders. Poor people are indeed hardest hit, in that they have the tightest budgets, so even a small increase in what they have to pay for energy knocks a big hole in their finances.

The people who use the most energy, however, are the rich. They travel more, have bigger houses to heat, drive bigger cars, and in the realms of the super-rich have their own private aircraft. Subsidizing energy – and this is what we are effectively doing by not charging for the external costs of greenhouse gas emissions, and in the UK by charging a reduced rate of VAT on domestic energy – overwhelmingly benefits the rich and the well off. So subsidizing energy is an inefficient way of making energy affordable for the poorest people in society, who use the least energy and so get the least benefit.

This is where the Second Theorem of Welfare Economics comes into play – referred to by economics journalist Tim Harford[3] as the 'head start theorem'. In a nutshell it says that if you want to help a group of people in society, you are better off just giving them a financial head start than by creating subsidies that distort their economic preferences in the marketplace.

Applied to energy prices, this means the best way to help people out of 'fuel poverty' is (at least in the short term) to give them more money, rather than subsidize fuel. That way, as an added benefit, they are more likely to invest in energy efficiency, rather than just spend more on fuel. Or if they prefer, they can spend the extra money on food and clothing – also good ways of keeping warm. In fact you would do better to give everyone in the country a lump-sum benefit – a sort of reverse poll tax – and put up energy prices than to carry on subsidizing fuel. At least this way the poor would get the same benefit as the rich, whereas now they get less.

So in the short term the best way to help fuel-poor people and families is actually to increase the price of energy for everyone, but to give some of that money back to poor people – for example, through an increased pensioners' winter fuel supplement, or more generally by way of child benefit, tax credits and pensions – so that the people who stand to suffer most from higher energy prices end up better off, and get to choose how to spend their extra money themselves.

In the longer term, Kyoto2 aims specifically to address the needs of the poor not just in the UK but globally by increasing their access to energy (while making sure that the energy comes from clean sources) and by making the poor and less well off the first and major beneficiaries of domestic energy efficiency and conservation programmes.

Is there not a danger that imposing Kyoto2 could push the global economy into recession, or at least severely impact economic growth?

Kyoto2 would raise a sum of approximately $1 trillion per year. This is a lot of money, make no mistake, but no, it would not trigger a global recession. On the contrary, it would provide a long-term stimulus to the global economy and make it far more sustainable. As Nicholas Stern put it, 'Tackling climate change is the pro-growth strategy for the longer term, and it can be done in a way that does not cap the aspirations for growth of rich or poor countries. The earlier effective action is taken, the less costly it will be.'[4]

To put the sum of $1 trillion in context, this is roughly equal to worldwide annual military expenditure, and is about half the cost of recent increases in the price of oil. Moreover, this is not money that would be taken out of the economy and thrown away. It would all be spent on addressing the causes and the consequences of climate change – as set out in Chapter 7 – and would thus be recycled into the global economy. Many of the investments would be highly labour intensive and bring employment opportunities to remote rural areas that have largely been left behind in recent decades.

Furthermore, one important effect of Kyoto2 would be to bring an end to existing economic inefficiencies created by market failures. For example, tighter regulations on energy efficiency (whether in buildings, consumer electronics, industry or vehicles) would have the effect of giving people more product (such as housing, warmth, light, music, goods, food or travel) for lower cost. The overall effect would not be to 'cost' growth or jobs, but to redirect growth and jobs into a more sustainable and less polluting direction.

In general, the fossil fuel sector would do less well than it has been doing in recent years (in which high fuel prices have made it, and the oil sector in particular, spectacularly profitable), while the renewable energy sector would benefit. Other sectors that would benefit include civil engineering in connection with adaptation works. This would trigger considerable growth in its own right, and because it would be based on renewable resources rather than declining fossil reserves this growth would be sustainable for the long term.

There would also be a net transfer of wealth from richer to poorer countries, which would again have positive economic consequences. At present the global economy is dangerously dependent on the USA as the 'consumer of last resort' – a position made increasingly unsustainable by the high level of indebtedness in the USA at almost every level, personal, corporate, state and federal. By increasing purchasing power in countries that are now too poor to participate fully in the consumer economy, the global economy would be greatly strengthened and its dependency on the US consumer diminished.

This would in turn help the rich countries as new export markets opened up – much as the Marshall Plan, while being financed by the US economy in the years after the Second World War to the tune of several per cent of GDP, underpinned the USA's economic boom of the 1950s as European economies came back to life and provided growing markets for US exports and rich opportunities for US investments.

We also know that rich countries enjoy many opportunities for reducing greenhouse gas emissions at low and negative cost. In November 2007 McKinsey reported[5] that the USA could cut its emissions by 3–4.5Gt per year by 2030 at marginal costs of under \$50/tCO_2 eq, of which 40 per cent (1.2–1.8Gt) would be achieved at negative cost. So one effect of Kyoto2 would be encourage reductions in emissions that are actually profitable in their own right, and so boost corporate profitability and household disposable incomes.

See also Chapter 4.

Given that rich countries are enjoying the fruits of fossil-fuelled prosperity achieved over decades of industrialization (and are responsible for 70 per cent of the atmosphere's accumulated CO_2 burden), how can this be accounted for to the satisfaction of countries that still consider themselves underdeveloped?

It is hard to apply a retrospective tax to historic greenhouse gas emissions because for most of the time that these emissions were going on, no one knew about global warming. Indeed, our whole knowledge and understanding of the 'greenhouse effect' is the result of rich countries' industrial and scientific development. From the time that global warming was widely recognized as a real danger, though not yet an actual phenomenon, it was less than a decade before the Climate Convention was agreed in 1992 at the Earth Summit. As Jim Hansen writes,

> The threat of global warming did not become clear until the present generation. Empirical evidence of warming was masked by weather fluctuations, and warming was kept small, temporarily, by the inertia of deep oceans. We cannot blame our ancestors for burning fossil fuels in an uncontrolled way. They worked hard to bring themselves and their children a better life. Their greenhouse emissions are small in comparison to ours. Any effect of their emissions on our climate is truly inadvertent. Ignorance is no excuse for us. There is overwhelming scientific evidence of global warming, its causes, and many of its implications. Today's generations will be accountable, and how tall we stand remains to be determined.[6]

The question of the historic burden of emissions is addressed in the Climate Convention's Principle 1, which states that 'the developed country Parties should take the lead in combating climate change and the adverse effects thereof', and Principle 2, which states: 'The specific needs and special circumstances of developing country Parties [...] should be given full consideration.' These principles apply now and any new climate agreement will have to apply them (see the Summary).

In the context of Kyoto2 these principles are reflected in the fact that most of the money raised from the auction of permits will ultimately derive from developed-country economies, and that most of the spending will take place in developing countries. Part of the investment programme (see Chapter 6) is to increase access to energy in developing countries that are 'energy poor' – but making sure that the energy derives from clean sources. Adaptation expenditures and programmes to maintain and restore forests and other ecosystems will also transfer funds to developing countries, while also protecting their populations and environmental resources against the impacts of climate change.

Does the global cap supersede all the various national targets that countries have, such as the UK's 2050 target?

No. The UK and other countries could maintain national targets, at the same time as the world as a whole is operating a global cap. In maintaining a national target, the UK would not be reducing global greenhouse gas emissions; it would, however, be reducing overall demand for permits and so depressing their market price. Thus the UK might want to complement its own reductions with the voluntary purchase and 'retirement' of permits, effectively tightening the global cap.

Given that Kyoto2 primarily passes on the cost of carbon through the price mechanism, is it compatible with other national-level schemes such as 'personal carbon allocations', 'Cap and Share' or 'Cap and Dividend'?

The two systems (global and national) could go on simultaneously, with separate caps applying globally and nationally; the overall volume of emissions would not be altered, however, since this is determined by the global cap. The main benefit would be in making people more directly aware of their impact on the climate than is possible through a purely economic carbon signal, which would not be clearly distinguishable from other cost elements, and in reducing the cost of permits.

If funding is to be given to the victims of climate change, how might this be assessed? Would this involve calculating the human fingerprint on each extreme weather event somehow?

There is no secure scientific basis for assessing whether any particular climate event is the 'result' of climate change. The IPCC says, however, that we should expect a general increase in, and increased severity of, extreme weather events, including intensely hot periods, droughts, floods, cyclones and hurricanes.[7] Under Kyoto2 there would be no direct funding to victims of climate change. There would, however, be considerable spending on adaptation, and specific funding for emergency disaster relief, which would supplement existing humanitarian efforts to provide better and more immediate respite (see Chapter 6) based on a fixed percentage of climate change responsibility. Longer term, increases in the frequency and severity of such disasters would strengthen the climate link and a higher percentage might become appropriate. Where significant damage to buildings, homes and infrastructure was caused by extreme weather events, adaptation funding could also be provided to help the reconstruction effort, provided that this was done in a way to increase resilience against such events in the future.

Assuming the whole world does not sign up to Kyoto2 at once, how would countries who have signed up trade with countries who have not?

In effect the world would be divided into two trading zones – those within Kyoto2 and those outside. When energy was imported, such as gas, oil, coal, etc., into the 'Kyoto2 zone', the importer would be in the position of producer and would have to obtain and surrender permits in the same way. Of course, energy and thus greenhouse gas emissions are also embodied in products and materials, and the importing country would have to levy an appropriate number of permits to cover those emissions too, to avoid giving the exporting country an unfair competitive advantage. Conversely, when goods and energy were being exported from the Kyoto2 zone, the associated permits would need to be credited back to exporters in order to maintain competitive parity.

The question of how best to do this was addressed by Ismer and Neuhoff in 2004 (updated in 2007), and their conclusion is that 'border tax adjustment (BTA) can be both feasible and compatible with WTO constraints' on both import duties and export subsidies, provided it is done right:

> BTA for the emissions trading scheme is an economically viable approach to address leakage effects. It is in conformity with WTO law where the adjustment level does not exceed the upper bound of the amount payable for production in the area covered

by emission trading using best available technology. To make the scheme implementable, we propose a processed-materials approach where these are in turn evaluated at the level of best available technology.[8]

Intriguingly, EC president Manuel Barroso suggested in early 2008 that the EU should 'require importers to obtain allowances alongside European competitors' – that is, force importers to buy EUAs to cover the emissions associated with energy-intensive products such as steel, aluminium and cement, to protect domestic producers, unless the producer countries have equivalent carbon-pricing systems in place.[9]

Why not just have a modest $2 carbon tax on fossil fuels and industrial gases and spend the money on low-carbon energy research – as Bjorn Lomborg advocates?[10]

In effect Kyoto2 incorporates Bjorn Lomborg's idea – in that the amount of money that Kyoto2 proposes to allocate to renewable and other clean energy research, for example in efficient energy storage, long-distance transmission and nuclear fusion, is almost exactly the same as that proposed by Lomborg.

But is this enough? Lomborg's proposal supposes that greenhouse gas emissions can continue to increase for a further few decades, before declining sharply as new technology gets cheaper. But this 'trajectory' would add a huge extra burden of atmospheric greenhouse gases. It will moreover involve large-scale building of fossil-fuel-based infrastructure, such as coal-fired power stations, with a lifetime of fifty or more years, and these will not be suddenly scrapped immediately solar power becomes a better investment for new power generation. The IEA and the IPCC are agreed that any realistic trajectory of emissions reductions leading to a 450ppm CO_2 eq stabilization (or less) means that emissions need to peak ideally in 2012 and at latest by 2015 – not to carry on rising until 2025 or beyond.

Lomborg's proposal also fails to address other key areas – such as protecting the world's forests, grasslands, soils and peatlands, helping countries vulnerable to climate change to adapt to all the many impacts that are now unavoidable, from rising sea levels to flood and drought, and accelerating the actual deployment of clean energy technologies, rather than just doing the R&D. So, we do need to do what Lomborg proposes – and everything else as well.

Why not just back Contraction and Convergence (C&C)? Surely it's a good plan that has made a lot of headway and you are just complicating things?

C&C has a lot going for it (see Chapter 3). It rightly focuses on the need for an effective global cap on greenhouse gas emissions that contracts over time – something the Kyoto Protocol does not deliver. It also focuses justifiably on the principle of convergence, if we take that to mean that the quality of life – access to energy, water, food, medicine, medical care, clothing, housing, warmth, lighting, security, justice, education, information, entertainment and other good things – should become more equal across the globe.

But convergence of greenhouse gas emissions makes less sense. No one starts the year thinking they want to cause so many tonnes of carbon dioxide emissions in the twelve months ahead. They do want the good things we currently get as a result of emitting greenhouse gases, such as warmth, travel, light, food and hot showers. But if they can get those good things without the emissions, no one is going to complain. Kyoto2 is about increasing global access to energy in particular, but also access to water, good housing, food and security, in spite of global warming, and doing it in a way that solves the problems of global warming rather than adding to them.

At a practical level, redistributing money among governments – and this is what the 'convergence' part of C&C comes down to – is not going to achieve any of these things. The money spent on permits to produce greenhouse gases should not just be passed around between governments, but invested so as to address both the causes and the consequences of global warming

– researching and deploying renewable energy sources, rebuilding forests and other ecosystems, relocating populations, roads, railways, power stations and other infrastructure at risk from sea flooding, and so on.

So C&C delivers only half of the solution, and it wastes the opportunity to deliver on the other half. Kyoto2 aims to deliver a complete package of solutions.

Another problem with C&C is that politically it can never happen. Governments that see a benefit will want it (hence the support for C&C from the Africa group of nations). Governments that will face large bills will oppose it, all the more so as their expenditures would do nothing to address the problems of climate change. In short it is a zero-sum game. Kyoto2 is a positive-sum game in that all countries (or national economies) contribute financially, all will benefit from expenditures, and the expenditures will directly tackle the problems of global warming to everybody's ultimate benefit.

How does Kyoto2 reflect the restoration of global equity, which must surely be a key part of any new climate agreement?

Equity is indeed key – any new climate agreement must be equitable. Kyoto2 addresses this theme as follows:

- Contributing to the cost. People contribute to tackling the problems of climate change in proportion to their contribution to creating the problem – as measured by the greenhouse gas emissions for which they are responsible. From an equity point of view it does not matter where the contribution is levied, but for practical reasons Kyoto2 levies the contribution 'upstream' – that is, at or close to the source of greenhouse gases – and the cost is then either absorbed in the supply chain or passed on to the end purchaser of products and services. This is in accord with the widely accepted 'polluter pays' principle.
- Compensation and restoration. The funds raised by the sale of permits, expected to be of the order of $1 trillion per year, would be spent on addressing the problems of climate change

– both the causes and the consequences. This differs from other systems such as C&C (see above), which are based on a per capita entitlement, and reflects the principle of 'to each according to their needs'. This would apply most particularly to expenditures to assist adaptation to climate change – an essential way of improving the lot of 'climate change victims', who under present arrangements are largely left to suffer their fate.

- Inter-generational equity. If we do not restrain climate change most of its impacts will be felt by future generations – our grandchildren, their grandchildren, and beyond. The key thing to do for future generations is not to try to compensate them for the impacts they will suffer, but to act now to stabilize the climate and forestall the possibility of a badly damaged planet.
- Major areas of expenditure include reforestation and the wider restoration of native ecosystems, sustainable agriculture, clean energy R&D and the large-scale deployment of clean energy, bringing the benefits of improved access to energy, water, food and other natural resources to hundreds of millions or billions of people. In this way Kyoto2 would help to restore many of the iniquities that characterize the world today.

Why does Kyoto2 propose geo-engineering the planet? Surely that could have unforeseen consequences and undermine efforts to cut greenhouse gas emissions?

Kyoto2 does not propose geo-engineering at this stage. Although there are indications that a 'runaway greenhouse effect' may be taking place, this is not (yet) conclusive. What is proposed is to research possible geo-engineering approaches in case they become necessary (see Chapter 6). Unforeseen consequences are always a danger – global warming is one example of this, and the depletion of stratospheric ozone another. This is one reason why research is necessary – precisely to try to avoid unforeseen consequences of this kind if we do need to resort to geo-engineering to maintain climate stability.

There is indeed a danger that if geo-engineering measures prove successful, people and companies would argue that we no longer need to cut greenhouse gas emissions. But this would be wrong. For example, making the ocean clouds more reflective, or reflecting more sunlight from a sulphate aerosol in the upper atmosphere, would do nothing to prevent the acidification of the oceans by excess CO_2, which could threaten many marine species and eat away at coral reefs. One particular danger[11] is that higher CO_2, especially when combined with overfishing, may shift the balance of oceanic ecology away from fish and small shelled organisms and towards jellyfish.

With diminishing reserves of oil we also need to research renewable energy alternatives to maintain a thriving global economy. And we also need to address the problems of deforestation, ecosystem degradation and declining soil quality – not only to stabilize climate but also to safeguard our planet's biodiversity, and to secure sustainable access to water, food, timber and other resources for a growing world population.

Kyoto2 proposes research into geo-engineering purely so that the world is prepared in the case of dire necessity – and then only to be used as a short-term palliative measure, not as a substitute for building a sustainable low-carbon economy.

Why does Kyoto2 propose to charge for the production of greenhouse gases from fossil fuels and other concentrated industrial sources, but not for greenhouse gases emitted from forestry, agriculture and other diffuse land-based sources? Is this fair?

It probably is not 'fair'. There is a strong case for saying that all greenhouse gas emissions should be treated equally. Emissions from deforestation and wider land use cannot, however, be treated in the same way as industrial emissions, because forested developing countries simply would not accept this approach. Their argument is: 'you rich countries cut your forests down to make farmland, and you canot stop us doing the same'. On the other hand they will be quite happy to keep their forests, peatlands and so on if they are paid to do so.

On a practical level, it is also hard to measure diffuse emissions arising from land use, whether CO_2, methane or nitrous oxide, and impossible to measure with accuracy. Satellite imaging is a powerful tool but it is hard to derive a precise measure of carbon fluxes from forests or other ecosystems from space. Furthermore, it is impossible to distinguish with certainty between natural wildfires (an essential component of many ecosystems), accidental fires (which may become more frequent in the drier conditions associated with climate change) and intentional fires designed to clear land for farming or ranching (the fires one might wish to penalize).

Hence the Kyoto2 approach: to sell permits for the emission of industrial greenhouse gases, and to apply a large part of the proceeds to forests, farming and wider land use: to reduce emissions, enhance sinks, increase sustainablity and raise production, all in the face of climate change and growing human demands.

What would happen to the carbon market under Kyoto2?

It would get a lot bigger. In October 2006 the World Bank revealed that the global carbon market was worth $21.5 billion, having doubled in value in the preceding nine months form the 1995 turnover of $11 billion.[12] Some $19 billion of this was traded under the EUETS. Under Kyoto2, some $1 trillion of permits would be sold at auction. If we assume that each permit will be sold, on average, once on the secondary market (reflecting the fact that some will be sold many times over, and others not at all), that indicates that the carbon market will turn over around $1 trillion per year, a fifty-fold increase over 2006. Of course, it could well be a lot more than that.

What about the 'carbon entrepreneurs' now producing emissions reductions under the Clean Development Mechanism (CDM)? Would they all go bust under Kyoto2?

The nature of their business would change, but the expertise they have developed would be highly sought after and their business would grow rather than shrink. One specific idea in

Kyoto2 is that national governments be granted budgets from the Climate Change Fund to 'buy in' emissions reductions generated within their territories (see Chapter 6), in specific sectors and at prices reflecting fair cost, effectively mobilizing the private sector's entrepreneurial flair to fill the gaps left by the main spending programmes. But even without this, in putting a price on greenhouse gas emissions all companies everywhere in the world would be redoubling their efforts to reduce their use of fossil fuels and of other industrial greenhouse gases, and the obvious place to turn to for ideas and expertise in achieving these reductions would be the companies already generating emissions reductions under the CDM.

What would be the role of 'voluntary carbon offsets' under Kyoto2? And could people in effect create their own voluntary offsets by buying permits, and retiring them?

When buying goods or services under Kyoto2, you would already be paying, in effect, to 'offset' the associated greenhouse gas emissions. But you might reasonably want to finance further emissions reduction projects as an extra contribution, over and above your compulsory contributions to the Climate Change Fund, and this should be welcomed. These projects would be of particular value if they clearly addressed sustainable development issues, and tackled land-based emissions, which are not part of the main Kyoto2 mechanism.

There is a clear role for the voluntary offset sector in providing this opportunity. The sector – or at least the better companies within it – has so far played a useful role in getting people to think constructively about climate change and what they can do about it, and in harnessing entrepreneurial creativity to bring about innovative solutions. It could generate additional benefits in the future by demonstrating novel approaches to reducing emissions, or enhancing sinks, that could be taken up more widely.

As for the voluntary retirement of permits, that would have the effect of tightening the cap, raising the permit price and putting more money into the Climate Change Fund, and it is hard to substantiate any objection to that. Either strategy, or indeed a combination of the two, would contribute to the achievement of the Climate Convention's objective.

You don't say much about nuclear power – why not? Surely it's an essential part of our response to climate change?

Under Kyoto2 there would be nothing to prevent the building of new nuclear power stations. Indeed, companies wishing to do so would have the benefit of a long-term carbon price signal, which would make it far easier to raise finance secure in the knowledge of a reliable advantage relative to electricity generated from fossil fuels. It appears likely that at least some new nuclear power stations would be built as a consequence. There are, however, considerable doubts as to the ability of nuclear power to contribute substantially to world energy needs. These arise from multiple factors including:

- solving technical problems associated with, and the financing of, the long-term safe storage or disposal of nuclear waste;
- the existence of sufficient uranium reserves at affordable cost – both economically and in terms of the greenhouse gas emissions associated with the energy-intensive mining, processing and enrichment of nuclear fuel, and other emissions in the nuclear fuel cycle;
- the considerable carbon footprint associated with nuclear power station construction, mainly from concrete and steel, and from decommissioning;
- the danger that nuclear power stations, or other elements of the nuclear fuel cycle, could be targets for military or terrorist attack;
- if 'fast breeder' reactors are used on a large scale to generate additional plutonium fuel, the associated routine emissions of radioactivity in reprocessing, and the danger of plutonium leaking into nuclear weapons manufacture;
- the availability of the required scientific, managerial and engineering expertise to build and operate many new nuclear

power stations, especially but not only in developing countries;
- liability issues in relation to nuclear accidents;
- the willingness of investors to finance new nuclear build, in view of the above factors and other risks, such as cost and time overruns in construction.

This is not the place to go into these questions in detail – it is rather for global capital markets to decide whether investments in nuclear reactors will be rewarding. But given the immense investments made in the last sixty years in nuclear power, amounting to many hundreds of billions ($), there is no need at this stage to provide any additional support for nuclear fission beyond the carbon price signal. New energy funding should rather go into areas that have been historically neglected by comparison, such as renewable energy, electricity storage, distributed and decentralized generation, demand management, fuel cells, hydrogen storage and nuclear fusion.

What form might the move you want towards renewable energy take?

The biggest available gains in the short term will probably come from expanded wind power, both land-based and offshore, as this is now a mature and effective technology. We can also expect the large-scale development of Concentrated Solar Power (CSP) stations, which are already in operation at several dozen plants in California, Spain and other sunny locations. A particular advantage of CSP is that it allows solar heat to be stored during the day, to generate electricity when demand is highest. It is likely to be developed on a large scale in hot, sunny locations such as North Africa, and the electricity transmitted to faraway markets by high-voltage DC power lines. It will have an important balancing role in a grid that includes a large proportion of intermittent generation, from wind and solar photovoltaic (PV).

In 2004 Frederick Morse, chairman of the US Solar Energy Industries Association, described how 354MW of CSP capacity had been working reliably for fifteen years, declaring that CSP had produced over 50 per cent of all solar electricity to date.[13] He went on to propose a programme to build 5GW of CSP worldwide over ten years at a cost of $10 billion, and argued that economies of scale and technical advances would halve the current cost of CSP to make it 'fully competitive with fossil based mid-load power'.

Solar PV is currently too expensive for mass power generation without expensive support; this is likely to change, however, over the coming decade or so as the technologies mature and production volumes increase. PV is initially likely to play a growing role in embedded power generation – for example, on factory, office and domestic roofs, as is already happening in Germany thanks to generous incentives (the country has over 300,000 PV systems, 55 per cent of the world's PV panels, capable of generating 3GW when the sun shines). Current experience suggests that costs drop 20 per cent every time manufacturing capacity doubles, and production forecasts suggest parity of cost between solar- and fossil-powered capacity between 2015 and 2020.[14]

Solar thermal is another essential technology, capable of producing hot water efficiently in homes, offices, factories, swimming pools and other applications. In the developed world the widespread development of solar thermal capacity will directly reduce fossil fuel use, and in the developing world it will improve quality of life by providing hot water on tap where it is now not available, and reduce pressure on forests and woodlands, which currently provide much domestic fuel for water heating.

Tidal power also offers considerable potential, both through developing large power stations in locations such as the UK's Severn Estuary (where a 8.6GW power station could be built, to produce 17TWh [terawatt-hour] per year, about 5 per cent of current UK electricity demand) and from tidal stream turbines (like wind turbines, but underwater). Wave power will also have a role, probably in offshore 'energy parks' which generate electricity from a combination of wind, wave and tidal stream. By combining the three, electricity supply will be smoothed, making it more valuable and reducing the need for back-up generation capacity, while expensive grid connections can be shared. An increasing proportion of intermittent renewable energy from wave, wind, tide and solar PV raises the prospect of surplus electricity that will need to be used up, and one way of using it is to electrolyze water to produce hydrogen, which may be used as an automotive fuel.

There is a also a big role for biofuels made from biomass such as farm and forestry waste (as opposed to first-generation biofuels derived from food) and purpose-grown energy crops. Biomass may be directly burnt for heat and to generate electricity, but a higher-value route may be to pyrolyze biomass to produce 'bio-oil' (a liquid with about half the energy density of mineral oil) and 'bio-char' (fine charcoal dust). The bio-oil can be produced in rural areas and used in place of mineral oil in boilers, or carried away in tankers for further processing into automotive fuels such as methanol. The bio-char is a valuable soil conditioner, improving soil structure and water and nutrient retention (see Chapter 6), and represents a means of effective long-term carbon sequestration. Alternatively it may be made up into briquettes for burning – taking pressure off natural forests that are being exploited for charcoal, an important fuel in the developing world and especially in Africa.

Geothermal energy will be locally important, where geological heat sources are accessible. In 2005 geothermal generation capacity worldwide amounted to some 9GW (electricity) in twenty-four countries and 27GW (thermal) in seventy-one countries,[15] showing that this is a mature technology that would be capable of considerable expansion in the correct economic climate.

If we are facing a future of fossil fuel scarcity, do we really need Kyoto2? If accessible and economic oil and coal simply run out, as many people think they will, won't that solve the problem?

Probably not. It would be highly unwise to rely on fossil energy supply shortages to bring about the changes we need to go through as this would bring about an 'energy crunch' characterized by high prices, economic instability and global security dangers. And one likely outcome would be that energy companies would move to exploit ever dirtier, lower-quality fossil energy resources – such as the 800 billion barrels of oil equivalent (more than three times Saudi Arabia's claimed reserves) contained in oil shales over 40,000 square kilometres of Colorado, Utah and Wyoming, the Alberta tar sands and the Orinoco heavy tars – at huge cost, both economic and environmental. This would certainly bring greenhouse gas emissions to dangerous levels.

So Kyoto2 (or something like it) is the win-win option. If fossil fuels turn out to be abundant, then it will moderate the rate at which we burn them, and protect us from a runaway greenhouse effect. If they are in short supply, it will moderate the rate at which we burn them, so they will last longer. And part of 'scarcity premium' from fossil fuels will finance the shift to a low carbon economy, so when supplies really do tighten we will have a whole clean energy infrastructure to supply our needs.

As Jim Hansen comments, 'We have to figure out how to live without fossil fuels some day anyhow – so why not sooner?'[16]

What if climate scientists are wrong and the world is not really warming up after all? Then Kyoto2 would be a huge waste of time, effort and money, wouldn't it?

No. Fossil fuels are a valuable but finite resource that will run out sooner or later no matter what. Kyoto2 could extend their lifetime so that they last far longer, and are used to deliver far greater human benefits than from burning them all up as fast as we can. After they have taken hundreds of millions of years to form, can we really justify using them all up in a matter of a century or two? Remember too that fossil fuels are worth far more to industry than their energy value alone.

So given that we are going to have to give up on fossil fuels anyway within (roughly speaking) the next hundred years, it makes sense to do it on our own terms and timetable, managing the rate at which fossil fuels are exploited and developing the alternative energy sources that will replace them. The alternative is an unstable and insecure world of energy shortages and punitive price hikes as fossil fuel production deficits hit energy markets, often unpredictably, without any alternatives in place.

The securing, production, transport and combustion of fossil fuels are also hugely damaging processes – as anyone who has witnessed open-cast coal mines in Colombia, Australia, Bulgaria or Wales, mountain-top removal in Appalachia, oil-sodden rainforest in Ecuador, flare-contaminated communities in Nigeria, Alaskan beaches buried in oil and tar, seabirds trapped in oil slicks, ash-filled lakes in Oxfordshire, petroleum smog in Mexico City or Los Angeles, the fume-ridden air of Beijing, medieval cathedrals in Poland corroded by sulphate from coal, dead forests in Germany killed by acid rain, New Mexico, Colorado and Alberta landscapes devastated by tar sand and shale exploitation, political murders along oil pipelines in Colombia, the burning of Kuwait's oilfields in the first Gulf War, or the unspeakable aftermath of Operation Iraqi Liberation (OIL), will surely know. Reduce energy demand and move from fossil fuels to renewable energy sources, and all these environmental and human rights abuses will decline.

Surely global warming is not altogether bad? Without global warming caused by human emissions, we might be going into an ice age by now.

Small variations in global average temperature are not in themselves a bad thing. People in some parts of the world win from modest temperature rises and others lose, and it may even be that a small temperature increase from pre-industrial levels is generally beneficial. It is also undeniable that human civilization would find it very difficult to adapt to an ice age, and that without the warming caused by human activities an ice age would probably be upon us within some hundreds or thousands of years. The degree of warming caused by our activities to date, however, and that to which we are already committed, is getting close to propelling the world into a 'hothouse Earth' state lasting for thousands of years which would lead to the extinction of much of its life, very likely including human life. Provided that we manage to avoid this it is true that a time may come when humanity faces the ice age question – that is: should we engineer the global climate to keep it in its present interglacial state, and so avoid all the destruction, disruption and expense that a new ice age would entail? It may well be that a future world would indeed decide to prevent or postpone an impending ice age. But for now our task is to make sure our descendants have that choice to make.

How might Kyoto2 actually happen?

Ideally the member countries of the Climate Convention will pick up on Kyoto2 and agree among themselves that this is the best way forward after the Kyoto Protocol's current phase expires in 2012. This cannot be relied upon, however.

Alternatively, and more probably, individual countries or the EU could apply a Kyoto2-like system as their domestic policy. Although the EU's Emissions Trading Scheme (EUETS; see Chapter 2) has suffered from severe problems in its phase 1 (2003–07), it has improved considerably as it enters its phase 2 (2008–12) and there is further scope for improvement in its phase 3, projected to run from 2013 to 2020. It appears to be moving the right way, with a higher proportion of allowances being auctioned, and there is a prospect that it may at the same time move away from national allocations and towards a single EU-wide auction of allowances. The EUETS is also expanding its scope to encompass more of the EU's emissions, and logic suggests that it should ultimately cover all emissions, not just a subset. In order to do this it may have to move to an 'upstream' system.

The EUETS is also the world's biggest carbon market, bigger than the Kyoto Protocol's 'compliance market'. Other countries, and states in the USA and Canada, have also expressed an interest in joining in a 'greater EUETS'. So it may be that the EUETS represents the best way forward for Kyoto2. The approach could subsequently 'globalize' through the Climate Convention once established in a greater EUETS.

Another possible route is the Climate Neutral Network, formed in early 2007 by the UN Environment Programme as a coalition of countries, cities, businesses and others dedicated to achieving zero net carbon emissions (see Chapter 2). CNN member countries might choose to adopt Kyoto2 (or a variant) as a means of harmonizing their activities.

But ultimately Kyoto2 will advance only if it wins popular support – from citizens, from charities and campaign organizations, and from business – strong enough to make a political impact. So whether Kyoto2 happens, or not, is really up to you.

Notes

Introduction

1 Hans Christian Andersen, *The Snow Queen*, trans. Naomi Lewis, 1968/1979.

2 Nicholas Stern, Gurukul Chevening Lecture, LSE, 7 November 2006.

3 Michael R. Raupach et al., 'Global and regional drivers of accelerating CO_2 emissions', *PNAS*, 104(24), 12 June 2007, pp. 10288–93.

4 Gwyn Prins and Steve Rayner, 'Time to ditch Kyoto', *Nature*, 449, 25 October 2007, pp. 973–5.

5 Jack Cogen, speaking at an International Emissions Trading Association/World Bank event, Montreal, 5 December 2005.

6 Barbara Haya, *Failed Mechanism: How the CDM is subsidizing hydro developers and harming the Kyoto Protocol*, International Rivers, November 2007.

7 Florian Bressand et al., *Curbing Global Energy Demand Growth: The energy productivity opportunity*, McKinsey Global Institute, May 2007.

8 Prins and Rayner, 'Time to ditch Kyoto'.

9 James Hansen et al., 'Target atmospheric CO_2: where should humanity aim?', pre-publication draft, February 2008.

10 Nicholas Stern, *Stern Review on the Economics of Climate Change*, HM Treasury, 2006.

1 *What's the problem?*

1 International Energy Agency, *World Energy Outlook 2007*.

2 Margaret Thatcher, Speech opening Hadley Centre for Climate Prediction and Research, 25 May 1990.

3 Tim Lenton, 'Tipping elements in the Earth's climate system', *Proceedings of the National Academy of Sciences*, 105(6), 12 February 2008, pp. 1786–93.

4 Prince Charles, Speech to the European Parliament, 14 February 2008.

5 James Hansen et al., 'Target atmospheric CO_2: where should humanity aim?', pre-publication draft, February 2008.

6 *Climate Change 2007: Synthesis Report*, IPCC, 2007.

7 *IPCC Second Assessment Report: Climate Change 1995*.

8 S. Rahmstorf et al., 'Recent climate observations compared to projections', *Science*, 316(5825), 4 May 2007, p. 709.

9 Ibid.

10 Dian J. Seidel et al., 'Widening of the tropical belt in a changing climate', *Nature Geoscience*, 2, December 2007.

11 James Lovelock, 'Climate

change on a living Earth', Royal Society public lecture, London, 29 October 2007.

12 James Hansen, Testimony to the Iowa Utilities Board, 22 October 2007.

13 James Hansen, 'Scientific reticence and sea level rise', *Environmental Research Letters*, 2, 2007, p. 24002.

14 Martin Redfern, 'Antarctic glaciers surge to ocean', BBC News, 24 February 2008.

15 Eric Rignot et al., 'Recent Antarctic ice mass loss from radar interferometry and regional climate modelling', *Nature Geoscience*, 1, 3 January 2008, pp. 106–10.

16 Edward Hanna et al., 'Increased runoff from melt from the Greenland Ice Sheet: a response to global warming', *Journal of Climate*, 21(2), January 2008, pp. 331–41.

17 Hansen, 'Scientific reticence'.

18 Ibid.

19 S. Rahmstorf, 'A semi-empirical approach to projecting future sea level rise', *Science*, 315, 19 January 2007, pp. 368–9.

20 Fred Pearce, 'Climate warning as Siberia melts', *New Scientist*, 11 August 2005.

21 F. Stuart Chapin, 'Policy strategies to address sustainability of Alaskan boreal forests in response to a directionally changing climate', *PNAS*, 103(45), 7 November 2006, pp. 16637–43.

22 George Marshall, *Carbon Detox*, Octopus, October 2007.

23 Josep Canadell et al., 'Contributions to accelerating atmospheric CO_2 growth from economic activity, carbon intensity, and efficiency of natural sinks', *PNAS*, 25 October 2007.

24 Ibid.

25 Kenneth J. Feeley et al., 'Decelerating growth in tropical forest trees', *Ecology Letters*, 10, June 2007, pp. 461–69; Douglas Fox, 'CO_2: don't count on the trees', *New Scientist*, 27 October 2007.

26 Kerry H. Cook and Edward K. Vizy, 'Effects of twenty-first-century climate change on the Amazon rain forest', *Journal of Climate*, 21(3), February 2008, pp. 542–60.

27 Corinne Le Quéré et al., 'Saturation of the Southern Ocean CO_2 sink due to recent climate change', *Science*, 316(5832), 22 June 2007, pp. 1735–8.

28 Lenton, 'Tipping elements'.

29 Ibid.

30 Stefan Rahmstorf, 'Abrupt climate change', *Weather Catastrophes and Climate Change – the state of science*, Munich Re, 2004.

31 Lovelock, 'Climate change'.

32 International Energy Agency, *World Energy Outlook 2007*.

33 Ibid.

34 *Limiting global climate change to 2 degrees Celsius: The way ahead for 2020 and beyond*, Commission of European Communities, Brussels, 2007.

35 Hansen et al., 'Target atmospheric CO_2'.

36 Ibid.

37 Andrew J. Weaver et al.,

'Long term climate implications of 2050 emission reduction targets', *Geophysical Research Letters*, 34, 6 October 2007, L19703.

38 *Climate Change 2007: Synthesis Report.*

39 Hansen et al., 'Target atmospheric CO_2'.

40 Ibid.; Jim Hansen, 'Global warming – the perfect storm', Lecture to the Royal College of Physicians, 29 January 2008.

41 Hansen et al., 'Target atmospheric CO_2'.

42 Jim Hansen, 'Averting our eyes', 28 November 2007, <www.columbia.edu/~jeh1/>.

43 Stern, *Stern Review on the Economics of Climate Change.*

2 *The policy response*

1 Margaret Thatcher, Speech at 2nd World Climate Conference, Palais des Nations, Geneva, 6 November 1990.

2 Jim Hansen, Testimony to the Iowa Utilities Board, 22 October 2007.

3 President George Bush Senior, Address to the United Nations Conference on Environment and Development, Rio de Janeiro, Brazil, 12 June 1992.

4 Richard Wing, Letters, *New Scientist*, 22 December 2007.

5 Dieter Helm, Robin Smale and Jonathan Phillips, *Too Good to be True? The UK's Climate Change Record*, pre-publication draft, 10 December 2007.

6 John Kay, 'Why the key to carbon trading is to keep it simple', *Financial Times*, 9 May 2006.

7 White House news release, 11 June 2006.

8 Netherlands Environmental Assessment Agency, June 2007.

9 Raupach et al., 'Global and regional drivers of accelerating CO_2 emissions', *PNAS*, 104(24), 12 June 2007, pp. 10288–93.

10 Barbara Haya, *Failed Mechanism: How the CDM is subsidizing hydro developers and harming the Kyoto Protocol*, International Rivers, November 2007.

11 Ibid.

12 Kevin Smith, 'Carbon trading and the limits of free-market logic', *Ecologist*, October 2007.

13 'Jindal steel claims CDM benefits', *Down to Earth*, June 2006.

14 Christoph Sutter and Juan Carlos Parreño, *Does the Current Clean Development Mechanism Deliver Its Sustainable Development Claim?*, Paper presented to the international conference: 'Climate or development?', Hamburg Institute of International Economics, 28/29 October 2005.

15 Christoph Böhringer, Ulf Moslener and Bodo Sturm, 'Hot air for sale: a quantitative assessment of Russia's near-term climate policy options', Centre for European Economic Research (ZEW) Discussion Paper no. 06-016.

16 'Prime Minister calls for global action on climate change', Speech to WWF, 19 November 2007.

17 Norwegian Institute for Air Research, 6 October 2006.

18 Michael Wara, 'Is the global carbon market working?', *Nature*, 445, 8 February 2007.

19 Smith, 'Carbon trading'.

20 Ibid.

21 Wara, 'Is the global carbon market working?'

22 'Climate policy uncertainty and investment risk', IEA, 2007.

23 Intertanko/IMO, 22 October 2007.

24 IEA statistics, website, 2008.

25 IPCC, *Aviation and the Global Atmosphere*, Cambridge University Press, 1999.

26 Carey Newsom and Sally Cairns, *Predict and Decide – Aviation, climate change and UK policy*, Environmental Change Institute, University of Oxford, September 2006.

27 Nicholas Stern, *Stern Review on the Economics of Climate Change*, HM Treasury, 2007.

28 Scott Barrett, 'Towards a better climate treaty', *Nota di Lavoro*, 54, July 2002.

29 Fred Pearce, 'How the climate drama unfolded in Bali', *New Scientist*, 22/29 December 2007.

30 Raupach et al., 'Global and regional drivers'.

31 'An investment framework for clean energy and development: progress report', World Bank, 5 September 2006.

32 *Status Report on the Climate Change Funds*, Global Environment Facility, 19 May 2006.

33 *Tiempo*, 65, October 2007.

34 Ibid.

35 William Nordhaus, *After Kyoto: Alternative Mechanisms to Control Global Warming*, Paper prepared for a joint session of the American Economic Association and the Association of Environmental and Resource Economists, Atlanta, Georgia, 4 January 2001.

36 *Forests Declaration*, Friends of the Earth International, January 2008.

37 Deepak Rughani and Almuth Ernsting, 'REDD alert', *China Dialogue*, 22 January 2008.

38 David Steven, 'In Bali – radical commitments', *Open Democracy*, December 2007.

39 Deepak Rughani, 'Bali: the truth is sobering', *Green World*, Winter 2008.

40 John Kay, 'Why the key to carbon trading is to keep it simple', *Financial Times*, 9 May 2006.

41 Ed Crooks, 'Watchdog wants £9bn windfall electricity profits clawed back', *Financial Times*, 17 July 2008.

42 Ed Crooks, 'Green policies push up energy prices', *Financial Times*, 16 January 2008.

43 'Reducing the climate change impact of aviation', SEC(2005) 1184, European Commission, 27 September 2005.

44 Quoted by Kevin Smith in 'The case against carbon trading', *Celsias*, 10 January 2008.

45 'EU plans carbon trading overhaul', *Reuters News*, 23 January 2008.

46 D. W. Fahey, *Twenty Questions and Answers about the Ozone Layer: 2006 update*, UNEP, 2006.

47 Press release, Netherlands

Environmental Assessment Agency, 5 March 2007.

48 Guus J. M. Velders et al., 'The importance of the Montreal Protocol in protecting climate', *PNAS*, 104(12), 20 March 2007, pp. 4814–19.

49 Press release, Netherlands Environmental Assessment Agency, 5 March 2007.

50 UNEP press release, 14 September 2007.

51 UNEP website, January 2008.

52 Velders et al., 'The importance of the Montreal Protocol'.

53 Ronald Steenblik, *Biofuels – At What Cost? Government support for ethanol and biodiesel in selected OECD countries*, Global Subsidies Initiative, September 2007.

54 *World Development Report 2008: Agriculture for Development*, World Bank.

55 Steenblik, *Biofuels*.

56 David Pimentel, 'Ethanol production using corn, switchgrass, and wood; biodiesel production using soybean and sunflower', *Journal of Natural Resources Research*, 14(1), March 2005.

57 'Biofuel, horsepower and hectares', *The Land*, Summer 2006.

58 Paul Crutzen et al., 'N_2O release from agro-biofuel production negates global warming reduction by replacing fossil fuels', *Atmospheric Chemistry and Physics Discussions*, 7, 2007, pp. 11191–205.

59 *Assessment of CO_2 emissions from drained peatlands in South-east Asia*, Wetlands International, 21 December 2006.

60 Ibid.

61 Joseph Fargione et al., 'Land clearing and the biofuel carbon debt', *Science*, 7 February 2008.

62 George Monbiot, 'An agricultural crime against humanity', *Guardian*, 6 November 2007.

63 *World Development Report 2008: Agriculture for Development*.

64 Steenblik, *Biofuels*.

65 *Today*, BBC Radio 4, 14 January 2008.

66 Timothy Searchinger, 'Use of US croplands for biofuels increases greenhouse gases through emissions from land use change', *Science*, 7 February 2008.

67 Alan Clendenning, 'Amazon destruction rises sharply in 2007', Associated Press, 24 January 2008.

68 Matthew L. Wald, 'Is ethanol for the long haul', *Scientific American*, January 2007.

69 *Renewable Energy*, National Audit Office, February 2005.

70 Steven Sorrell and Jos Slim, 'Carbon trading in the policy mix', *Oxford Review of Economic Policy*, 19(3), Autumn 2003.

71 House of Commons Select Committee on Environmental Audit, *Ninth Report*, October 2007.

72 'Ofgem puts forward new approach to funding green generation', Ofgem, 22 January 2007.

73 Ed Crooks, 'Green policies push up energy prices', *Financial Times*, 16 January 2008.

74 Fiona Harvey and Rebecca Bream, 'Setback for UK wind farm

push' and 'Inflated energy bills fail to boost market', *Financial Times*, 4 February 2008.

75 'Renewable Energy', National Audit Office, February 2005.

76 Oliver Tickell, 'Treasury hijacks funds meant for green causes', *Independent*, 10 December 2005.

77 *Acid News*, September 2007, p. 20.

78 Arnold Schwarzenegger, 'Cool thinking', *New Scientist*, 20 January 2006.

79 'UNEP unveils the Climate Neutral Network to catalyze a transition to a low carbon world', UNEP press release, 10th Special Session of the Governing Council/ Global Ministerial Environment Forum, Monaco/Nairobi, 21 February 2008.

3 *The atmospheric commons*

1 Peter Barnes, *Capitalism 3*, Berrett-Koehler, November 2006.

2 Aristotle, *Politics*, trans. Benjamin Jowett, Clarendon Press, Oxford, 1885.

3 Garrett Hardin, 'The tragedy of the commons', *Science*, 13 December 1968.

4 Ibid.

5 George Monbiot, 'The tragedy of enclosure', *Scientific American*, January 1994.

6 Hardin, 'The tragedy of the commons'.

7 Margaret Thatcher, Speech opening Hadley Centre for Climate Prediction and Research, 25 May 1990.

8 Aubrey Meyer and Nicholas Hildyard, 'Climate and equity after Kyoto', Corner House Briefing 3, December 1997.

9 Ibid.

10 Michael Grubb, 'The Greenhouse Effect: negotiating targets', *International Affairs*, 66(1), January 1990, pp. 67–89.

11 Michael Jacobs, *The Green Econony*, Pluto Press, London, 1991, p. 191.

12 Karl Marx, 'The Duchess of Sutherland and slavery', *The People's Paper*, 45, 12 March 1853 (in *Articles on Britain*, Progress Publishers, Moscow, 1971).

13 Thomas Devine, 'The Highland Clearances', *Refresh*, 4, Spring 1987.

14 William Nordhaus, *After Kyoto: Alternative Mechanisms to Control Global Warming*, Paper prepared for a joint session of the American Economic Association and the Association of Environmental and Resource Economists, Atlanta, Georgia, 4 January 2001.

15 Charlie Kronick, Personal communication, 14 December 2007.

16 Simon Fairlie, Personal communication, January 2008.

17 *Briefing on Aid in 2004*, Development Initiatives, 2005.

18 *Cap & Share: A fair way to cut greenhouse emissions*, Draft Feasta working paper, January 2008.

19 Mark Lynas, 'If the cap fits, share it', *New Statesman*, 31 January 2008.

20 Peter Barnes, *Carbon Capping: A citizen's guide*, Tomales Bay Institute, 2007.

21 Lynas, 'If the cap fits'.

4 *Applying market economics*

1 Interview with Jeremy Paxman, *Newsnight*, BBC2, 1 October 2007.

2 Margaret Thatcher, BBC World Service phone-in with Oliver Scott, 3 June 1990.

3 Nicholas Stern, *Stern Review on the Economics of Climate Change*, HM Treasury, 2006.

4 Ibid.

5 Bali Communiqué, December 2007.

6 *OECD Environmental Outlook to 2030*, OECD, 5 March 2008.

7 Ibid.

8 Stern, *Stern Review*.

9 *Climate Change 2007: Synthesis Report*, Table SPM.6 and Figure SPM.11, IPCC, 2007.

10 George Monbiot, *Heat: How to stop the planet burning*, Allen Lane, 2006.

11 Nick D. Hanleya et al., 'The impact of a stimulus to energy efficiency on the economy and the environment: a regional computable general equilibrium analysis', *Renewable Energy*, 31(2), February 2006, pp. 161–71.

12 Geoffrey Heal, 'New strategies for the provision of global public goods: learning from international environmental challenge', *Global Public Goods*, UNDP, 1999.

13 Peter Barnes, *Carbon Capping: A citizen's guide*, Tomales Bay Institute, 2007.

14 Stern, *Stern Review*.

15 Gerard Wynn, 'Carbon market windfall profits', Reuters, 24 August 2007.

16 Peter Barnes, *Capitalism 3*, Berrett-Koehler, November 2006.

17 Peter Cramton and Suzi Kerr, 'Tradeable carbon permit auctions – how and why to auction not grandfather', *Energy Policy*, 30, 2002, pp. 333–45.

18 Scott Milliman and Raymond Prince, 'Firm incentives to promote technological change in pollution control', *Journal of Environmental Economics and Management*, 17(3), November 1989, pp. 247–65.

19 Cameron Hepburn, Michael Grubb, Karsten Neuhoff, Felix Matthes and Maximilien Tse, 'Auctioning of EU ETS phase II allowances: how and why?', *Climate Policy*, 6, 2006, pp. 137–60.

20 Ibid.

21 Ibid.

22 Stern, *Stern Review*.

23 *Reducing US Greenhouse Gas Emissions: How much at what cost*, McKinsey & Co., November 2007.

24 Brian C. O'Neill and Michael Oppenheimer, 'Climate change impacts are sensitive to the concentration stabilization path', *PNAS*, 101(47), 23 November 2004, pp. 16411–16.

25 Martin L. Weitzman, 'Prices vs. quantities', *Review of Economic Studies*, 41(4), October 1974, pp. 477–91.

26 Marc J. Roberts and Michael Spence, 'Effluent charges and licenses under uncertainty',

Journal of Public Economics, 5, 1976, pp. 193–208.

27 Ibid.

28 Cameron Hepburn, 'Regulation by prices, quantities or both: a review of instrument choice', *Oxford Review of Economic Policy*, 22(2), 2006.

29 Barnes, *Carbon Capping*.

30 Hepburn, 'Regulation by prices'.

31 Ibid.

32 Stern, *Stern Review*.

33 U. Thara Srinivasan et al., 'The debt of nations and the distribution of ecological impacts from human activities', *PNAS*, 22 January 2008.

34 Stern, *Stern Review*.

35 *Climate Change 2007: Synthesis Report*.

36 Roger Harrabin, 'UK "to ignore" EU pollution plea', BBC News, 23 January 2008.

37 *Climate Change 2007: Synthesis Report*.

38 *World Energy Outlook 2007*, IEA.

39 Stern, *Stern Review*.

40 R. J. Nicholls et al., *Ranking port cities with high exposure and vulnerability to climate extremes: exposure estimates*, OECD Environment Working Papers no. 1.

41 Ibid.

42 International Energy Agency R&D statistics, 2006.

43 Arthur Pigou, *The Economics of Welfare*, Macmillan, London, 1920, pt II, ch. 9.

44 Ibid.

45 Adam Smith, *An Inquiry into the Nature and Causes of the Wealth of Nations*, 1776; Modern Library, New York, 1937, p. 423.

46 Pigou, *The Economics of Welfare*.

47 David Pearce, 'The role of carbon taxes in adjusting to global warming', *Economic Journal*, 101(407), July 1991, pp. 938–48.

48 Barnes, *Capitalism 3*.

49 A. L. Bovenberg and R. A. DeMooij, 'Environmental levies and distortionary taxation', *American Economic Review*, 84(4), 1994, pp. 1085–9.

50 Bovenberg and Goulder, 'Optimal environmental taxation in the presence of other taxes: general-equilibrium analyses', *American Economic Review*, 86(4), 1996, pp. 985–1000.

51 Ian Parry, 'Pollution taxes and revenue recycling', *Journal of Environmental Economics and Management*, 29, 1995, S64–S77.

52 Jesse Schwartz and Robert Repetto, 'Nonseparable utility and the double dividend debate: reconsidering the tax-interaction effect', *Environmental and Resource Economics*, 15, 2000, pp. 149–57.

53 Ronald Coase, 'The problem of social cost', *Journal of Law and Economics*, 3, October 1960, pp. 1–44.

54 Ibid.

55 Ibid.

56 Ibid.

57 Paul Klemperer, 'What really matters in auction design', *Journal of Economic Perspectives*, 2002.

58 Ibid.

59 Ibid.

60 *Auction Design for Selling CO_2 Emission Allowances under the Regional Greenhouse Gas Initiative*, RGGI, 2007.

61 Peter Cramton and Suzi Kerr, 'Tradeable carbon permit auctions – how and why to auction not grandfather', *Energy Policy*, 30, 2002, pp. 333–45.

62 Ibid.

63 Ibid.

64 *Auction Design for Selling CO_2 Emission Allowances.*

65 Vilfredo Pareto, *Manuale di economia politica*, 1906.

66 Coase, 'The problem of social cost'.

67 Paul Klemperer, 'Awkward questions on behalf of our children', *Financial Times*, 11 May 2007.

68 Michael Jacobs, *The Green Economy*, Pluto Press, 1991.

69 Ibid.

70 Klemperer, 'Awkward questions'.

71 Stefan Rahmstorf, 'Abrupt climate change', *Weather Catastrophes and Climate Change – the state of science*, Munich Re, 2004.

72 Martin L. Weitzman, review of 'The Stern Review of the Economics of Climate Change', *JEL*, 31 April 2007.

73 Stern, *Stern Review*.

74 Weitzman, review of 'The Stern Review'.

75 Martin L. Weitzman, *On Modeling and Interpreting the Economics of Catastrophic Climate Change*, Unpublished draft, 5 December 2007.

76 Nicholas Stern, Gurukul Chevening Lecture 2006, LSE, 7 November 2006.

5 *Non-market solutions*

1 Jim Hansen, Testimony submitted to the Iowa Utilities Board, 22 October 2007.

2 Kevin Smith, 'The case against carbon trading', *Celsias*, 10 January 2008.

3 Nicholas Stern, Gurukul Chevening Lecture 2006, LSE, 7 November 2006.

4 *Reducing US Greenhouse Gas Emissions: How Much at What Cost?*, McKinsey, November 2007.

5 Ibid.

6 Florian Bressand et al., *Curbing Global Energy Demand Growth: The energy productivity opportunity*, McKinsey Global Institute, May 2007.

7 Ibid.

8 Nicholas Stern, *Stern Review on the Economics of Climate Change*, HM Treasury, 2007.

9 *Reducing US Greenhouse Gas Emissions.*

10 Sir Mark Moody Stuart, *Today*, BBC Radio 4, 4 February 2008.

11 *Synthesis Report of the IPCC Fourth Assessment Report*, IPCC, November 2007.

12 *Greenhouse Gas Emission Trends and Projections in Europe 2003*, European Environment Agency.

13 *Energy Efficiency and Climate Change: Considerations for On-Road Transport in Asia*, Asian Development Bank, 2006.

14 'World's cheapest car goes

on show', BBC News, 10 January 2008.

15 George Monbiot, *Heat: How to stop the planet burning*, Allen Lane, 2006.

16 Intertanko press release, 22 October 2007.

17 Ban Ki-moon, United Nations Secretary-General, 'Act ozone friendly, stay sun safe', 16 September 2007 (20th anniversary of the Montreal Protocol).

18 Michael Wara, 'Is the global carbon market working?', *Nature*, 445, 8 February 2007.

19 President George Bush Senior, Speech at the Goddard Space Flight Center, 1 June 1992.

20 Prince Charles, Speech to the European Parliament, 14 February 2008.

21 *Synthesis Report of the IPCC Fourth Assessment Report.*

22 Frédéric Achard et al., 'Improved estimates of net carbon emissions from land cover change in the tropics for the 1990s', *Global Biogeochemical Cycles*, 18, 2004.

23 Stern, *Stern Review*.

24 *World Development Report 2008: Agriculture for Development*, World Bank, 2007.

25 Nicolas Gruber et al., 'The vulnerability of the carbon cycle in the 21st century: an assessment of carbon-climate-human interactions', in C. B. Field and M. R. Raupach (eds), *The Global Carbon Cycle: Integrating humans, climate and the natural world*, 2004.

26 *Synthesis Report of the IPCC Fourth Assessment Report.*

27 *World Development Report 2008: Agriculture for Development.*

28 *Adaptation to climate change in agriculture, forestry and fisheries*, FAO, 2007.

29 *World Development Report 2008: Agriculture for Development.*

30 *World Energy Outlook 2007*, International Energy Agency.

31 Stern, *Stern Review*.

32 Hansen, Testimony submitted to the Iowa Utilities Board.

33 James Hansen et al., 'Target atmospheric CO_2: where should humanity aim?', Pre-publication draft, February 2008.

34 Cement Sustainability Initiative website, 2007.

35 Rachel Nowak, 'Hopes build for eco-concrete', *New Scientist*, 26 January 2008.

36 Bressand et al., *Curbing Global Energy Demand Growth.*

37 *State Aid Scoreboard, Autumn 2007 Update*, European Commission, 2007.

38 *Commission staff working document – Annex to the Communication from the Commission to the European Parliament, the Council, the European Economic and Social Committee and the Committee of the Regions – Commission Report on the Application of Council Regulation (EC) No. 1407/2002 on State Aid to the Coal Industry, COM(2007) 253 final*, European Commission, 2007.

39 Andrew Simms et al., *The Price of Power*, New Economics Foundation, 2004.

40 Thomas R. Casten, 'Recycling energy to reduce costs

and mitigate climate change', in Michael C. MacCracken, Frances Moore and John C. Topping Jr (eds), *Sudden and Disruptive Climate Change*, Earthscan, 2008.

41 Bressand et al., *Curbing Global Energy Demand Growth.*

42 Ronald Coase, 'The problem of social cost', *Journal of Law and Economics*, 3, October 1960, pp. 1–44.

6 *Allocating resources*

1 Editorial, *Nature*, 31 January 2008.

2 Dr Margaret Chan, Director-General of the World Health Organization, 'Climate change and health: preparing for unprecedented challenges', The 2007 David E. Barmes Global Health Lecture, Bethesda, MD, USA, 10 December 2007.

3 *Synthesis Report of the IPCC Fourth Assessment Report*, IPCC, November 2007.

4 *Reducing US Greenhouse Gas Emissions: How Much at What Cost?*, McKinsey & Company, November 2007.

5 'Analysis of carbon capture and storage cost-supply curves for the UK', DTI, January 2007.

6 *World Factbook*, CIA, 2007.

7 Nicholas Stern, *Stern Review on the Economics of Climate Change*, HM Treasury, 2006.

8 *World Energy Outlook 2007*, IEA, November 2007.

9 Linda Bilmes and Joseph E. Stiglitz, 'Iraq War will cost more than $2 trillion', *Milken Institute Review*, December 2006.

10 'War at any price', Report by the Joint Economic Committee Majority Staff, November 2007.

11 *SIPRI Yearbook 2007*, Stockholm International Peace Research Institute.

12 Andrew Simms et al., *The Price of Power*, New Economics Foundation, 2004.

13 Jennifer Kent and Norman Myers, *Perverse Subsidies: How Tax Dollars Can Undercut the Environment and the Economy*, Island Press, 2001.

14 *Newsnight*, BBC2, 24 January 2008.

15 Stern, *Stern Review.*

16 Ibid.

17 Ibid.

18 *Climate Change 2007: Impacts, Adaptation and Vulnerability*, IPPC, 2007.

19 Mark Lynas, *Six Degrees*, Fourth Estate, London, 2007.

20 David Satterthwaite, 'Climate change and cities', *Tiempo*, 66, January 2008.

21 R. J. Nicholls et al., *Ranking port cities with high exposure and vulnerability to climate extremes: exposure estimates*, OECD Environment Working Papers no. 1, December 2007.

22 Ibid.

23 'Adapting to climate change – what's needed in poor countries, and who should pay', Oxfam Briefing Paper 104, 29 May 2007.

24 Ibid.

25 *An investment framework for clean energy and development: progress report*, World Bank, 5 September 2006.

26 *World Development Report 2008: Agriculture for Development*, World Bank, 2007.

27 Jim Hansen, 'Global warming – the perfect storm', Lecture to the Royal College of Physicians, 29 January 2008.

28 'Climate change FAQs', World Bank website.

29 *An investment framework for clean energy and development.*

30 Stern, *Stern Review.*

31 *World Energy Outlook 2007.*

32 John Carey and Adam Aston, 'Solar's day in the sun', *Business Week*, 15 October 2007.

33 'Ministers generally endorse World Bank's plans on clean energy investments', World Bank press release, 19 April 2007.

34 'Financing clean energy: a framework for public private partnerships to address climate change', Speech by Paul Wolfowitz, London, 13 March 2007.

35 *An investment framework for clean energy and development.*

36 Tom Doggett, 'Bush to commit $2 billion to climate change fund', *Reuters News*, 29 January 2008.

37 Florian Bressand et al., *Curbing Global Energy Demand Growth: The energy productivity opportunity*, McKinsey Global Institute, May 2007.

38 Brenda Boardman, *Home Truths: A low-carbon strategy to reduce UK housing CO_2 emissions by 80% by 2050*, Environmental Change Institute, University of Oxford, November 2007.

39 *World Energy Outlook 2007.*

40 IEA energy R&D database, 2006.

41 Gwyn Prins and Steve Rayner, 'Time to ditch Kyoto', *Nature*, 449, 25 October 2007, pp. 973–5.

42 *World Energy Outlook 2007.*

43 Jim Giles, 'Physics reels as the financial axe falls', *New Scientist*, 19 January 2008.

44 David Strahan, 'Coal: bleak outlook for the black stuff', *New Scientist*, 19 January 2008.

45 'US pulls the plug on flagship clean coal project', *New Scientist*, 9 February 2008; 'Come clean on coal', *New Scientist* editorial, 9 February 2008.

46 Bjorn Lomborg, 'An inconvenient voice', *New Scientist*, 27 October 2007.

47 Dr Seuss, *The Lorax*, Random House, 1971.

48 *Synthesis Report of the IPCC Fourth Assessment Report.*

49 *Global Forest Resources Assessment 2005 – progress towards sustainable forest management*, FAO Forestry Paper 147.

50 'Report on the second workshop on reducing emissions from deforestation in developing countries', Climate Convention, 26th session of the Subsidiary Body for Scientific and Technonological Advice in Bonn, 7–18 May 2007.

51 *Ecosystems and human well-being: synthesis*, Millennium Ecosystem Assessment, 2007.

52 *Peat CO2: Assessment of CO_2 emissions from drained peatlands in South-east Asia*, Wetlands International, 21 December 2006.

53 Fred Pearce, 'Bang bang, and the world warms', *New Scientist*, 12 August 2006; A. R. Yallop et al., 'The extent and intensity of management burning in the English uplands', *Journal of Applied Ecology*, 43(6), 2006, pp. 1138–48; Pat H. Bellamy et al., 'Carbon losses from all soils across England and Wales', *Nature*, 437, 8 September 2005, pp. 245–8.

54 Robert N. Stavins and Kenneth R. Richards, *The cost of US forest-based carbon sequestration*, Pew Center on Global Climate Change, January 2005.

55 C. D. Thomas et al., 'Extinction risk from climate change', *Nature*, 427(6970), 8 January 2004, pp. 145–8.

56 Emma Marris, 'The escalator effect', *Nature Reports*, 23 November 2007.

57 Jason S. McLachlan et al., 'A framework for debate of assisted migration in an era of climate change', *Conservation Biology*, 21(2), April 2007, pp. 297–302.

58 Bob Holmes, 'Assisted migration: helping nature to relocate', *New Scientist*, 6 October 2007.

59 James Lovelock, 'Climate change on a living Earth', Royal Society public lecture, London, 29 October 2007.

60 Fred Pearce, 'Climate change: one degree and we're done for', *New Scientist*, 27 September 2006.

61 Edward Goldsmith, 'How to feed people under a regime of climate change', *World Affairs Journal*, Winter 2003.

62 Ibid.

63 Steven R. Schroeder and Kenneth Green, *Reducing global warming through forestry and agriculture*, Reason Public Policy Institute, July 2001.

64 *Reducing US Greenhouse Gas Emissions.*

65 Johannes Lehmann, 'Bio-char sequestration in terrestrial ecosystems – a review', *Mitigation and Adaptation Strategies for Global Change*, 11, 2006, pp. 403–27.

66 Peter Aldhous, 'Could new GM crops please the greens?', *New Scientist*, 5 January 2008.

67 Allen G. Good et al., 'Engineering nitrogen use efficiency with alanine aminotransferase', *Canadian Journal of Botany*, 85(3), 2007, pp. 252–62.

68 Schroeder and Green, *Reducing global warming through forestry and agriculture.*

69 Martin Weitzmann, 'On modeling and interpreting the economics of catastrophic climate change', in draft, 5 December 2007.

70 A. J. Watson et al., 'Minimal effect of iron fertilization on sea-surface carbon dioxide concentrations', *Nature*, 371, 8 September 2002, pp. 143–5.

71 James E. Lovelock and Chris G. Rapley, 'Ocean pipes could help the Earth to cure itself', *Nature*, 449, 27 September 2007, p. 403.

72 Roger Angel, 'Feasibility of cooling the Earth with a cloud of

small spacecraft near the inner Lagrange point', *PNAS*, 103(46), 14 November 2006, pp. 17184–9.

73 Mikhail I. Budyko, *Climatic Changes*, American Geophysical Union, Washington, DC, 1977.

74 *Synthesis Report of the IPCC Fourth Assessment Report.*

75 John Latham, 'Control of global warming?', *Nature*, 347, 27 September 1990, pp. 339–40.

76 Keith Bower et al., 'Computational assessment of a proposed technique for global warming mitigation via albedo-enhancement of marine stratocumulus clouds', *Atmospheric Research*, 2006.

77 James Latham, 'Amelioration of global warming by controlled enhancement of the albedo and longevity of low-level maritime clouds', *Atmospheric Scence Letters*, 2002, pp. 52–8.

78 Ibid.

79 Ibid.

80 James Latham, Personal communication, November 2007.

81 Angel, 'Feasibility of cooling the Earth'.

82 IEA statistics, IEA website, 2007.

83 IPCC, 1999.

84 R. E. Dickinson, 'Climate engineering: a review of approaches to changing the global energy balance', *Climatic Change*, 33, 1996, pp. 279–90.

85 Paul Crutzen, 'Albedo enhancement by stratospheric sulfur injections: a contribution to resolve a policy dilemma?', *Climatic Change*, 77(3–4), August 2006.

86 *Climate Change 2007: Impacts, Adaptation and Vulnerability*, Working Group II Contribution to the Intergovernmental Panel on Climate Change, Fourth Assessment Report, 2007.

87 *Climate Change and the Financial Sector: An Agenda for Action*, WWF/Allianz Global Investors, June 2005.

88 *From Weather Alert to Climate Alarm*, Oxfam Briefing Paper 108, 25 November 2007.

89 John Bongaarts, 'Population growth and global warming', *Population and Development Review*, 18(2), June 1992, pp. 299–319.

90 *State of World Population 2004*, United Nations Population Fund, 2004.

91 Ibid.

92 Tom Dyson, 'On development, demography and climate change: the end of the world as we know it?', Paper prepared for Session 952 of the XXVth Conference of the International Union for the Scientific Study of Population, Tours, 18–23 July 2005.

93 Dr Margaret Chan, Director-General of the World Health Organization, 'Climate change and health: preparing for unprecedented challenges', 2007 David E. Barmes Global Health Lecture, Bethesda, MD, 10 December 2007.

94 Ibid.

95 *Climate Change and Health*, World Health Organization, 16 January 2008.

96 Ibid.

7 *The Great Dying*

1 Nicholas Stern, Gurukul Chevening Lecture 2006, LSE, 7 November 2006.

2 Michael J. Benton and Richard J. Twitchett, 'How to kill (almost) all life: the end-Permian extinction event', *Trends in Ecology and Evolution*, 18(7), July 2003.

3 Robert A. Berner, 'Examination of hypotheses for the Permo-Triassic boundary extinction by carbon cycle modeling', *PNAS*, 26 March 2002.

4 Benton and Twitchett, 'How to kill (almost) all life'.

5 C. V. Looy et al., 'The delayed resurgence of equatorial forests after the Permian-Triassic ecologic crisis', *PNAS*, 96(24), 23 November 1999, pp. 13857–62.

6 Ibid.

7 Ibid.

8 Benton and Twitchett, 'How to kill (almost) all life'.

9 Roland Mundil et al., 'Age and timing of the Permian mass extinctions: U/Pb dating of closed-system zircons', *Science*, 305(5691), 17 September 2004, pp. 1760–63.

10 Sandra L. Kamo et al., 'Rapid eruption of Siberian Flood-volcanic rocks and evidence for coincidence with the Permian-Triassic boundary and mass extinction at 251Ma', *Earth and Planetary Science Letters*, 214, 2003, pp. 75–91.

11 Luann Becker et al., 'Impact event at the Permian-Triassic boundary: evidence from extraterrestrial noble gases in fullerenes', *Science*, 291, 23 February 2001.

12 Richard Twitchett et al., 'Rapid and synchronous collapse of marine and terrestrial ecosystems during the end-Permian biotic crisis', *Geology*, 29(4), April 2001, pp. 351–4.

13 Kamo et al., 'Rapid eruption of Siberian Flood-volcanic rocks'.

14 Benton and Twitchett, 'How to kill (almost) all life'.

15 Kliti Grice et al., 'Photic zone euxinia during the Permian-Triassic superanoxic event', *Science*, 4 February 2005, pp. 706–9; Peter Ward, 'Precambrian strikes back', *New Scientist*, 9 February 2008.

16 Grice et al., 'Photic zone euxinia during the Permian-Triassic superanoxic event'.

17 Lee R. Kump et al., 'Massive release of hydrogen sulfide to the surface ocean and atmosphere during intervals of oceanic anoxia', *Geology*, 33(5), May 2005, pp. 397–400.

18 Evelyn S. Krull and Gregory J. Retallack, 'd13C depth profiles from paleosols across the Permian-Triassic boundary: evidence for methane release', *GSA Bulletin*, 112(9), September 2000, pp. 1459–72.

19 James Lovelock, 'Climate change on a living Earth', Royal Society public lecture, 29 October 2007.

20 A. Sluijs et al., 'The Palaeocene-Eocene Thermal Maximum super greenhouse: biotic and geochemical signatures, age models and mechanisms of climate change', *Deep Time Perspectives*

on Climate Change, Geol. Soc. London Spec., in press.

21 John A. Higgins and Daniel P. Schrag, 'Beyond methane: towards a theory for the Paleocene-Eocene Thermal Maximum', *Earth and Planetary Science Letters*, 245(3–4), 30 May 2006, pp. 523–37.

22 Euan G. Nisbet, 'Have sudden large releases of methane from geological reservoirs occurred since the Last Glacial Maximum, and could such releases occur again?', *Philosophical Transactions of the Royal Society* A, 360, 2002, pp. 581–607.

23 Ibid.

24 Ibid.

8 *Questions and answers*

1 Dr Margaret Chan, Director-General of the World Health Organization, 'Climate change and health: preparing for unprecedented challenges', 2007 David E. Barmes Global Health Lecture, Bethesda, MD, 10 December 2007.

2 David Strahan, 'Coal: bleak outlook for the black stuff', *New Scientist*, 19 January 2008.

3 Tim Harford, *The Undercover Economist*, Little, Brown, 2006.

4 Nicholas Stern, *Stern Review on the Economics of Climate Change*, HM Treasury, 2007.

5 *Reducing US Greenhouse Gas Emissions: How Much at What Cost?*, McKinsey, November 2007.

6 Jim Hansen, 'Averting our eyes', 28 November 2007.

7 *Climate Change 2007: Impacts, Adaptation and Vulnerability*, IPCC, 2007.

8 R. Ismer and K. Neuhoff, 'Border tax adjustments: a feasible way to support stringent emission trading', Cambridge Working Papers in Economics CWPE 0409/CMI Working Paper 36, 2004/2007.

9 Roger Harrabin, 'Barroso trade threat on climate', BBC News, 22 January 2008.

10 Bjorn Lomborg, *Cool It*, Cyan-Marshall Cavendish, 2007.

11 Debora Mckenzie, 'Why jellies love global warming', *New Scientist*, 11 December 2007.

12 *State and Trends of the Carbon Market 2006 – Update: January 1–September 30, 2006*, World Bank, 2006.

13 Frederick H. Morse, chairman of the US Solar Energy Industries Association, 'The Concentrating Solar Power Global Market Initiative (GMI) as a result of research and development', Renewables04 Conference, Bonn.

14 Bennett Daviss, 'Solar power: the future's bright'; 'A place in the sun' (editorial), both in *New Scientist*, 8 December 2007.

15 John W. Lund, *Successes and State of the Geothermal World 2005*, ENEL.

16 Jim Hansen, 'Global warming – the perfect storm', Lecture to the Royal College of Physicians, 29 January 2008.

Glossary

AAU – see *Assigned Amount Unit.*

Adaptation Fund (AF) – a fund under the *Kyoto Protocol* which exists to finance concrete adaptation projects and programmes in developing countries that are Parties to the Protocol. It is funded by a 2 per cent tax on transactions under the *CDM* except those arising from *least developed countries.*

AF – see *Adaptation Fund.*

Allowance – normally, shorthand for *European Union Allowance.*

Annex 1 – that part of the *Climate Convention* that lists industrialized countries with targets to limit their *carbon* emissions, under the Climate Convention itself and under the *Kyoto Protocol.* The term is used to describe the group of industrialized countries.

Assigned Amount Unit (AAU) – a tradable unit representing one tonne of *carbon dioxide* emissions under *Emissions Trading*, one of the *flexibility mechanisms* of the *Kyoto Protocol.*

Auction – in the context of this book, auction is a means of allocating *permits* to produce *greenhouse gases* up to a global cap to those willing to pay the highest price. The chosen auction method for Kyoto2 is a *uniform price sealed-bid auction*, subject to a *reserve* and a *ceiling* (or *safety valve*).

Biodiversity Convention – see *Convention on Biological Diversity.*

C&C – see *Contraction and Convergence.*

Cap – in the context of this book, a maximum number of *permits* made available in a given period, in order to limit *emissions* of *greenhouse gases* to that cap. Kyoto2 advocates a global cap, but caps may also be set on specific countries, industries, etc. Under Kyoto2 the cap is not firm in any given year as the *auction* of permits would be subject to *reserve* and *ceiling* prices.

Cap and Dividend – similar to *Cap and Share*, except that the *permits* would be retained by and sold by governments which would return the proceeds to citizens, for example by way of tax rebates, and perhaps by way of additional expenditures on energy efficiency and renewable technologies. C&D has been developed by Peter Barnes in the USA.

Cap and Rebate – largely synonymous with *Cap and Dividend.*

Cap and Share – a system for controlling *greenhouse gas* emissions through *permits*, under which *production authorization permits* (PAPs) up to a fixed cap are distributed to world citizens for them to sell on to polluters. A proportion of the PAPs would go to a *Global Atmosphere Trust*. The system is also applicable on a national basis, and may be incorporated into Ireland's climate policy. C&S is championed by *Feasta*.

Carbon – generally shorthand for *carbon dioxide* and other *greenhouse gases*. Where carbon dioxide is being measured in terms of its carbon content, remember that one tonne of carbon is contained in about 3.7 tonnes of carbon dioxide.

Carbon capture and storage (CCS) – a technology whereby emissions of carbon dioxide from power stations or other industrial plant are captured prior to emission and sequestered to safe underground or submarine reservoirs. The technology is as yet in an early stage of development and there remain numerous uncertainties over its long-term viability and safety.

Carbon credit – a general term for carbon-backed securities, whether *offsets* in the *voluntary market* or *emissions reductions* traded in the *compliance markets* of the *Kyoto Protocol* or the *EUETS*.

Carbon dioxide (CO_2) – the principal *greenhouse gas* responsible for *global warming*. Although not a very powerful greenhouse gas, it is important due to the immense volumes in which it is emitted, mainly from burning *fossil fuels*, and its long residence time in the atmosphere. CO_2 is also the reference gas for calculating the *global warming potential* of other gases, and thus has a *GWP* of 1.

Carbon market – a general term for the various markets which exist in *carbon* and carbon-backed securities. The carbon market divides into the *compliance market* and the *voluntary market*.

Carbon offset – a promise to remove from, or prevent the emission to the atmosphere of, a given quantity of *carbon dioxide* or an equivalent amount of other *greenhouse gases*. Carbon offsets are normally sold by the tonne of carbon dioxide or equivalent, and bought in order to neutralize or *offset* the emissions associated with a specific event, product or act. The term is normally applied to offsets in the *voluntary carbon market*, but is also sometimes applied to *carbon credits* traded in *compliance markets*.

Carbon tax – a tax applied to *carbon* emissions. Such a tax may be applied at different stages of the carbon *emission* process, for example upstream – at or close to where a *fossil fuel* is produced or imported – or at the actual point of emission, or somewhere in between. The term 'tax' normally specifies a flat-rate levy based on the amount of carbon.

Carbon trading – the trading of *carbon*-backed securities, within a *carbon market*. These include *carbon offsets* for the *voluntary carbon market*, *allowances* under the *EUETS*, and *emissions reductions* under the *flexibility mechanisms* of the *Kyoto Protocol*.

CCS – see *Carbon capture and storage*.

CDM – see *Clean Development Mechanism*.

CDM Executive Board (EB) the body within the *Climate Convention* which approves (registers) projects submitted for approval under the *Kyoto Protocol*'s main *flexibility mechanism*, the *CDM*.

CEIF – see *Clean Energy Investment Framework*.

Ceiling – in an auction of multiple identical items, a ceiling is the maximum selling price (the opposite of a *reserve*). If bids reach the ceiling, the *cap* on the number of items to be sold is lifted, so that as many items will be sold at the ceiling price as bid for. Kyoto2 proposes that its *uniform price sealed-bid auction* for *permits* should be subject to both *ceiling* and *reserve* prices. This would allow the cap to be stretched or contracted in any year, while the cap is adjusted accordingly in future years.

CER – see *Certified Emission Reduction*.

Certified Emission Reduction (CER) – a unit of *carbon* for the purpose of trading under the *Clean Development Mechanism* of the *Kyoto Protocol*, representing a tonne of *carbon dioxide* whose emission has been prevented or offset.

CFC – chemical shorthand for chlorofluorocarbon. CFCs are powerful *greenhouse gases*, but are better known for their role in catalysing the destruction of the *ozone layer*. The main uses of CFCs are as refrigerants, propellants and in blowing foams, but their use has declined following restrictions under the *Montreal Protocol*. Substitutes include *HFCs*, *HCFCs*, blends of hydrocarbons and *carbon dioxide*.

CH_4 – the chemical notation for *methane*.

Chlorofluorocarbon – see *CFC*.

Clean Development Mechanism (CDM) – the most important of the *flexibility mechanisms* of the *Kyoto Protocol*. Under the CDM, projects to reduce greenhouse gas emissions in developing countries can generate *Certified Emission Reductions* or *CERs*. It is intended to contribute to the sustainable development of the host country and to allow *Annex 1* countries to meet their *emissions* reduction targets in a cost-efficient way. In practice the CDM has been widely abused, with many projects being registered by the *CDM Executive Board* despite failing to meet the applicable criteria.

Clean Energy Investment Framework (CEIF) – a development framework, coordinated by the *World Bank*, which aims to increase access to energy, especially in sub-Saharan Africa; accelerate the transition to a low *carbon* economy; and adapt to climate variability and change. The CEIF estimates the necessary scale of energy investments at $165 billion per year for a decade.

Clearing price – described under *uniform price sealed-bid auction*.

Climate change – a term normally used to described *global warming* caused by humans, though in principle it could apply to any change in climate at any time.

Climate Convention – shorthand for the *United Nations Framework Convention on Climate Change* (UNFCCC).

Climate Neutral Network (CNN) – created in February 2007 in Monaco by *UNEP* and a founding group of cities and companies wishing to act seriously on *climate change*, in order to 'federate the small but growing wave of nations, local authorities and companies who are pledging to significantly reduce emissions en route to zero emission economies, communities and businesses'.

CNN – see *Climate Neutral Network*.

CO_2 – the chemical notation for *carbon dioxide*

Compliance market – that part of the *carbon market* that deals in *carbon* under the *flexibility mechanisms* of the *Kyoto Protocol* and the *EUETS*, as opposed to the *voluntary market*.

Compliance period – the period within the *Kyoto Protocol* during which *Annex 1* states are to comply with their obligations to limit their *emissions* of *greenhouse gases*. It runs from 2008 to 2012.

Contraction and Convergence (C&C) – a system for the global regulation of *greenhouse gas emissions* in which countries are allocated tradable permits to emit greenhouse gases up to a cap, pro rata to each country's population size. First presented by Michael Grubb in 1990, C&C has been further developed and promoted by the *Global Commons Institute*.

Contrail – the often visible trail of exhaust gas emitted by high-flying aircraft, which contains a potent mixture of *greenhouse gases* other than *carbon dioxide*, including *nitrous oxide* and *water vapour*.

Convention on Biological Diversity – international convention agreed at the 1992 Earth Summit, and coming into force in 1993. The CBD aims to conserve, ensure the sustainable use of, and bring about the fair and equitable sharing of the benefits arising from, biodiversity. The CBD secretariat is based in Montreal, under the *United Nations Environment Programme*.

EB – see *CDM Executive Board*.

EEC – see *Energy Efficiency Commitment*.

Emissions Reduction Unit (ERU) – an emissions reduction for trading under *Joint Implementation*, one of the *flexibility mechanisms* of the *Kyoto Protocol*. Each ERU represents one tonne of CO_2.

Emissions – refers to emissions of *greenhouse gases* to the atmosphere. Emissions are normally measured in tonnes of *carbon dioxide* equivalent.

Emissions Trading (ET) – one of the *Kyoto Protocol*'s *flexibility mechanisms* allowing *Annex 1* countries under-shooting their *Kyoto Protocol* emissions targets to sell their surplus rights to other Annex 1 countries who are exceeding their targets. These are denominated in *Assigned Amount Units* or *AAUs*. These emissions reductions are widely known as *hot air*.

Energy Efficiency Commitment (EEC) – a requirement on UK energy suppliers to invest in reducing energy demand by raising the energy efficiency of consumers.

ERU – see *Emissions Reduction Unit*.

ET – see *Emissions Trading*.

EU – the European Union, which operates the world's biggest carbon market, the *EU Emissions Trading Scheme*.

EUA – see *European Union Allowance*.

EU Allowance – see *European Union Allowance*.

EU Emissions Trading Scheme (EUETS) – the trading system for *greenhouse gas* emissions which applies within the EU. The world's biggest *carbon market*, the EUETS's *Phase 1* began to operate in January 2005, and is now in its *Phase 2*. Although the EUETS is deeply flawed, reforms are in process, and it will be somewhat better after 2012 in *Phase 3*.

EUETS – see *EU Emissions Trading Scheme*.

European Union Allowance (EUA) – a permit to emit a tonne of *carbon dioxide* under the *EUETS*.

Executive Board – see *CDM Executive Board*.

External cost – a cost attached to a process, action or activity, which is borne externally, that is by the environment, society as a whole or a particular set of people. Examples which we are concerned with include the social costs and environmental costs imposed by the emission of *greenhouse gases*.

Externality – see *external cost*.

FAO – see *Food and Agriculture Organization of the United Nations*.

Feasta – Ireland-based environmental *NGO*, founded in 1988, developing and promoting a number of interesting ideas including *Cap and Share*. In full, the Foundation for the Economics of Sustainability.

F-gases – fluorinated gases such as the *HFCs*, *PFCs* and *sulphur hexafluoride*, all powerful *greenhouse gases*.

Flexibility mechanisms – the mechanisms for the trading of reductions in *emissions* of *greenhouse gases* under the *Kyoto Protocol*. These are the *Clean Development Mechanism*, *Joint Implementation* and *Emissions Trading*.

Food and Agriculture Organization of the United Nations (FAO) – a UN agency whose mandate is to defeat hunger. Founded in 1945, it is based in Rome, Italy. In practice it promotes a largely industrial and commercial model of agriculture (and of forestry), and considers subsistence or near-subsistence farming to be anti-development.

Fossil fuel – a fuel mined or derived from fossil deposits. Fossil fuels all contain *carbon* in different proportions. The main fossil fuels are coal, oil and natural gas/methane, but novel fossil fuels are currently being developed including oil shales and tar sands. Collectively fossil fuels supply the great bulk of the world's energy, and the emissions of *carbon dioxide* produced by their combustion are the main contributor to *global warming*.

GDP – see *gross domestic product*.

GEF – see *Global Environment Facility*.

Global Atmosphere Trust – the body that would be set up under *Cap and Share* to sell some *production authorization permits* and so raise funds to spend on adaptation and other measures.

Global Commons Institute – the *NGO* set up to develop and promote *Contraction and Convergence*.

Global Environment Facility (GEF) – founded in 1991 to finance projects that would improve the global environment (including international waters, the *ozone layer*, biodiversity, land degradation, persistent organic pollutants and *climate change*, the GEF is the financial mechanism for the *Climate Convention* and the *Convention on Biological Diversity*. Based in Washington DC, the GEF is an independent organization but operates closely with its implementing agencies, including the *World Bank*, *UNDP* and *UNEP*, and has an annual budget of about $1 billion per year. The GEF operates the *Special Climate Change Fund* and the *Least Developed Countries Fund* and was selected to host the interim secretariat for the *Adaptation Fund* at the Bali meeting of the *Climate Convention* in 2007.

Global heating – as *global warming* except that the word 'heating' is chosen to sound less pleasant.

Global warming – this term is now used, specifically, to describe the process by which the Earth is heating up as a result of human emissions of *greenhouse gases* into the atmosphere.

Global warming potential (GWP) – a measure of the warming potential of a given mass of a *greenhouse gas*, relative to the same mass of *carbon dioxide*, over a given period of time, 100 years if not otherwise specified.

GNI – see *gross national income*.

GNP – see *gross national product*.

Greenhouse effect – the mechanism whereby *greenhouse gases* in the atmosphere maintain a generally equable global temperature, but which, due to the emission by humans of large volumes of greenhouse gases, is now causing *global warming*.

Greenhouse gas – a gas that allows high-temperature solar radiation to enter the Earth's atmosphere unhindered, but blocks the lower-temperature re-radiation of heat from the planetary surface. So called due to their contribution to the *greenhouse effect*.

Gross domestic product (GDP) – the total market value of all final goods and services produced within a country in a given year.

Gross national income (GNI) – the *gross domestic product* of a country, plus income received from other countries minus similar payments made to other countries in the year in question. Similar to *gross national product*, but applies to the territory of a country.

Gross National Product (GNP) – the gross domestic product of a country, plus the income earned by citizens abroad, minus the income earned by foreigners in the country, in the year in question. Similar to *gross national income*, but applies to the citizens of a country.

GWP – see *global warming potential*.

HCFC – chemical shorthand for hydrochlorofluorocarbon. The HCFCs are an important group of *greenhouse gases*, developed following the *Montreal Protocol* as very weakly ozone-depleting alternatives to *CFCs*. One of the major HCFCs in use is *HCFC-134a*.

HCFC-134a – a member of the *HCFC* group of gases, used as a refrigerant. It is a powerful greenhouse gas with a *GWP* of 1,300. Although still widely used in mobile air conditioning and other applications, new controls will soon come into force under the *Montreal Protocol*.

HFC – chemical shorthand for hydrofluorocarbon. The HFCs are an important group of *greenhouse gases*, developed following the *Montreal Pro-*

tocol as non-ozone-depleting alternatives to *CFCs*. One of the most important HFCs is *HFC-23*.

HFC-23 (CHF_3) – a member of the *HFC* group of gases, HFC-23 is a powerful *greenhouse gas* with a *GWP* of 11,700. As well as having applications as a refrigerant, HFC-23 is a by-product of the manufacture of *HCFC-134a*.

Hot air – a colloquial and disparaging term for *Emissions Trading*.

IEA – see *International Energy Agency*.

IMF – see *International Monetary Fund*.

Intergovernmental Panel on Climate Change (IPCC) – a global scientific organization founded in 1988 by the World Meteorological Organization and the *United Nations Environment Programme* to evaluate the risk of climate change caused by humans and present climate policy options to world leaders.

International Energy Agency (IEA) – founded by the *OECD* in 1974, the IEA is an international organization dedicated to preventing disruption in the supply of fuels, developing alternative energy sources, promoting energy security and rational energy policies, fostering international energy technology cooperation and environmental protection, and publishing statistics and other information on energy markets. The IEA is based in Paris, France.

International Monetary Fund (IMF) – set up in 1944, the IMF is one of the Bretton Woods institutions to harmonize the world financial system. The role of the IMF is to loan emergency funds to states suffering balance of payments deficits. The reputation of the IMF has suffered due to its frequent insistence on harsh packages of neoliberal economic reform as a condition of its loans. The importance of the IMF has recently declined as governments have turned to alternative sources of funding.

International Union for Conservation of Nature (IUCN) – the world's largest global environmental network, founded in 1948 and based in Gland, Switzerland, its objective is to 'influence, encourage and assist societies throughout the world to conserve the integrity and diversity of nature and to ensure that any use of natural resources is equitable and ecologically sustainable'.

IPCC – see *Intergovernmental Panel on Climate Change*.

IUCN – see *International Union for Conservation of Nature*.

Joint Implementation (JI) – one of the *Kyoto Protocol*'s *flexibility mechanisms*. It operates in the same way as the *Clean Development Mechanism* but between *Annex 1* countries, to produce *Emissions Reduction Units* or

ERUs. Typically JI projects take place in transition economies such as those of the former Soviet Union where emissions reductions can be obtained at lowest cost.

Kyoto Protocol – signed in 1997 and coming into force in 2005, the Kyoto Protocol supplements the *Climate Convention*. Its principal creations are its *flexibility mechanisms* for *carbon trading* between countries, including the *CDM*, *JI* and *Emissions Trading*. Despite having created a flourishing global *carbon market*, it has so far proved unsuccessful in limiting actual *greenhouse gas* emissions.

LDC – see *least developed country*.

LDCF – see *Least Developed Countries Fund*.

Least Developed Countries Fund (LDCF) – this fund was created in 2001 to help *LDCs* to prepare and implement *national adaptation programmes of action*. The LDCF is operated by the *Global Environment Facility*, and funded by voluntary contributions.

Least developed country (LDC) – a country with a very low Human Development Index, based on low per capita income, human resource weakness and economic vulnerability. There are currently forty-nine of these 'Fourth World' countries, of which thirty-three are in Africa.

Methane (CH_4) – a *greenhouse gas* with a *GWP* of about 30. It has a relatively short atmospheric lifetime, being oxidized to carbon dioxide over a decadal timescale. It is emitted from swamps and wetlands (including rice paddies) from the stomachs of ruminant animals, from the burning of biomass, from coal mines, and leaks of *natural gas*. Methane plays a huge role in the global climate system.

Montreal Protocol – shorthand for the 'Montreal Protocol on Substances that Deplete the Ozone Layer', an international treaty under the *Vienna Convention for the Protection of the Ozone Layer* which came into force in 1989. It uses a direct regulation approach to phase out chemicals responsible for depleting the *ozone layer*, backed up by a *Multilateral Fund* to help developing countries meet their obligations. Its secretariat is provided by *UNEP*.

Multilateral Fund – a fund created by the *Montreal Protocol* to finance the efforts of developing countries to phase out the manufacture and use of chemicals responsible for depleting the *ozone layer*.

N_2O – the chemical notation for *nitrous oxide*.

NAPA – see *national adaptation programmes of action*.

National adaptation programmes of action (NAPA) – plans of adaptation to *climate change* that address the most urgent needs of the *least developed* *countries*, funded under the *LDCF*.

Natural gas – the name applied to *methane* of fossil origin when supplied as a *fuel*.

NFFO – see *Non Fossil Fuel Obligation*.

NGO – see *non-governmental organization*.

Nitrous oxide (N_2O) – a *greenhouse gas* with a *GWP* of about 300, produced from various sources including the bacterial decomposition of nitrate fertilizer and of nitrate of natural origin, the combustion of *fossil fuels*, and nylon manufacture.

Non Fossil Fuel Obligation (NFFO) – the UK's mechanism for the support of renewable energy which was brought to an end in favour of the *Renewables Obligation*.

Non-governmental organization (NGO) – a term normally used for a civil society organization working to progress good causes in the field of environmental and social protection or development.

OECD – see *Organisation for Economic Co-operation and Development*.

Offset – see *carbon offset*.

Organisation for Economic Co-operation and Development (OECD) – an international organization of countries committed to representative democracy and a free market economy. OECD was founded in 1948 and is based in Paris, France.

Ozone (O_3) – a form of oxygen in which each molecule contains three oxygen atoms. In the *ozone layer*, ozone protects the Earth from UV radiation, but also acts as a *greenhouse gas*.

Ozone layer – the *ozone* in the stratosphere which protects the Earth's surface from dangerous UV-B ultraviolet solar radiation. The ozone layer is vulnerable to damage caused by the catalytic destruction of its ozone ultimately caused by human emissions of CFCs and other gases, now controlled by the *Montreal Protocol*.

PAP – see *production authorization permit*.

Perfluorocarbon – see *PFC*.

Permit – in the context of this book, a permit to produce *greenhouse gases*, or *fossil fuels*, resulting in an emission of 1 tonne of *carbon dioxide*, or equivalent, under the Kyoto2 system.

PFC – chemical shorthand for perfluorocarbon. The PFCs are powerful *greenhouse gases* with long atmospheric lifetimes. One major source of PFCs is aluminium smelting, however new technologies have rendered these emissions unnecessary.

Phase 1 – in *carbon market* terms, this refers to Phase 1, or the first trading period, of the *EUETS*, which ran from January 2005 to December 2007.

Phase 2 – this likewise refers to Phase 2 of the *EUETS*, which began in January 2008 and runs until December 2012, coinciding with the *compliance period* of the *Kyoto Protocol.*

Phase 3 – this likewise refers to Phase 3 of the *EUETS*, due to run from January 2013 until (probably) 2020.

PIGG – see *potent industrial greenhouse gas.*

Potent industrial greenhouse gas (PIGG) – a powerful *greenhouse gas* of industrial origin. Examples include *CFCs, HCFCs, HFCs, PFCs, sulphur hexafluoride* and *nitrous oxide.*

Production authorization permit (PAP) – the term used for a permit to produce/emit a tonne of CO_2 under the *Cap and Share* system of regulating *greenhouse gas* emissions.

REDD – see *Reducing Emissions from Deforestation and Degradation.*

Reducing Emissions from Deforestation and Degradation (REDD) – refers to measures to reduce *greenhouse gas* emissions from the destruction and degradation of forests and of other *carbon*-rich biomes and their underlying soils. The term is largely used in the context of the *carbon market*, and the creation of *carbon credits* arising from REDD as tradable instruments within the *compliance market* of the *Kyoto Protocol* in a post-2012 form.

Regional Greenhouse Gas Initiative (RGGI) – originating in 2003, this is an initiative of ten states in the northeast USA, which aims to implement a cap and trade system for *greenhouse gas* emissions from power plants.

Renewables Obligation (RO) – the UK's much-criticized mechanism to encourage an increase in the proportion of electricity generated from renewable sources. It is characterized by its high cost to consumers, its complexity, and its ineffectiveness in encouraging new investment. See also *Renewables Obligation Certificate.*

Renewables Obligation Certificate (ROC) – a certificate given to generators of renewable energy under the UK's *Renewables Obligation*, which they can sell on to electricity suppliers for them to demonstrate their degree of compliance with the applicable targets.

Reserve – in an *auction*, the reserve or reserve price is a price which must be met before the item or items are sold. In the context of the *uniform price sealed-bid auction* proposed by Kyoto2, the number of *permits* sold may be reduced to the number for which at least the reserve price has been bid.

RGGI – see *Regional Greenhouse Gas Initiative.*

RO – see *Renewables Obligation.*

ROC – see *Renewables Obligation Certificate.*

Safety valve – alternative term for *ceiling* in an auction.

SCCF – see *Special Climate Change Fund.*

SDR – see *special drawing rights.*

SF_6 – chemical notation for *sulphur hexafluoride.*

Social cost – a cost imposed on society by some action or activity. Social cost is normally taken to include environmental cost. Social costs are an example of an *externality* or *external cost.*

Special Climate Change Fund (SCCF) – a fund which exists to finance projects relating to adaptation, technology transfer, capacity building, energy, transport, industry, agriculture, forestry, waste management, and economic diversification. The SCCF is operated by the *Global Environment Facility*, and funded by contributions from the GEF's donors.

Special drawing rights (SDR) – the currency used by the *International Monetary Fund*, representing a weighted basket of the US dollar, the euro, the Japanese yen and the pound sterling, according to the role of each currency in international trade and finance.

Stern Review – shorthand for the *Stern Review on the Economics of Climate Change*, published by HM Treasury in 2007. The principal author is the economist and banker Nicholas Stern. The Stern Review was and continues to be highly influential, in presenting serious action to prevent, mitigate and adapt to climate change as the economically preferable option for long-term growth.

Sulphur hexafluoride (SF_6) – a very powerful *greenhouse gas* with a *GWP* of 22,200, used during magnesium casting.

UNDP – see *United Nations Development Programme.*

UNEP – see *United Nations Environment Programme.*

UNFCCC – see *United Nations Framework Convention on Climate Change.*

UNFPA – see *United Nations Population Fund.*

Uniform price sealed-bid auction – the preferred *auction* system for *permits* under Kyoto2. Under this system, bidders submit their bids in secret and the bids are opened only at the auction close. A *clearing price* is determined at which all the permits would be sold, at the clearance price itself or at a higher price. The winners are those bidding at or more than the clearing price, and they all buy the permits at the clearing price. Under Kyoto2 the auction is also subject to a *reserve* and a *ceiling* price.

United Nations Development Programme (UNDP) – founded in 1965, the UNDP is the largest multilateral source of development assistance with an annual budget of some $4.5 billion. Based in New York, it is answerable to the United Nations General Assembly. The UNDP works to achieve the Millennium

Development Goals, and has a focus on poverty reduction, HIV/AIDS, democratic governance, energy and environment, crisis prevention and recovery, the protection of human rights, and the empowerment of women. It is an implementing agency of the *GEF*.

United Nations Environment Programme (UNEP) – the coordinator of United Nations environmental activities, founded in 1972 and based in Nairobi, Kenya. UNEP, together with the World Meteorological Organization, established the *Intergovernmental Panel on Climate Change* (IPCC) in 1988. UNEP also provides the secretariat for the *Montreal Protocol* and the *Convention on Biological Diversity*, and is one of the implementing agencies for the *Global Environment Facility* (GEF).

United Nations Framework Convention on Climate Change (UNFCCC) – negotiated at the Earth Summit in Rio de Janeiro in 1992, the UNFCCC came into force in 1994. Its objective is the 'stabilization of greenhouse gas concentrations in the atmosphere at a level that would prevent dangerous anthropogenic interference with the climate system'. In 1997 the UNFCCC was supplemented by the *Kyoto Protocol*. In this book we use the term *Climate Convention*.

United Nations Population Fund (UNFPA) – founded in 1969 as the Fund for Population Activities, UNFPA was renamed the United Nations Population Fund in 1987. It operates supports programmes in the field of reproductive health, including family planning, safety in pregnancy and childbirth, avoidance of sexually transmitted disease, preventing volence against women, and promoting the equality of women. Its annual budget amounts to about $600 million per year.

Vienna Convention – shorthand for the *Vienna Convention for the Protection of the Ozone Layer*.

Vienna Convention for the Protection of the Ozone Layer – agreed in 1985 and coming into force in 1987, this is the international environmental treaty that gave rise to the *Montreal Protocol*.

Voluntary carbon market – that part of the *carbon market* which trades outside the formal or *compliance market*, generally in *carbon offsets*.

Water vapour – the *greenhouse gas* with the single biggest contribution to *global warming*. Both atmospheric water vapour and cloud play a huge part in global climate, but their future role under conditions of rising concentrations of other greenhouse gases is one of the great unknowns of climate science. Stratospheric water vapour from aircraft *contrails* is a significant cause of warming.

World Bank – formed in 1945, the World Bank is one of the Bretton Woods institutions intended to harmonize the world financial system and stimulate development. The World Bank is active in developing *carbon markets* and *REDD*. It is also an implementing agency of the *Global Environment Facility*, and coordinator of the *Clean Energy Investment Framework*.

World Trade Organization (WTO) – international organization, founded in 1995 as the successor to GATT (the General Agreement on Tariffs and Trade), designed to liberalize international trade and police member countries' adherence to WTO agreements. It is based in Geneva, Switzerland.

WTO – see *World Trade Organization*.

WWF – originally the World Wildlife Fund but now known only by its acronym, WWF is an international *NGO* that campaigns on a wide range of environmental issues, including *global warming*. Founded in 1961 and based in Gland, Switzerland, it is the world's largest conservation organization with over 5 million supporters worldwide.

Index

Printed in the United States
215853BV00001B/1/P